MAIN STREET
READY-MADE

Arnold R. Alanen & Joseph A. Eden

MAIN STREET
READY-MADE

The New Deal Community of Greendale, Wisconsin

Wisconsin Historical Society Press

In memory of Joseph Shiflett (Eden), 1946-1998

The Library of Congress has cataloged the hardcover edition as follows:

LIBRARY OF CONGRESS CATALOGING IN PUBLICATION DATA:

Alanen, Arnold R.
Main Street Ready-Made.

Bibliography: p. 135. Includes index.

1. Greendale (Wis.)—History.
2. New Towns—Wisconsin—Milwaukee Region—History.
I. Eden, Joseph A. [co-author].
II. Title.

F589.G72A42   1987   977.5'94   87-10828

ISBN 0-87020-251-0

PREFACE

MY interest in planned and model communities began while I was an undergraduate and graduate student at the Universities of Minnesota and Helsinki, Finland. It was during this period that I became intrigued by a number of "intentional places"— communities that represented the goals, objectives, and occasionally the idealism of a sponsoring individual, company, or organization. I maintained a focus on these communities during the years (1974-2009) that I served as a faculty member in the Department of Landscape Architecture at the University of Wisconsin-Madison—and I continue to follow these interests today. Besides Greendale, I have made in-depth assessments of several planned company towns—Kohler and Montreal, Wisconsin; Morgan Park, Minnesota; and Gwinn, Michigan—and one of the world's best-known post-war garden city suburbs: Tapiola, Finland.

During my thirty-five years of full-time academic life at the UW-Madison, I regularly taught a large introductory landscape history course to undergraduate students; this class always included a presentation on Greendale, a subject that the Wisconsin students typically seemed to find interesting. I also was rather surprised, upon arriving in Wisconsin, to realize that no scholarly book had yet been written about this iconic town. Therefore, in 1977 I began exploring the possibility of preparing such a volume, initially by offering a graduate seminar on planned communities that featured Greendale. During the span of that single semester, the six students and I explored the community on foot, conducted interviews with residents, and delved into the collection of historical materials that were stuffed into boxes and files in the basement of Greendale's small community library. The results of our efforts clearly convinced me that a detailed story of Greendale was well worth telling, but I also realized that this task could be completed only by making a close inspection of New Deal-related documents and sources sequestered in several archives outside of Wisconsin.

During the late 1970s and early 1980s, I applied for and received several grants that allowed me to undertake numerous studies of planned communities in the Midwest. Fortunately, Joseph Eden, an excellent graduate student in our department, was available to work as a research assistant on the Greendale section of the project. After completing further historical research, we wrote an article about Greendale that was accepted and published by the *Journal of the American Planning Association*, a leading American planning journal. We then began preparing a book-length manuscript for submission to the State Historical Society of Wisconsin (now the Wisconsin Historical Society) for publication consideration. The manuscript was reviewed and accepted in 1985, and following some revisions, *Main Street Ready-Made: The New Deal Community of Greendale, Wisconsin*, appeared in 1987. We were pleased when, in 1988, the book received both the Gambrinus Prize from the Milwaukee County Historical Society, and the scholarly book award from the Council for Wisconsin Writers.

Chapters Three through Seven of *Main Street Ready-Made* give considerable attention to the three years of intensive work—land acquisition, community planning, landscape and architectural design, town construction, resident selection, and social and economic programming—that preceded Greendale's opening. Chapter Eight, which documents the community's existence as a "government town," is followed by a discussion of the transition to private ownership that began in 1952 and continued for three tumultuous years thereafter. Chapter Nine explores the development of Greendale from 1955 to 1985. The remainder of this preface provides a brief overview of the community since the mid-1980s.

Change and Stability in Greendale's Built Environment

If someone had departed Greendale's residential area in 1938, and returned three quarters of a century later, she or he would have no problem recognizing the community. Some relatively minor alterations have been made to a number of Greendale's original houses since the 1950s—the application of synthetic siding to exterior walls, the substitution of original windows with vinyl or aluminum replacements, the modification or elimination of single-car garages, and the enclosure of once-open porches. Nevertheless, even now, during the second decade of the twenty-first century, the overall integrity of Greendale's housing districts remains remarkably intact and well maintained.

The most obvious changes to Greendale's physical fabric, some of which began before 1985, may be seen along the Broad Street commercial corridor. The street's eastern flank, originally parkland, was converted into a linear grouping of small businesses between 1959-61; four years later, the former tennis courts were used as the site for a large grocery store that was later converted into office and retail space. These modifications were utilitarian in nature and appearance and served the functional needs of a growing community. As noted in Chapter Nine, the commercial district faced its major challenge in 1970 when the huge Southridge Shopping Center, still the largest facility of its kind in Wisconsin, opened about one mile northwest of the Village Hall. Soon a steady stream of shop and store closings began occurring along Greendale's business corridor, events that were exacerbated by the inaction and hands-off approach of an out-of-state landlord who owned all of the Broad Street properties. By the early 1990s, just a few years after Greendale's fiftieth anniversary celebration in 1988, only seven of twenty-nine rental sites were occupied.[1]

Concentrated efforts to revitalize Greendale's commercial district began at this time, much of it sponsored by Roy Reiman, a locally based publisher whose company produced thirteen national magazines—most with "rural," "down home," or "lifestyle" themes—for millions of subscribers. Because a steady stream of visitors, most of whom wished to observe the magazines' products and publication process, constantly descended upon company headquarters, the entrepreneurial owner opened the Reiman Publications Visitor Center at the intersection of Broad Street and Northway in 1995. The facility included a test kitchen, a space for showing a video of the company's history, a "bargain basement" of Reiman catalog items, and a display of Norman Rockwell's *Saturday Evening Post* covers.[2] Although Reiman Publications was sold to the Readers Digest Association in 2002, the building still maintains most of its original Reiman functions; it was renamed the Greendale Visitor Center in 2011.

In 1997, Reiman organized the Grandhaven Investment Company, which purchased all of the remaining commercial structures located along both sides of Broad Street. Shortly thereafter, the Milwaukee architectural firm of Uihlein-Wilson prepared a plan for the preservation and renovation of the buildings; construction work was completed in 1998. The linear appearance of many existing buildings (termed "monotonous" by some) was modified by the application of varied rooflines and gabled parapets, while each end of the street was punctuated by a hip-roofed tower. The smaller southwestern tower identifies the entrance to Greendale's Municipal Building (the site of the original cooperative store), which, since its opening in late 1990, has accommodated the public library, local historical society, and health department. The northeastern end of Broad Street is anchored by a two-story clock tower connected to the visitor center.

The renovation plan also called for "putting the green back in Greendale," which resulted in the placement of new trees along Broad Street (along with "nostalgic" lamp posts), the addition of three thousand flowering trees throughout the community, and the planting, each spring, of more than 37,000 annuals in flower beds, baskets, window boxes, and pots. An article by Roy Reiman in a 1997 issue of his *Country* magazine asked readers to send daffodil bulbs to Greendale, where they would be planted in Dale Park, thereby making it "Daffo*dale* Park"! Although the organizers hoped to receive at least 7,000 bulbs, they were overwhelmed when 54,000 arrived; the excess 47,000 bulbs were then distributed to eager Greendale residents. Daffodils now bloom throughout the park and community each spring, covering the surface of Greendale with a blaze of vivid color. Dale Park and the Village Center were also connected by an attractive passageway that emerged following the removal of two small buildings along the eastern side of Broad Street, and the construction of a pedestrian bridge over Dale Creek.[3]

A notable 1988 addition to the western side of Broad Street is "Eleanor's Courtyard," which marks the 1936 visit that First Lady Eleanor Roosevelt made to Greendale during the early stages of town construction. The courtyard, located in front of the former post office—a well-preserved example of Greendale's original public architecture—offers a pleasant space with outdoor seating. The focal point is a round fountain, installed in 1998 and placed in a low, brick-faced circular pool; set in the middle of the fountain is a diminutive bronze sculpture of two children standing under a rain umbrella. Metal plaques surrounding the fountain present a brief chronology of Greendale's history. The intersection of Northway and Broad Street, just across from the Village Hall, serves as the site of another new outdoor seating area: the centerpiece of this installation is a circular planter that displays seasonal flowers and a small bronze sculpture of a young girl who is laughing as she sprinkles the flowers with her watering can.

Besides the former post office, two other Broad Street buildings still retain much of their 1930s character. One is the Greendale Village Inn, which functions as a family-oriented tavern that features one of Wisconsin's signature culinary events: a Friday-evening fish fry. At the northern terminus of Broad Street is the Greendale Village Hall, a well-designed and recently remodeled Colonial Revival style building that continues to accommodate the community's administrative offices and council chamber.

Elsewhere in the Village Center are three properties that have remained unchanged since the 1930s. One is the flagpole sculpture located on the mall that stretches west of Broad Street; designed and executed by Alonzo Hauser, it remains an excellent example of New Deal-era sculptural expression. The two other properties, both now vacant, are the former police and fire station and the grounds building and hose tower (often termed the public works building).

Economics and Demographics

As noted in *Main Street Ready-Made*, Greendale was initially populated by a relatively small group of moderate income people who moved into the community during the late 1930s. Over time, however, Greendale's socio-economic profile has both changed and remained remarkably constant, especially after the transition from public to private ownership occurred during the early 1950s; this growth took place when large areas of undeveloped land were converted into residential subdivisions from the 1950s to the 1970s. The plans and designs for the neighborhoods and housing that emerged during the 1950s and 1960s—typically one and one-half story ranch houses built along curving streets and roadways at an average density of eleven units per acre—reflected suburban preferences and practices of the post-war era. On the other hand, the appearance and much greater size of the 1970s-era housing that appeared in the Overlook Farms and Overlook West districts of western Greendale (1.5 units/acre) differed appreciably from those built earlier. Even today, one of the most striking contrasts in the community's physical appearance and economic differentiation is provided by a comparison of homes in Overlook and the original Village Center.

The overall quality of Greendale's housing, parks, and community services has always attracted solid middle-class residents. Nevertheless, Greendale's overall population count has fallen slowly but steadily over the past three decades—from 16,930 people in 1980, to 15,130 in 1990, to 14,405 in 2000, and finally, 14,045 in 2010. This downward trend is typical of many older suburbs in America, although Greendale is somewhat of an anomaly because the value of its housing and residential environment has not fallen over time. Rather, Greendale's population numbers are due to an overall decline in family size and the aging of its residents. Indeed, the median age of a Greendaler increased from 32.2. years in 1980 to 45.9 in 2010; during this same period, the median age of the entire Milwaukee Metropolitan Statistical Area (MSA) increased less dramatically–from 29.8 to 36.9 years.[4]

In 1980, the median family income of Greendale's residents ($26,327) was quite similar to that of the Milwaukee MSA ($23,635), but by 2010 the differential had become more pronounced: $80,143 and $68,787, respectively. The gap in median housing values, however, has narrowed appreciably. A difference of $46,400 separated the two in 1980 (Greendale $119,800; MSA $73,400), but narrowed to $10,500 by 2010 (Greendale $215,300; MSA $204,800).[5]

Since all of the original residents were selected by public administrators and social workers, the demographic and racial profiles of these Greendalers were very similar. Although Greendale still remains a predominantly white community, it has become more racially diverse over time. Greendale's minority population, barely evident in 1980, has now expended to some ten percent of the community: the Hispanic/Latino population of 667 constituted 5 percent of the community (MSA 9.5 percent) in 2010, while the 430 Asians represented 3.1 percent (MSA 2.9 percent) of Greendale's residents. The African American presence, however, remains extremely low, even though slight growth did occur over the three decades—from 23 in 1980, or less than 0.2 percent of Greendale's population, to 143 in 2010, still only 1.0 percent of all residents (MSA 16.4 percent). But it must be noted that Greendale's characteristics do not differ greatly from many other suburban communities in the Milwaukee metropolitan area.[6]

Greendale as a National Historic Landmark

Soon after Greendale and its sister communities in Maryland (Greenbelt) and Ohio (Greenhills) emerged during the 1930s, historians and critics of town planning, landscape architecture, and architecture quickly recognized their significance. The more comprehensive books that would feature the Greenbelt towns, written from the 1970s to the early 2000s, were also part of the growing scholarly discourse that, since the 1960s, has given considerable attention to American suburbs and suburban phenomena.[7]

In 2002, the National Park Service published a bulletin that provided context and guidelines for evaluating and documenting America's historic residential suburbs. This bulletin has aided local and state preservation agencies in determining the significance of suburbs nominated for either National Register or National Historic Landmark (NHL) designation. Since then, numerous suburbs have been added to the national register, while the NHL list now includes a few exceptional examples, including Greenbelt, Maryland, already approved in 2001.[8] Because of its much more rigorous selection and evaluation criteria, the NHL program, which considers only those places that "possess exceptional value or quality in illustrating or interpreting the heritage of the United States," includes fewer designations. (When considering all listings the National Register count now exceeds 87,000, whereas the NHL program has fewer than 2500.)[9]

The National Register of Historic Places nomination for the Greendale Historic District was approved by the Secretary of the Interior in 2005. Since the documentation clearly identified Greendale's iconic town planning status, pursuit of National Historic Landmark designation was initiated soon thereafter. Substantial reviews and revisions of the draft document were subsequently undertaken by National Park Service and Wisconsin Historical Society staff members and other experts in 2010-11; the NHL nomination was submitted to the Secretary of the Interior for approval in 2012.[10]

Greendale's significance and eligibility as a National Historic Landmark are based on two primary criteria. First is its association with highly important activities initiated by the federal government in coping with the Great Depression: providing a better life for working-class Americans by offering construction work to the unemployed, and utilizing modern design principles and economical building methods and materials in home construction. The second criterion involves Greendale's superior town planning qualities, notably its "innovative, cost-saving measures of group housing and large-scale home construction." When considering the built environment that characterizes Greendale today, the nomination noted that the historic village core still "retains a high degree of historic integrity," and the housing units "generally show very good integrity." Because numerous changes have occurred along the Broad Street commercial corridor, only a few of its buildings are considered as "contributing" features: the historic section of the Greendale Tavern (high integrity), the old post office (fair integrity), the rear elevations of the Greendale theatre block (good integrity), and the Village Hall (excellent integrity). The nearby flagpole structure, former police and fire station, and the grounds building and hose tower are also identified as contributing elements. The Greendale Historical Society is spearheading a fund-raising effort to save the grounds building and hose tower as a community center, but the fate of the original police and fire station remains uncertain.[11]

Today, Greendale represents one of the nation's most outstanding examples of New Deal town planning and building activity. Greendale's reputation and importance will only continue to grow into the future, given that significant numbers of the 65,000 buildings originally constructed by New Deal agencies are destroyed each year. In Greenhills, Ohio, for example, fifty-two apartment units were torn down in 2008 alone because of deterioration and maintenance shortcomings. Robert Karo, who has written masterfully about the New Deal construction projects supervised by New York "Power Broker" Robert Moses, laments the destruction of this legacy. "We should be preserving them and honoring them," he stated in 2008. "They serve as monuments to the fact that it is possible to combine infrastructure with beauty."[12]

The high quality of Greendale's contemporary environment is based on the genius of the planners and designers who created a special place during the 1930s that has now endured for three-quarters of a century. But equally important are the generations of residents who have made Greendale their home and the local officials who guided the community through difficult periods in its history. These people were recognized and honored during Greendale's fiftieth anniversary in 1988.[13] Greendale also received the American Society of Landscape Architecture Medallion Award in 1999. Additional recognition will occur once again in 2013 when seventy-five years of Greendale history are celebrated. We can only hope that future residents and government officials will honor this legacy by respecting and maintaining the features that make Greendale such a special and noteworthy place.

I am indebted to the following reviewers who provided comments on an earlier version of this preface: Lynn Bjorkman, Kathy Borkowski, Rachel Cordasco, Kathleen Hart, Ted Mainella, and Daina Penkiunas.

JOSEPH SHIFLETT (EDEN), 1946-1998

JOSEPH Earl Shiflett was born on 16 June 1946 in Springboro, Ohio. After receiving a B.A. from Wittenberg College (Ohio) in 1968, Joe joined the Peace Corps and spent two years in Malaysia. His experiences there, which left him with a life-long respect and love for Malaysia and its people, included work on water and sanitation projects sponsored by the World Health Organization. After returning to the United States, Joe enrolled as a graduate student at Miami University in Ohio, where he completed an M.A. thesis in anthropology (1973) that dealt with the myths and rituals of the Pacific Coast's Kwakiutl Indians.[1] After earning another M.A. degree, this one in Southeast Asian Studies from Ohio University in 1976, Joe taught anthropology and comparative religions at Warren Wilson College in Swannanoa, North Carolina.

Joe arrived at the University of Wisconsin-Madison in 1979, where his research thesis, a Master of Arts in Landscape Architecture (1981), focused on the planning of Greendale, Wisconsin.[2] (By this time, he had changed his name to Joseph Anfield Eden in recognition of his maternal great-grandfather.) In 1983, a co-authored article that he and I prepared for an issue of the *Journal of the American Planning Association* offered an overview of Greendale from its inception to 1980, whereas our book-length manuscript—*Main Street Ready-Made: The New Deal Community of Greendale, Wisconsin*—published in 1987, provided a much more comprehensive assessment of town planning activities and the subsequent evolution of this iconic settlement.[3]

After leaving Madison, Joe eventually moved to the University of North Carolina, where he had been accepted as a Ph.D. student by the Department of Geography. While there, Joe was a highly popular teaching assistant, and he received a Fulbright Fellowship that allowed him to undertake a year of dissertation research in Malaysia. His dissertation, an in-depth study of the urban social geography of Malaysian women, was completed in 1989.[4]

During the early 1990s, Joe taught at Sonoma State University in California and then, due to health concerns, moved to Venice, Florida to live with his parents. Joe returned to teaching in 1997, taking a position in Bangkok, Thailand. The next year, while visiting Calcutta, India, on a return to the U.S. from Bangkok, he became seriously ill. After a two-month-long period of recuperation in India, he appeared well enough to continue the long journey back to Florida. Unfortunately, he had a relapse while traveling and died on 3 November 1998 in a Sarasota hospital, as Joseph Earl Shiflett (having earlier returned to his original birth name).

In my thirty-five years at the University of Wisconsin-Madison, I was privileged to advise many talented graduate students, but Joe stands out as one of the most hard-working and intellectually gifted. His academic path offers a portrait of a scholar who was endlessly curious and ever willing to explore new disciplines and ideas. Finally, I would be remiss in failing to mention Joe's gentle spirit and demeanor. His kindness and thoughtful outlook were evident throughout a full, but all too brief, life.

Arnold R. Alanen
Professor Emeritus
University of Wisconsin-Madison

[1] Joseph Shiflett, "Social and Structural Aspects of Southern Kwakiutl Myths and Rituals," MA Thesis (Oxford, Ohio: Miami University, 1973).

[2] Joseph A. Eden, "The Aging of a Greenbelt Town: A Planning History of Greendale, Wisconsin," MALA Thesis (Madison: University of Wisconsin-Madison, 1981).

[3] Joseph A. Eden and Arnold R. Alanen, "Looking Backward at a New Deal Town: Greendale, Wisconsin, 1935-1980," *Journal of the American Planning Association* 49 (Winter 1983): 56-74; Arnold R. Alanen and Joseph A. Eden, *Main Street Ready-Made: The New Deal Community of Greendale, Wisconsin* (Madison: State Historical Society of Wisconsin, 1987).

[4] Joseph Anfield Eden, "Female Labor and Regional Economic Development in Malaysia," Ph.D. dissertation (Charlotte: University of North Carolina, 1989); also see Joseph Eden, "Life Cycle Strategies of Female Assembly Line Workers in Malaysia: Demographic Profiles of a Dual Work Force," *Urban Anthropology and Studies of Cultural Systems and World Economic Development* 18 (Summer 1989): 153-85; and "Mobilisation and Employment of Female Labourers in Malaysia," *Pacific Viewpoint* (1991).

ACKNOWLEDGMENTS

THIS study could not have been completed without the generous assistance of several individuals, agencies, and organizations. The College of Agricultural and Life Sciences at the University of Wisconsin, Madison, played the key role in getting the study underway when they awarded a U.S. Department of Agriculture (Hatch) grant to Arnold R. Alanen for the assessment of various planned and resource communities in the Upper Midwest. The grant made it possible to begin the archival investigation that provided the basis for this volume, and to undertake a survey of Greendale residents and thereby determine their evaluations of various community features. More recently, the College of Agriculture and Life Sciences provided further support to cover the costs for cartography and photographic duplication. Additional funding from the Graduate School of the University of Wisconsin, Madison, allowed us to complete the archival work, as did the assistance provided while Professor Alanen was a National Fellow (1980–1983) of the W. K. Kellogg Foundation.

A special challenge that must be met in studying a greenbelt town stems from the many changes in ownership and legal status that each town has undergone. Although this study has confined itself to one of the three completed projects, it was, nonetheless, necessary to use several major archival holdings, primarily in Greendale and Milwaukee, Wisconsin; in Washington, D.C.; and in Lexington, Kentucky. The assistance of specialists, cordially rendered, at each of those repositories has been indispensable. The staffs to whom thanks must be given are those at the Greendale Village Library in Greendale; the Milwaukee County Historical Society Library in Milwaukee; the Natural Resources Branch and the Industrial and Social Branch of the Records Service of the National Archives and Records Administration in Washington, D.C.; the Special Collections Division of the University of Kentucky Library in Lexington; and the Morton Arboretum Archives in Lisle, Illinois. The newspaper microfilm collection of the State Historical Society of Wisconsin in Madison also was indispensable in providing insight to the daily progression of activities in Greendale.

Within Greendale itself, many people were most helpful in agreeing to help us with our efforts. Several of Greendale's original pioneers provided reminiscenses of their early years in the community, while Victor J. Jacoby reviewed those portions of the manuscript that discussed the years he served on the Greendale Village Board (1958–1966). Patricia Goetsch, former president of the Greendale Historical Society, deserves special mention for the many photographs and personal memories she kindly supplied, and for providing us with inspiration to complete the project.

At the State Historical Society of Wisconsin it has been Paul Hass who assumed primary responsibility for guiding the manuscript through the publication process. Not only did he secure the comments of outside reviewers who supplied us with many useful suggestions for improving the original manuscript, but his many recommendations, from beginning to end, have made this a much more readable volume. We are also indebted to the Department of Landscape Architecture at the University of Wisconsin for providing the space and facilities to carry out this project; to Carol Ahlgren and Jacqueline Bettinger for their conscientious efforts in word processing the manuscript and its revisions; and to Frank E. Martin who helped to track down sources and to verify the references. Any errors of interpretation, of course, are the responsibility of the authors.

CONTENTS

ILLUSTRATIONS
follow page 84

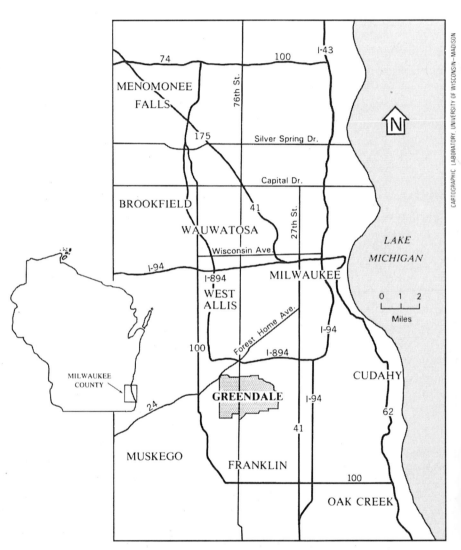

Greendale, Wisconsin, in relation to Milwaukee County
highways and communities, c. 1987.

CHAPTER ONE
The Recovery of Community Life in America

THE decline of the city in America is an old and enduring theme of social criticism.[1] The awareness of an urban crisis gave impetus to the American city planning movement during the first decades of this century—a time when rapid technological change threatened to obliterate the beauty and the liveability of urban areas. Planned cities, of course, were scarcely new to this continent. On the grand scale, there were the rather imaginative plans of various colonial cities such as Savannah, Georgia; Williamsburg, Virginia; Philadelphia, Pennsylvania; and Annapolis, Maryland. The formative years of the Republic also displayed specific planning ideals in such cities as Washington, D.C.; Detroit, Michigan; Madison, Wisconsin; and several others.[2] Another tradition, and one infused with the paternalistic motives of industrial entrepreneurs, has left behind numerous company towns: Lowell, Massachusetts; Pullman, Illinois; and Kohler, Wisconsin, among others. As was true of the earlier planned cities in America, the company towns borrowed widely from examples of earlier planned towns in Europe, but whereas the colonial communities often drew upon classical and medieval schemes, the later philanthropic towns of American capitalists derived, in large part, from contemporary housing experiments in England and on the European continent. The purpose of these public and private ventures was to provide healthful and attractive housing for city workers, and the most popular model community of the day was the self-supporting satellite suburb, or garden city, complete with its own farms, industry, and community services.[3]

The English garden city was perhaps foremost in the minds of Americans when they turned to suburban planning. At the turn of the twentieth century, the Englishman Ebenezer Howard—court stenographer, journalist, and publicist of housing reform—attracted the support of financiers, politicians, and architects with his proposal for a network of satellite centers around the urban hub of London. Howard and his cohorts (chief among them the architects Raymond Unwin and Barry Parker) wished to provide factory workers and clerks with an alternative to the grim confines of inner London. As Howard explained in his famous tract of 1898, *To-morrow: A Peaceful Path to Real Reform* (reissued in 1902 as *Garden Cities of Tomorrow*), each rigidly geometric town plan would nest in the center of

1

an agricultural district and include both factories and cooperatively run shops to sustain the economic life of the community. Land was to be a shared commodity with ownership rights vested in a quasi-public authority. In 1903, the garden city of Letchworth (4,500 acres) was built, followed by Welwyn (3,100 acres) in 1919. Both were promptly hailed in America as the consummation of Howard's proposed "marriage of town and country."[4]

While American planners and reformers were actively promoting the English concept of the garden city, a critique of industrialization in America was being pressed from other quarters. Two groups of thinkers, in particular, extolled the virtues of America's diverse rural landscapes and people. Together, these exponents of American regionalism laid the intellectual foundations for much of the New Deal national planning movement. Perhaps the most literary of the two streams of regionalism in America was represented by such acclaimed Southerners as William Faulkner and Robert Penn Warren. Less well known, but quite as influential in his day, was the astute scholar-planner Howard Odum. During the 1920's, Odum argued against the evils of the city's economic and spiritual domination over agrarian societies and cultures. In his books and from his lectern at the University of North Carolina, he advocated a many-sided technological and artistic renaissance in the South that eventually would provide a mosaic of diverse cultural landscapes.[5]

This fear of homogenization through urban industrialization motivated another group of regionalists as well, although they, unlike the Southerners, aimed to save the city from itself. Indeed, the Regional Planning Association of America (RPAA) began as an offshoot of the metropolitan planning movement in New York City. At the center of this genteel but fiercely committed clique sat Lewis Mumford, a multi-talented social and cultural critic, historian, planner, philosopher, and housing reformer. Mumford, more than anyone else in the early 1920's, propagated the ecological teachings of Patrick Geddes, the Scottish biologist and town planner, in American circles.[6] Joining Mumford in the RPAA were Benton MacKaye, forester and conservationist; Henry Wright, Clarence Stein, and Frederick Bigger, architects; Tracy Augur and Earle Draper, landscape architects; Catherine Bauer, housing expert; and Alexander Bing, financier and philanthropist.[7]

Comprehensive in its approach, the RPAA promoted "territorial" planning to enhance the bio-social interdependencies within a particular geographic region—a unit often defined by a river basin. In their publications,

RPAA members implied a threshold of urban growth and congestion beyond which health and social relations were thought to deteriorate. The alternative recommended by Mumford and the rest was an approximation of the self-sustaining garden city complete with farms, factories, shops, common ownership and taxation of land-holdings, elimination of commercial competition from the new town, and, most apparent, the preservation of a greenbelt to shield the town from undesirable urban sprawl.[8]

In addition to a flood of ink on the subject, the proposals of the RPAA led to several experiments in community planning, the most famous of which was Radburn, New Jersey. Heralded as a "town for the motor age" by its planners, Henry Wright and Clarence Stein, Radburn was no more (and no less) than an attractive suburb with critical innovations in site planning. It was distinguished by the siting of row houses in "superblocks"—large units of land without through streets; by connecting large areas of open space in each superblock to form a continuous park; and by providing a variegated street system which separated vehicular from pedestrian traffic while conforming to the natural contours of the land.[9]

With the apparent collapse of world capitalism in the 1930's, critics of the American economic system began to call for sweeping reforms in all sectors, and decent housing for everyone became the goal of the liberal planning movement. In this atmosphere of optimism mixed with desperation, Franklin D. Roosevelt's New Deal elevated to national prominence a man who was destined to become a prototype for the planner as a canny, can-do, yet principled crusader: Rexford Guy Tugwell. In 1933, Tugwell left behind a professorship in economics at Columbia University to serve as advisor to President Roosevelt. Schooled at the Wharton School of Finance, yet possessing a broad interest in land resources, Tugwell soon made his way into Roosevelt's inner sanctum. Along with a few select others, such as Raymond Moley and William Wooden, Tugwell was identified by the press as a member of Roosevelt's "Brains Trust."

Displaying a tenacity that was worthy of his name, Tugwell won presidential favor for a series of comprehensive land reforms. Once the confluence of urban and rural problems became clear to Tugwell, he seized upon the garden city-satellite model of the RPAA as a means to correct severe imbalances among people and resources and as a vehicle for an experiment in participatory planning. The garden city of the New Deal would be, according to Tugwell's plans, the setting for "grassroots democracy," a phrase borrowed from David Lilienthal of the Tennessee Valley Authority (TVA) to emphasize the return of economic and political power to communities through federal controls on big business and through the development of the region's natural and human resources.[10]

In the tradition of institutionalist economics, Tugwell believed that the exploitation of the nation's resources could be regulated and marshaled so as to benefit directly the ordinary citizen. Yet any broad restructuring of industrial democracy in America would, ironically, demand centralization as well as decentralization of political authority, since individual freedom demanded the discipline of collective action.[11] Tugwell was, by all accounts, a man who genuinely loved the rural landscape and who possessed a scholarly appreciation of its past and its problems. But he also was an urbane connoisseur who valued the role of cities as centers of culture. In the city, Tugwell and his colleague, Howard C. Hill, stated, "Free or cheap public advantages for education are available; food and sanitation are inspected; newspapers, motion pictures, and contacts with other minds exist."[12] The golden mean of policy was to be forged between the isolated farmstead and the crowded city. It was, according to Tugwell, located in the moderate concentrations of a new multicellular metropolis: "In fact the loft and the sweatshops ought to be transformed and moved bodily to become the nucleus, along with the schools, of our projected farming villages."[13]

The "greenbelt towns"[14] program proposed by Tugwell came to assume goals far beyond make-work relief employment and low-cost housing. It was, in fact, a bold crusade against the invisible and ill-understood economic and social forces that were undermining the dignity and self-worth of Americans while destroying that fabric of interdependence which had bound together families and communities. With the greenbelt town, the New Deal cautiously backed into the future.

CHAPTER TWO
Garden Cities for America

THE public works of the Roosevelt years generally were undertaken in haste, their primary aim being unemployment relief. The greenbelt towns were no exception. But what began as a rather modest rural land reclamation scheme ballooned into a major commitment. Rexford Guy Tugwell, Undersecretary of Agriculture from 1934 to 1935, decided that the government ought to purchase some 15,000 acres of submarginal land near the National Agricultural Research Station at Beltsville, Maryland, a site that was less than a thirty-minute drive from the nation's capital. Tugwell took the idea to John S. Lansill, an old friend who was director of the Land Utilization Division of the Federal Emergency Relief Administration (FERA). After inspecting the tract in February, 1935, Lansill cleared the way for its acquisition. In the next few weeks, however, the character of the Beltsville project changed dramatically after Congress passed, on April 8, an Emergency Relief Appropriations Act making $4 billion available for public works.[1]

During his February tour of the Beltsville area with Lansill and Wallace Richards, Tugwell had casually mentioned the possibility of building a community housing project on the site for workers at the federal research facility. When jockeying for federal funds began, it was this town-building aspect of the Beltsville project, by then known as Maryland Special Project No. 1, which Tugwell emphasized to the President.[2] The proposal was surely the right one at the right moment of the New Deal. It held the possibility of jobs for thousands of men while creating something of lasting worth. And the program did not have to be limited to a solitary project. New towns could be built for workers outside major centers of industry across the country—a strategy that could serve not only to alleviate the national housing crisis but also to regulate the haphazard sprawl of cities.[3]

Since Roosevelt was never one to reject any reasonable means of helping people to live outside of cities, Tugwell's idea earned his enthusiastic support.[4] The suburban program that ensued was handed over to Tugwell's new Resettlement Administration—basically a rural relief agency that assumed the rehabilitation and conservation programs begun by Harry Hopkins' Federal Emergency Relief Administration and the Subsistence Homesteads Development Division, a much-maligned farm colony program authorized by the National Industrial Recovery Act of 1935.[5] It was

5

another of those instances when agrarian rehabilitation and industrial recovery fell within the purview of the same agency, and because of this, the suburban program of the Resettlement Administration had little in common with other resettlement programs except for its place within Tugwell's vast administrative complex. Unfortunately, a consequence of lumping all resettlement projects together was a confusion between rural and suburban that plagued the greenbelt towns program throughout much of its existence and caused it to suffer unfavorable comparisons with the other "Tugwelltowns," which were rural, largely agricultural communities and homesteads.[6] This same confusion, in fact, would exist in Milwaukee after initial plans were announced for Greendale, Wisconsin, in late 1935.

The greenbelt towns program officially began on April 30, 1935, when Roosevelt signed Executive Order 7027, Section A of which authorized the resettlement of "destitute and low-income families from rural areas." Tugwell had managed to satisfy all the requisites of relief: land rehabilitation was taken care of by the working farms that were to be retained in the greenbelt, the poor were to be housed, and the jobless were to be given jobs. This was logical enough in theory, but the proposal was rife with practical difficulties. First, there was the matter of buying large amounts of land outside every city targeted for a satellite project. But even more perplexing was the question of how, in the wording of the executive order, "to administer approved projects . . . including the establishment, maintenance, and operation, in such connection, of communities in rural and suburban areas."[7]

This objective was never clear, even to the planners. Valuable time was lost in futile attempts to coordinate town life and the marginal agrarian economies of each project. Over the course of a hectic summer, four men were primarily answerable for policy: John Lansill, who in 1935 was named Director of the Suburban Resettlement Division of the Resettlement Administration; the economist Warren J. Vinton, Lansill's colleague in the FERA and Chief of the Suburban Division's Research Section; Frederick J. Bigger, an architect-planner who proved instrumental in hiring well-qualified professionals to take charge of designing the towns; and finally Tugwell himself, who in July presided over a distinguished seminar consisting of, among others, Ernest J. Bohn, president of the National Association of Housing Officials, the economist Stuart Chase, the philosopher-educator John Dewey, and a more anonymous mass of child-care specialists and social workers. Tugwell reportedly asked these assembled experts to help him "breathe life" into the new resettlement communities.[8]

Besides these central figures, there were numerous others who helped shape the final program. Most important were several planning consultants from the ranks of the moribund Regional Planning Association of America (RPAA), as well as several young disciples of the Association's founding members. Frederick Bigger, for example, was one of a clique that included such eminent leaders of the planning profession as Henry Wright and Clarence Stein, planners of the model community of Radburn, New Jersey, and other garden city adaptations; Tracy Augur and Earle Draper, site planners attached to the Tennessee Valley Authority; John Nolen, doyen of American landscape architects; and Jacob Crane, recently appointed state planning consultant for Wisconsin and Illinois by the National Resources Committee (NRC). Largely through the persuasions of these planners, and the suggestions of housing experts such as Catherine Bauer, another veteran of the RPAA, the greenbelt towns program was scaled down from sixty-odd to four exemplary projects designed to serve as models of community planning.[9] One such project was to be located just southwest of Milwaukee, Wisconsin.

Nonetheless, the emphasis on speed nearly outweighed all other concerns at the beginning. Tugwell, believing that building styles and site plans would have to be standardized, initially assigned a team of engineers—many of whom were holdovers from the controversial Subsistence Homesteads Division—to draft the town plans. When it became apparent that they had no flair for such work, Vinton and others in the program prevailed upon Lansill to recruit more qualified individuals. On October 14, 1935, Lansill appointed Frederick Bigger to coordinate greenbelt town planning and architecture. A separate planning staff was soon assembled for each project in order to ensure a variety of town plans appropriate to local laws and customs. This upgrading of planning talent and uniform "spread of responsibilities" appealed to Vinton, who by this time was facing the chore of selling the resettlement idea to local officials in each project city—a task that might have been impossible had the pedestrian plans of the engineers been accepted. In October, 1935, Vinton's office became the epicenter of a planning apparatus as Wright, Stein, Crane, Augur, Bauer, and architectural consultant Henry Churchill conferred with Vinton on every phase of the program, from architecture to rental rates.[10]

The new slant to the program—a concern for the quality of design—was further impelled by a chauvinistic desire on the part of the consultants, and Lansill as well, to catch up with the rest of the Western world. Judging from experiments in England, Germany, and especially Sweden, the wave of the future appeared to be the garden city with its blending of rural amenities, a centralized metropolitan planning authority, and the social and economic interdependencies of the neighborhood. The Suburban Resettlement Division proudly declared that one of its primary purposes was "to set up models which will stimulate private builders to erect planned communities of their own."[11] Besides farsightedness, budgetary limitations and uncertainties also weighed in the decision to build only a few towns. Not until September 13, 1935, did Roosevelt agree to an initial expenditure of $31 million, with a dubious guarantee of $37 million more whenever Congress would allocate additional funds for relief programs. As Lansill put it, "the necessity in 1935 was to make jobs, and quickly." Roosevelt demanded that ground be broken at every project by December 15, 1935, and that all construction work be completed by June, 1936.[12]

Each of the planning sections chosen by Bigger consisted of three units: Town Planning, Architecture, and Engineering. John Nolen was no doubt influential in shaping this tripartite structure. In 1934, Nolen, then technical advisor to the Subsistence Homesteads Division, had urged the hiring of landscape architects and architects, in addition to civil engineers. According to Nolen, the chief planner on such a team would be the landscape architect, thereby ensuring "the proper placing of the plan upon the ground. . . ."[13] During much of the New Deal period the omnipresent landscape architect, in projects located throughout the country, "became indispensable to the reordering of the land." Besides the Resettlement Administration, landscape architects were evident in the Works Progress Administration (WPA), the Civilian Conservation Corps (CCC), the Tennessee Valley Authority (TVA), and the Soil Conservation Service (SCS). Landscape architects also found employment in two other agencies that, while predating the New Deal period, received massive infusions of financial support during the 1930's depression era: the National Park Service (NPS) and the United States Forest Service (USFS).[14]

Attached to each section of every greenbelt town planning staff were scores of support personnel and consultants. The Greendale staff, for example, comprised over 100 people, eight of them full-time consultants on such diverse matters as wildlife management, farming practices, and real estate trends. The creative responsibilities, however, were left to a few leaders—the landscape architects, town planners, and architects on each project team. Incongruously, these principals were ensconced with their assistants in the Washington mansion of one of the city's more flamboyant and colorful characters, Lady Evalyn Walsh McLean.[15]

According to a tacit rule of the Suburban Division, the leaders of each planning group were appointed, in part at least, on the basis of some familiarity with the geographic region. In charge of site design at Greendale was Elbert Peets, a graduate of Harvard's Department of Landscape Architecture who possessed a well-proved scholarly and practical mastery of European Renaissance and Colonial American town-planning principles. Peets had worked in and around Milwaukee shortly before and after World War I and had collaborated with the well-known German town planner, Werner Hegemann, on a number of ventures. Prior to American involvement in World War I, Hegemann and Peets had prepared plans for Kohler, Wisconsin, where a partially realized version of a company town emerged, and for Washington Highlands, a prestigious suburb outside of Milwaukee. Most notably, the two had co-authored a compendium of world architecture and civic design entitled *The American Vitruvius*, published in 1922.[16]

Peets was joined at Greendale by Jacob Crane, who retained his position with the National Resources Committee while devoting twenty days a month to Greendale throughout 1936 and 1937. Crane had spent much of his professional life as a city-planning consultant in Chicago, but he also was at ease in larger theaters. In 1931, for example, Crane was engaged briefly by the State Planning Commission of the Soviet Union. (As was true of most American planners who ventured to Russia at this time, Crane returned ideologically unscathed by his exposure to totalitarian town planning.) In 1934 Crane was elected president of a reorganized American City Planning Institute.[17] The two Greendale town planners, between themselves, spanned the temperamental latitudes of an eclectic profession. Crane, according to Peets, was the "contact man upstairs," and Peets seems to have been the prima donna of the planners, keenly in tune with bygone eras of town planning in Europe and America.[18]

Dedicated to serving the needs of the average American worker, the planners found little room for the avant-garde in site planning. Much the same can be said for the architecture, although the Bauhaus influence was evident in the Maryland and Ohio towns. Some 150 young architects, along with the entire library of the New York Housing Study Guild, an association with direct links to the RPAA, moved into the drafting rooms of the Suburban Division during the winter of 1935 and 1936. The migration was of such proportions as to stir the editor of the *American Architect* to warn: "The detrimental cheapening of the professions by such agencies (e.g., the Resettlement Administration) will require renewed effort to effect a better status for architects." Henry Hubbard, president of the American Society of Landscape Architects and editor of *Landscape Architecture*, issued a similar warning from his own professional podium.[19]

At Greendale, the principal architects—Harry H. Bentley, who designed the homes, and Walter G. Thomas, who was responsible for public buildings—certainly did nothing to cheapen their craft, but neither did they do much to advance it. Bentley, self-consciously eschewing the international styles of his day, came closest of all the greenbelt architects to a version of the English cottage. Thomas, his colleague, indulged a love for the Beaux-Arts style and borrowed unabashedly from the recent reconstruction of Colonial Williamsburg, Virginia. Perhaps more than any other greenbelt town staff, the one at Greendale strived, in the words of architectural consultant Henry S. Churchill, to combine "those amenities characteristic of early colonial villages with the advantages of our mechanical era."[20] Even so, the planners were seldom firmly in control. Important decisions often were made deep within the swollen ranks of bureaucrats— the administrators, economists, accountants, realtors, lawyers, and clerks, who, with the planners, comprised the Suburban Division, the planning arm of the Resettlement Administration.

Besides the town planning, architectural, and engineering sections for each project, there also were general sections for land acquisition (a Land Section under Tilford Dudley took charge of the purchase of all project sites) and for social and economic research (Warren Vinton's Research Section). Legal and administrative support came from the office of attorney Frank H. Osterlind in Milwaukee, from Fred Naumer, executive officer of the Greendale project, and from B. I. Nowell, regional coordinator of the Resettlement Administration. Beyond the confines of the Suburban Division, the lines of authority blurred, and, consequently, the planners (represented by on-site liaisons) often clashed with the no-nonsense engineers of the Construction Division of the Resettlement Administration. (Several of the latter, in fact, had been demoted by Lansill and Vinton from the drawing boards to the field.)[21] In addition to animosity, there were frequent snarls in the red tape generated by the Management Division, an agency in charge of tenant selection at all resettlement communities—both farm and non-farm. The Management Division eventually assumed control over rent collections and the resolution of local tax arrangements in the three fledgling greenbelt towns. Far more amicable relations prevailed between the planners and Adrian Dornbush, director of a Special Skills Division, who commissioned a handful of sculptors and artists through the Works Progress Administration (WPA) for incidental chores.[22]

Clearly, by the time actual planning began in late 1936, the Suburban Division was a hydra-headed and highly specialized organization. It was unarguably over-qualified and over-salaried for what had initially been promoted as an attack on the housing problems of the poor. Moreover, in the hermetic setting of the Suburban Division, the planners talked mainly among themselves, well beyond earshot of political rumblings.

CHAPTER THREE
From Farm Land to Federal Land

WHILE the planners were at work on early drafts of land use and architectural plans, construction crews and land agents of the Resettlement Administration were encountering a complicated world. The Construction Division commenced work on the Beltsville, Maryland, site (later named Greenbelt) almost immediately after Roosevelt officially authorized the Division's budget in late September, 1935. Unfortunately, town planning had scarcely begun before relief laborers from Washington were sent out to the site, and to keep them busy, foremen put the men to work digging a lake. Meanwhile, the land agents attached to Dudley's section were struggling desperately to beat an early December deadline which Lansill had set for land acquisition. In the final weeks of September and in early October, there were four projects besides the one in Maryland under consideration. Two of these were more or less certain—Greenbrook near Newark, New Jersey, and Greenhills near Cincinnati, Ohio. Two other cities were still in close competition for a greenbelt town—St. Louis, favored by both Dudley and Vinton, and finally, Milwaukee.[1]

In all four cities, land agents were working almost around the clock, seven days a week.[2] By way of contrast, the Research Section under Vinton had proceeded with all due caution in narrowing the choice to four or five cities. Beginning in June, 1935, the Section had compiled crude economic and social profiles for twenty-five metropolitan areas in order to determine which of them might best accommodate a project. The objective was to locate those urban areas having a stable manufacturing base, where outlying land was cheap and available and, very importantly, where the political climate likely would favor public works. In Cincinnati, for example, the political competence of the city and county planning department, in addition to the predominantly German-American character of the city, were among the advantages noted by the Research Section. According to one agency report, Germanic peoples in general exhibited such commendable characteristics as industriousness, thrift, love of music, art, drama, and horticulture, and displayed "maternal efficiency."[3]

Milwaukee also was highly considered because of its Teutonic heritage, though a whole host of other factors entered into the final choice. In particular, a sympathetic reception for the resettlement project seemed assured in a city notable for the socialist orientation of its labor councils and political machinery. Daniel W. Hoan, the astute mayor of the city, presided over a reformist government with broad support among labor groups, although the Research Section may have stretched the truth slightly when it observed in its report on Milwaukee: "The friendly attitude of the local government is largely responsible for the fact that violence has been almost entirely absent from Milwaukee strikes."[4] In fact, Milwaukee was just as prone to labor disturbances as any other city in the Midwest. In 1934, for example, streetcar workers in Milwaukee had won a contested contract by demolishing dozens of cars and trolley poles with the help of unemployed workers.[5]

Perhaps the greatest advantage Milwaukee had was its reputation for metropolitan planning. In 1923, socialist Milwaukee had been one of the first municipalities in America to help finance and plan an inner city public housing project made up of single-family dwellings. Termed Garden Homes, the project was laid out according to English garden city principles (even many of the street names were those of planned communities in England). Milwaukee also was among the first places to adopt a county-wide zoning ordinance in 1927. With the onset of the national recession in the 1930's, Mayor Hoan had petitioned Washington for federal assistance in a public housing program that would follow the example of the Garden Homes.[6] These hopes were raised briefly in 1934 when Milwaukee played host to an international tour of housing experts, including Americans Ernest J. Bohn and Henry Wright, and the English garden city planner Sir Raymond Unwin. During a pre-luncheon discussion with Milwaukee planners, Unwin expressed the prevalent opinion that "this tendency to move out is very healthy and I think there is infinitely more danger in trying to bolster up a desire to live in the center than doing a little too much to live on the outside . . . . To me, the desirable life is to live in a one-family house with a garden."[7]

Eager though Milwaukee was for more public housing—and federal funds to construct such units—civic leaders also were anxious to retain local control. Between February and July of 1935, for example, a Milwaukee engineer working with the FERA, Mendel Glickman, presented a series of proposals for one or two cooperative farms to be located on one of fourteen sites outside the city. Ideally the sites were to be situated along an eighty-one-mile stretch of a projected county parkway then under construction with the help of federal relief labor.[8] C. B. Whitnall, a tireless housing reformer and planning advocate in Milwaukee, extracted a number of concessions from Glickman, including the agreement that the project should be thought of as "garden homesteads." These were to be designed by landscape architects in the county's planning department and were to house low-income workers, rather than the urban unemployed. Finally, however, the idea was dropped when Whitnall and others began to fear that this experiment in collectivism would not succeed among those "who have suffered all their life through exploitation."[9]

Whereas Glickman tried, without success, to work with official committees, the Resettlement Administration entered the city by the back door. Harold Gelnaw, acting on Dudley's orders, studiously avoided contact with local planners in the county courthouse as well as with officials in city hall. Dudley suspected, and rightly so, that once word was out on the massive federal land purchase, prices throughout Milwaukee County would soar.[10] Between July 26 and August 5, 1935, Gelnaw lived a monkish existence in Milwaukee. Headquartered in a downtown hotel, and telling no one of his assignment, Gelnaw nevertheless managed to complete an extensive report on the Milwaukee metropolis, including its housing, labor situation, transportation, and real estate structure.[11]

Like Gelnaw, the land agents were truly a breed apart from the rest of the Suburban Division personnel. As Dudley later recalled, all of his negotiators were professional real estate brokers; none were interested in government careers; and most, probably all, were skeptical about the New Deal. Nevertheless, according to Dudley, they had the "know how to get things done . . . . They were primarily men of powerful persuasion—men who knew how to get people to do what they didn't want to do—men who worked hard to achieve difficult goals." Throughout the acquisition phase, Gelnaw was the sole government negotiator, assisted by two local real estate firms.[12]

Vinton, however, remained unsure about the appropriateness of Milwaukee for a greenbelt town. With regard to need, Vinton doubted that Milwaukee's well-publicized housing shortage was as serious as in other cities. Moreover, Vinton, Tugwell, and Lansill were anxious to avoid any semblance of competition with Harold Ickes, Director of the Progress Works Administration (PWA), who had established a small housing fiefdom in Milwaukee with one project—Parklawn Apartments—underway and another planned.[13]

After conferring for an afternoon and an evening with Jacob Crane in Chicago, Vinton and Dudley visited Gelnaw in Milwaukee on August 5, 1935. They found him in his hotel room, which by this time was cluttered with the debris of two weeks' reconnaissance. But Vinton was less interested in the maps and charts than in the political ambiance of Milwaukee. Dudley watched in dismay as Vinton left the hotel on his way to City Hall.[14] The project's cover, if not blown, was at least askew.

Mayor Hoan, for once caught off guard, greeted Vinton cordially and promptly directed him to the county building where the federal official met A. E. Howard, an engineer and planner for Milwaukee County. During the next few hours, Vinton and Howard drove around the city discussing a likely spot for the resettlement project. Finally, Howard showed Vinton one of the spots under consideration for Glickman's homesteads. It was a section of rolling, pond-studded dairy farms eight miles southwest of the central city—nearly equidistant from major industrial concentrations and remote from the apartment project of the PWA. Unbeknownst to Vinton, Gelnaw was driving around the same area with Dudley, who also thought the land attractive and well-suited to a resettlement effort. In order to avoid undue speculation around Milwaukee, Vinton persuaded Gelnaw to

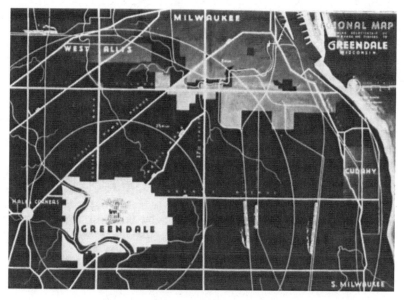

As indicated by this 1936 Resettlement Administration map, Greendale offered the scenic and sanitary benefits of the countryside as well as accessibility to the downtown and industrial areas of Milwaukee. *Source: Greendale Historical Society.*

introduce him to a local real estate agent as a representative of an anonymous Chicago investment firm that intended to purchase land in the vicinity. It was not until that evening, while on the train back to Washington, that Dudley and Vinton discovered the coincidence of their chosen sites.[15]

For the next two weeks, Dudley and Gelnaw shuttled between Milwaukee and Washington to confer on land prices and the logistics of securing land options. While the Milwaukee project was expected to require about 5,000 acres of land, twice that amount was scheduled to be optioned. The realtors, commissioned by Gelnaw, started to work at once. Nine days after Lansill's official authorization on August 20 a total of 273 acres already were under option by the government.[16]

From late August to late November of 1935, Gelnaw prodded his realtors in the field and complained to Dudley that he needed more help. Certainly Gelnaw had his hands full, but more agents would have served no purpose, for the real obstacle in the way of land acquisition was the recalcitrance of landowners. Convinced that their lands were about to be snapped up for speculative purposes, the farmers played hard to get. Land that the government had predicted could be purchased for one or two hundred dollars per acre soared to asking prices of over four hundred dollars an acre. Gelnaw himself admitted that sometimes he had to spend from one to five hours at a time trying to extract a signature from an unwilling landowner.[17] A few owners claimed illiteracy; some mentioned sentimental ties to their land; others cited family obligations, such as one spinster who was willing to sell but could not persuade any of her fourteen half-siblings. But in only one instance did Gelnaw completely give up. After intermittent efforts over seven months to encourage Herman Bohn, an elderly farmer, to lower his asking price, the government's ace admitted "the futility of any further attempts." Gelnaw recommended, shortly thereafter, that the government meet Bohn's demands.[18]

Faced with such headstrong resistance (which Dudley quickly attributed to the German ancestry of many of the farmers), the government considered condemnation proceedings, but that tactic was ruled out because it would have meant several years spent in the courts. Gelnaw discovered, however, that the mere threat of condemnation was usually enough to convince a landowner to sell. The Land Section at Milwaukee also resorted to numerous administrative shortcuts in order to speed the proceedings. Agents, for example, were permitted to use local option forms instead of the more complicated federal documents that, in any event, had not yet been approved by the Legal Division when land acquisition began. Dudley gave credit to Lansill for his "fierce fighting" on behalf of the Land Section whenever its casual methods met with the censure of "the red tape artists" and the "visionless" bureaucrats in the Resettlement Administration.[19]

Finally Gelnaw doggedly maneuvered his land-purchasing agents to surrounding a core of hold-outs in the center of the tract. Nearly 3,500 acres of land had been optioned by September 23, 1935. Then word came from Washington that the Milwaukee project had been suspended in favor of the one in St. Louis. Gelnaw was reassigned in short order, first to Cincinnati, then to St. Louis. His replacement in Milwaukee was John Bay, who formerly had appraised land for railway companies in St. Louis and San Francisco. Agent Bay had been in Milwaukee for less than a month when Gelnaw arrived back on the scene with a new set of marching orders. Conflict with real estate interests in St. Louis had forced the Resettlement Administration to abandon its project there and, instead, to intensify its efforts in Milwaukee County. Greenbelt parcels to the south and west of the proposed parkways were now cut from the acquisition map, and the negotiating team, bolstered by several agents from the moribund St. Louis project, concentrated on a tract outlined by the county highway system and parkway.[20]

The increasingly frenetic pace of the Land Section and its Machiavellian approach to land acquisition contributed to an early, albeit temporary, breakdown of rapport with local planners. On September 5, 1935, Charles Bennett, a nationally known Milwaukee city planner, wrote to Tugwell asking what projects the Resettlement Administration intended for Milwaukee County. Tugwell, at a loss for a reply, delayed until Vinton was able to contact Howard by telephone in October and question him on the matter of leaks—of which there had been several. In the meantime, Gelnaw moved to another hotel. It is remarkable, considering the enormity of the land deal, that Gelnaw managed to maintain such a low profile. Reportedly not even the legal counsel of the Resettlement Administration in Wisconsin had any notion of "who and where" Gelnaw was.[21]

Telegrams criss-crossed the country: the planners in Washington advised the purchase of more land, and agents in Milwaukee asked for permission to trim the total. Meanwhile, Gelnaw planted conflicting rumors to the effect that low-cost apartment housing would be built in the area or that the government needed land for a munitions factory—rumors that presumably would appeal either to the cupidity of landowners or to their patriotism. Indeed, such tactics left some farmers with bitter feelings toward the federal government. One woman, in 1976, recalled the loss of her family's farm four decades earlier, and stated bluntly: "We were deceived into selling our land." She contended that the agents had duped her father by telling him the property was needed for a new veterans' home; the agents asked him, as a patriotic gesture, to sell the farm for a reduced price. It was only later, after the announcement appeared in the newspaper, that her father determined the true purpose of the acquisition program.[22]

After spending a futile day in the field on November 25, Dudley, Gelnaw, and Bay bundled up their appraisals and reports and hurried to Washington on the evening train. Two days later Tugwell approved the purchase of a preliminary tract of 4,366 acres out of the 10,760 acres that had been optioned. Dudley estimated the cost at $1.55 million, or $356 per acre, a figure that was substantially lower than the $1.8 million established by an independent appraiser. After the first payment checks were mailed from Washington a week later, some local resistance began to fade, and a few landowners even consented to prices lower than the option figures. A savings of almost $7,500 was achieved in the final weeks of 1935, and as the deadline for ground-breaking approached, the legal formalities of the land purchase were given highest priority. Special clauses in the land titles gave government workers access to the properties while the arrangements for payment were being finalized.[23]

During the winter months of 1936, further reductions in both the total area and the prices brought the tract size down to 3,511 acres. Gradually, over the course of the summer, the parcel size was cut to 3,410 acres and the cost to $1,200,000, or an average per-acre price of some $372. This amounted to about $100 more per acre than the government paid at Greenhills, Ohio, and approximately $200 more per acre than at Greenbelt, Maryland. Its greater proximity to the central city explained, in part, the higher cost of land at Greendale, which was approximately three and one-half miles from the edge of Milwaukee. Greenbelt, Maryland, was twelve miles from Washington, D.C., and realized land costs of $165 per acre, while Greenhills, Ohio, was four and one-half miles from Cincinnati and had a price of $268 per acre. Also, the land at Greenbelt was almost entirely in possession of the federal government when the Suburban Division was inaugurated. Moreover, the brokerage contracts at Milwaukee were unusual. At St. Louis, at Bound Brook, New Jersey (the Greenbrook project), and in Cincinnati (Greenhills), real estate brokers collected their commissions from the individuals who sold the land. In Milwaukee, on the

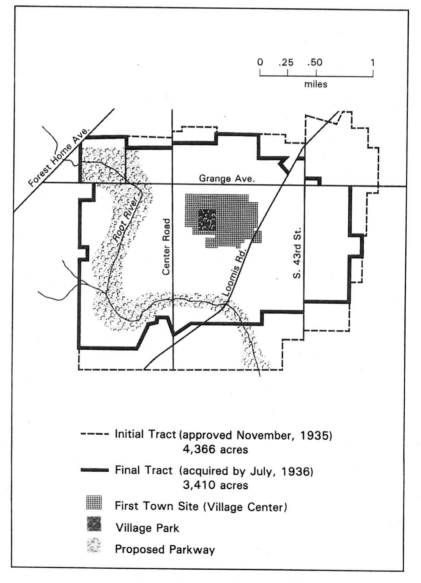

Land acquisition at Greendale, November, 1935, to July, 1936. *Source: Based on maps in J.S. Lansill Papers.*

other hand, commissions of 5 per cent were factored into the price of the land and paid directly to the real estate brokers by the government, both to alleviate accounting chores and "in order that the brokers might thus feel more loyal to the Government than to the owners." As a result, land prices at Greendale contained hidden brokerage fees. Salaries for the federal land agents at Greendale totaled about $20,640; salaries amounted to about $31,700 at Greenbelt, Maryland, $26,500 at Greenbrook, New Jersey, and $26,130 at Greenhills, Ohio.[24]

For months Vinton, Dudley, and Gelnaw had spent much of their waking and sleeping hours on trains. The government could have asked little more of its servants than it did of these men and the scores of assistants who gave their efforts to the greenbelt towns program. But it is obvious, too, that under the pressure of politically expedient deadlines, many Suburban Division personnel began to exhibit a curious paranoia. In the end, the land acquisition phase turned into a grim escapade with all the trappings of a military operation. Dudley, the head of operations, attributed much of the success of his Land Section to the perseverance of the staff: "Their enthusiasm was stubborn, their convictions certain. They had the will to win a great battle—to overcome red tape, delays, obstinate land owners, and intangible land values." Nonetheless, Dudley admitted that the covert nature of the operation had actually done little to lower prices. In 1934, Henry Wright already had touched upon a relevant truth while speaking to Milwaukee planners. "I am struck with the fact," he said, "that most of us who are most sincere are still chasing population around."[25]

CHAPTER FOUR

Public Policy and Local Opinion

THE Resettlement Administration was caught off guard on December 4, 1935, when the *Milwaukee Journal* inaccurately reported that a "Tugwelltown" project outside the city, containing "hundreds of small houses on two or three acre tracts," would be available on long-term amortized mortgages. One day later the *Journal* published a map showing the approximate boundaries of the government's tract southwest of Milwaukee, and provided an illustration of housing in a Tugwelltown (actually a community for subsistence homesteaders) already under construction at Elkins, West Virginia.[1] Shortly after the stories came out, Frank H. Osterlind, an attorney for the Resettlement Administration in Milwaukee, informed Rexford Tugwell that the source of the leak was "a group of officials from Washington" who had talked indiscreetly in the lobby of the Schroeder Hotel in Milwaukee. Osterlind urged Tugwell to send someone from Washington to Milwaukee to put the best face possible on the situation; however, the Washington office, a month before the "damaging articles" appeared, had already decided to let Harold Gelnaw deliver a formal announcement once all of the land had been optioned.[2]

Thus, on December 15, 1935, the crack negotiator found himself before an assembly of city and county officials, U.S. Congressman Raymond J. Cannon (a Democrat from Wauwatosa, Wisconsin), and the press. Gelnaw did his best to assure those gathered that the "government town" was a one-time experiment in middle-income housing, and not the harbinger of a national housing policy. In deference to the labor representatives on hand, Gelnaw spoke of the thousands of workers in the construction trades who would find employment on the project.[3] And clearly there was a need for such an impetus. After 1929, largely because of the economic depression, the Milwaukee County Regional Planning Department had reported a dearth of applications for suburban plats while a sparse demand for outlying homes was being satisfied primarily by "bungalow garages" priced at very modest levels.[4] Following Gelnaw's conference, scores of people lined the sidewalks outside the county building to apply for a home at Greendale, although no doubt many of the hopefuls were as confused about the nature of the project as were the mayors of two nearby industrial suburbs who tried to persuade Washington to locate such pro-

21

jects in their communities. One mayor wrote to assure Tugwell that factory foremen would give tenants sufficient time off to tend gardens.[5]

Compared to the stanch local resistance that had greeted the Suburban Division in St. Louis and Newark, the opposition in Milwaukee proved mild indeed. Of critical significance was the fact that, despite some grumblings about federal intervention in the private sector, neither the *Milwaukee Journal* nor the Milwaukee Real Estate Board took any concerted action against the project.[6] The Board, which had just endured the loss of its long-time president (who was, incidentally, a city planning enthusiast), vacillated for days after the announcement of the project. All six of its divisions—city planning, subdivision, taxation, builders, brokers, mortgages, and finance—parleyed and decided, in effect, to decide nothing—neither to support nor to condemn the resettlement town. The *Milwaukee Journal* published the charges made on the floor of the U.S. Senate by Michigan Senator Arthur Vandenberg—a grim critic of the New Deal—who stated that excessive amounts of money had been paid for certain parcels of land for the Milwaukee project. The *Journal*, however, admitted that it could uncover no evidence of wrongdoing.[7]

On January 2, 1936, Suburban Division officials and planners met with local builders and officers of the Milwaukee Building and Loan Association. At the session, John Lansill tried to establish a conciliatory tone by apologizing for the secretive land dealing. He then asked that Milwaukeeans consider "this a joint federal-county project" and promised "to avoid any hint of paternalism." But the builders and the bankers were in no mood for diplomacy. The president of the Milwaukee Building and Loan Association put some hard questions to Lansill and Crane concerning the tax liabilities of their new community, and intermittently the president of the Milwaukee Building and Trades Council pushed for some guarantees that mainly union men would be hired for construction work.[8]

In mid-January, Frank H. Osterlind, regional attorney for the Resettlement Administration, wrote in confidence to a Washington colleague that he perceived a "growing conspiracy" against the federal housing effort in Milwaukee. One identifiable enemy, the United Taxpayers Cooperative Association, was not to be taken seriously; the Resettlement Administration did see a "dangerous" foe in the Wisconsin Building and Loan League, particularly its Milwaukee affiliates, but Osterlind considered them "vulnerable" to investigations by Wisconsin's state banking commission or perhaps by federal tax authorities. In the weeks that followed, the Resettlement Administration remained confident that it could outlast its detractors in Milwaukee—provided the realtors in the city remained disunited. Regional coordinator Fred Naumer consulted with several brokerage firms in March and received the encouraging opinion that "any activity in the development of farm lands . . . has a stimulating effect on surrounding property and enhances its value."[9] If, indeed, this was the opinion of most realtors, then the Greendale plan was safe from that quarter.

When, on May 18, 1936, word reached Milwaukee of the defeat handed the Resettlement Administration in its Bound Brook, New Jersey, case, a group of Milwaukee realtors, city landlords, and a minority of the Milwaukee building and loan associations declared their joint intention to seek a similar restraining order against Greendale and Parklawn.[10] The Resettlement Administration still was unruffled and proceeded at Greendale and elsewhere as if nothing had happened. Construction activities begun in late March proceeded with increasing numbers of workers on the site. Throughout the summer of 1936 the *Milwaukee Journal* printed far more cheers than jeers for Greendale, while the *Milwaukee Sentinel* remained silent.[11] In fact, the first mention of the project did not appear in the *Sentinel* until December 16, 1935—almost two weeks after the initial *Journal* article.[12]

As officials had predicted, it was among the realtors in Milwaukee that the Resettlement Administration found its most ardent supporters, including the president of the organization. The most vocal backing, nevertheless, came from organized labor. Within forty-eight hours after news of the suit by the Milwaukee Building and Loan Association was released, the Federated Trades Council, the Building and Trades Council, the Milwaukee Federation of Labor, and the Polish Citizen's Club registered unanimous support for the greenbelt project in a flood of letters and telegrams to resettlement officials in Washington, D.C., and Madison, Wisconsin.[13] The American Legion Post in Hales Corners, the village adjacent to the project site, sent its endorsement directly to Roosevelt, with copies to Tugwell and members of Congress. On May 19, the *Milwaukee Leader*, a socialist paper with a circulation of about 50,000, and according to Vinton's Research Section, "the organ of organized labor," predicted a countersuit. Labor was joined in the pro-settlement movement by various Wisconsin Progressives, led by Governor Philip F. La Follette and his brother "Young Bob," U.S. Senator Robert M. La Follette.[14]

Finally, on August 29, 1936, a minority group of the Milwaukee Building and Loan Association filed a complaint against the Greendale project in the U.S. District Court of Washington, D.C. The suit was never argued, however, principally because the Resettlement Administration had skillfully defused the main issues. The Black-Bankhead Act, passed by Congress and subsequently signed by President Roosevelt on June 29, 1937, subjected Greendale and other resettlement projects to local taxes—fulfilling a payment-in-lieu-of-taxes (PILOT) pledge that Tugwell had made months earlier.[15] A second cause for complaint was the possible depreciation of local property values caused by an exodus of potential tenants and home buyers from the private market. The Resettlement Administration countered by recalling the city's housing shortage—the same that Vinton had once doubted so strongly. The Resettlement Administration also was able to quote the Acting Comptroller-General of the United States, who discounted the view that there was anything unconstitutional in making "available in suburban areas housing facilities and agriculture and gardening plots" to lower-income groups.[16]

The inconsequential attack upon resettlement in Milwaukee was hardly the "campaign of misrepresentation" that Tugwell later accused his critics of mounting. Nor could the opposition be fairly labeled as "curbstone critics," a description once made by city planners Charles B. Bennett and Richard B. Fernbach in the pages of the *Planners' Journal*.[17] Rather, the Resettlement Administration's bout in Milwaukee was above-board and was undertaken in a gentlemanly manner. Not so elsewhere, however. The *Chicago American*, for instance, devoted virtually an entire front page to a story on "the communistic town" that Tugwell was building only ninety miles from Chicago and just eight miles outside Milwaukee. The tabloid carefully edited an interview with Fred Naumer and painted a picture of communes and commissars at Greendale—guaranteed incomes for farmers, a despotic town-manager form of government, cooperative stores, and public ownership of all property.[18] While few contemporary accounts were as sensational as this one in the *Chicago American*, others in a more rational tone asserted that the greenbelt towns were setting a dangerous, even un-American precedent in real estate and property rights.[19] Hoping to divert such critics away from the program, Tugwell announced his decision to resign his government post in mid-November of 1936, shortly after he toured Greenbelt, Maryland, with the President.[20]

Although resettlement officials refused to accede to their critics, more than a modicum of truth was contained in some of the criticisms made of Greendale. Harold G. Siljan, president of the Milwaukee Real Estate Board in 1936, asserted that the government's housing activities had "resulted in failure because they have provided neither low rent nor housing for the low income group." Many Milwaukeeans sympathetic to the government's cause admitted the veracity of such comments. Milwaukee County planner and venerable garden city enthusiast C. B. Whitnall bared his disappointment when he mentioned Greendale and Parklawn before the Milwaukee Common Council in 1937: "The sad feature of all efforts made thus far is that they do not reach the family whose income is less than $1000 per annum."[21]

Whatever benefits Greendale and Parklawn had provided by way of relief labor, they contributed little to a broad program of housing reform. Mayor Hoan, a familiar supplicant at the doors of national housing agencies after 1932, temporarily despaired of help from Washington. In the pages of the *Architectural Forum* (May, 1937), Hoan commended local builder Frank Kirkpatrick, who was somehow staying solvent on profits from low-income rentals. "I am not as much interested in who is providing the capital," said Hoan, "as I am in seeing that such housing is provided."[22] More importantly, neither Greendale nor Parklawn was on the scale of federal aid required by Milwaukee and other American cities. Information released by the mayor's office in 1940 claimed that federal projects "did not make a dent in the housing situation." Instead, the vacancy rate in Milwaukee's rental market had fallen by 66 per cent from its level in 1938, the first year that both Parklawn and Greendale were in operation.[23] Future relations between Washington and city hall would have to be based upon earnest dialogue rather than paternalistic plans.

CHAPTER FIVE
A Design for Land and People

THE planners for the Greendale project began arriving in Washington shortly after the New Year of 1936. Walter Kroening, a supervising engineer on the Greendale engineering section, reminisced in 1948 about the pell-mell of planning against the backdrop of Victorian bric-a-brac that filled the Walsh mansion: "[There were] assorted cupids frolicking on the ceilings . . . . As our staff grew, it was necessary, on occasion, to utilize for a conference room what was once the commodious private bath of Lady McLean."[1] Until April of that year, day and night, the drafting boards of the Suburban Division were rarely without a staff member bending over, shirt sleeves rolled up, laboring over one of the myriad drawings that the Construction Division would require.

December in Wisconsin was hardly the best month and place in which to begin outdoor work, but the Suburban Division had little choice. On December 4, 1935, Gelnaw employed an engineering firm in Milwaukee and insisted that land surveys on the project site be completed as quickly as possible. The surveyors entered the area five days later, and Peets reconnoitered the site during the following week.[2] Severely cold weather and heavy snows, however, made accurate site analysis almost impossible. Drifting snow buried the site—in some spots up to depths of ten and twelve feet—and forced crews to suspend survey work in mid-February. Soil borings and aerial photographs of the site had to be retaken in the spring. In January, the planners were still anticipating a project area totaling about 5,250 acres—nearly one-third more land than was eventually purchased.[3]

In February, 1936, Frederick Bigger, the planning coordinator, met with all of the greenbelt town planners in Washington to prepare a preliminary budget for each project. This was the first indication of how many homes the towns would contain based upon available funds. It was decided that Greendale and Greenbrook each would receive just over $7 million out of the total budget of $31 million. Greenbelt, Maryland, and Greenhills, Ohio, together received somewhat less than half of the remaining $17 million. About $7 million would go to Greenbelt (under construction since October, 1935), while Greenhills was to receive $8.75 million. The reserve funds were later used to cover cost overruns and administrative operations. After the Greenbrook project was halted in May, 1936, the money allocated to it (except the $6,500 paid to land agents) was spread among the other projects.[4]

The number of dwelling units scheduled at each site was determined according to a variety of factors such as local wage scales, site topography, housing styles, and costs of materials. Greendale and Greenbrook were planned to receive an initial allotment of 750 units each, while Greenbelt and Greenhills were planned for 1,000 units each. The Greendale planners were unique in venturing an optimal size for their project—3,000 units contained in three primary residential groupings representing a population of roughly 12,000 persons.[5] The first sets of Greendale plans were

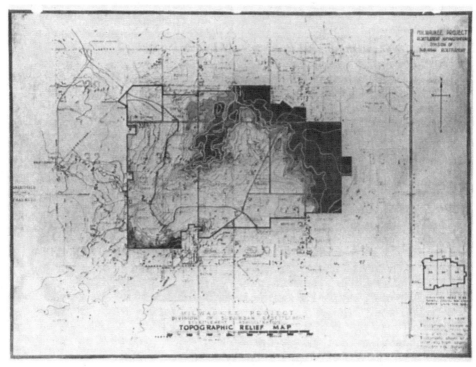

The hilly character of the Greendale project site (darker areas) was apparent in this 1936 topographic map.
Source: J.S. Lansill Papers.

completed in the final week of March, 1936, a few days before the planners received a corrected topographic survey. For amusement, they relaxed briefly with their spouses and selected a proper name for the town. According to a rigorous logic (born, perhaps, of fatigue), all streets, except for the main village thoroughfares, were named for botanical species arrayed alphabetically and ordered by housing blocks in a clockwise progression throughout the entire village area—Apple, Apricot, Basswood, Clover, and so on.[6]

The design of the greenbelt towns proceeded in tandem with social research on the housing preferences of blue-collar families. Early in 1936 the Research Section required Fred Naumer's regional office in Madison, Wisconsin, to distribute several thousand questionnaires among Milwaukee labor unions, churches, civic groups, and ethnic associations. About 2,200 questionnaires were returned, but the Research Section utilized only some 1,000 received from families whose reported annual incomes were between $1,000 and $2,000. It was calculated that within this income range, families spent, on the average, $21 to $28 per month in rent, a range that ultimately coincided rather closely with anticipated rents in Greendale.[7] The Suburban Division took an inordinate amount of time and paper to calculate a reasonable rent scale. Clarence Stein finished the first study of rents and operating costs in early December, 1935, and warned that unless "radical savings" could be gained for the tenants with regard to schools and the personal expense of commuting to and from jobs, and unless each of the towns was enlarged to house at least 4,000 people, then families with annual earnings of less than $1,250 would be effectively excluded.[8] The Research Section later determined that the income limit at Greendale could be substantially lowered for childless couples and single persons who might be assigned to two- and three-room apartments renting for $12 and $16 per month; nevertheless, it was believed that if total revenues ever were to match operating costs, then not more than ninety of these small units could be built out of a projected 750 units. In addition to the fiscal constraints of low-income housing, planners feared that deprived families would degrade the social life of the community. Peets, for example, observed that until the character of the project had been established, Greendale "was not the place to house the least fortunate economic group."[9]

On the basis of the survey returns, the Research Section was able to profile a typical Greendale family of four. Its principal wage earner (male, of course) traveled fifteen or twenty minutes to a skilled factory job that paid about $1,400 annually. The sample pool was younger than the general urban population of Milwaukee and of the United States as reported by the 1930 federal census. Nearly 70 per cent of the Greendale group was below the age of thirty-seven years, while over one-half the sample group was below the age of fourteen years. These figures were approximately 60 per cent higher than those reported either for Milwaukee or the urban United States.[10] This forecast of village age structures had strong implications for community planning: recreational facilities would have to be given high priority, larger homes would be required for growing families, and the cost of education would threaten to become a major stumbling block in financing town operations.

The survey did, however, calm initial fears that the workers would not have adequate access to places of employment. The planners shelved early considerations of some form of public transit—trolley or shuttle bus—primarily because Milwaukee's industry was scattered throughout such a wide zone of the metropolitan fringe. Fortunately, Vinton's survey showed that 61 per cent of the sample group owned automobiles, although only 28 per cent used their automobiles to commute to jobs.[11] Nonetheless, Vinton was convinced that Greendale would become a village of automobile users, if not owners. His calculations had proved that the car was the cheapest conveyance, and it was common knowledge, according to Vinton, that workers across the country were sharing rides. Consequently, 90 per cent of Greendale units were given garages.[12]

The questionnaires also suggested a wide variety of housing arrangements and community facilities. The tabulations provided a crude basis for judgments about such details as floor space and numbers of rooms. It uncovered, too, the pent-up longings of home-hungry apartment dwellers. Surely, the questionnaire was a wonder to the families who received it—a chance to fantasize gracious lives. Nearly everyone wanted a flower garden (94.5%), a vegetable garden (92.1%), and a library (86.1%). A majority wanted a swimming pool (78.8%), a hall (60.8%), and baseball fields (57.0%), while a large minority requested such facilities as a beauty parlor (45.8%), bowling alleys (45.5%), tennis courts (41.2%), and a tavern (34.9%).[13]

Several of the volunteered responses were deemed reasonable enough to be incorporated into the community plan; these included requests for an automobile service station, a movie theater, a drug store, health services, a barber shop, and village fire and police agencies. A few items, however, were clearly out of the question, such as a dance hall and communal

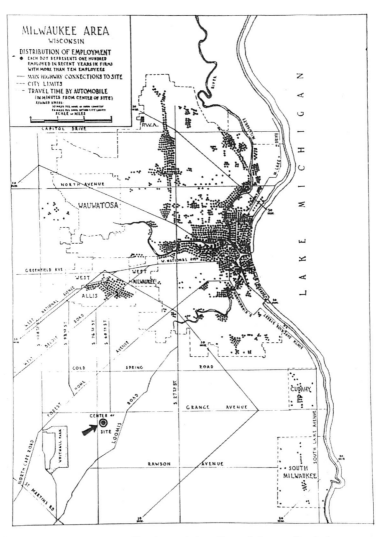

The planning staff estimated that Greendale was situated within twenty minutes' driving time from most of Milwaukee's industrial concentrations. *Source: J.S. Lansill Papers.*

chicken coops. The swimming pool also was eliminated, but not the tennis courts; nor was a rustic, earth-and-stone amphitheater, which later was fashioned near the community building.

The planners readily concurred with the one in three respondents who wanted a tavern in their Wisconsin village. On the other hand, they were forbidden by constitutional law from building churches on the project. The most that could be done for the many who specified religious affiliations—over 90 per cent of the sample—was to set aside future church sites.[14]

Despite the thoroughness of Vinton's work, however, the survey overlooked attitudes about living in such a singular housing project. Crane spoke about the "carefully appraised desires" of the future residents, and Bentley concurred that the questionnaire gave a "degree of reality and

Resettlement Administration diagram reflecting the agency's canvass of Milwaukee civic and labor organizations as to what features were most desired by working-class families. *Source: J.S. Lansill Papers.*

What Milwaukee's Prospective Tenants Want...

90% LIBRARY
80% SWIMMING POOL
66% COMMUNITY HALL
61% PLAY GROUND
56% BALL DIAMOND
48% BEAUTY PARLOR
44% BOWLING ALLEY
43% TENNIS COURT
33% TAVERN
29% FOOTBALL FIELD
27% BASKETBALL COURT
22% HANDBALL COURT
21% RESTAURANT
12% DAY NURSERY

individuality" to the people who wanted Greendale homes. The truth of
the matter was, as Peets noted, that the planners usually relied upon
agency guidelines and professional experience, and not upon the example
of a "folk-way" or some indigenous "pattern of home-building," as they
often contended.[15]

At the crux of the greenbelt town plan was the desire to demonstrate
frugality and balance in land use. Restraint in the allocation of property
for homes and streets acquired the highest priority, ahead of incidental
experiments in resident cooperatives and technical conveniences. The real
issue, then, was a conservationist land-planning model. Accordingly, the
total residential area at Greendale—both immediate and future—
amounted to less than 40 per cent of the total 3,511 acres, the size of the
tract in June, 1936. The village space included three discrete town units
(525 acres altogether), suburban homesites (475 acres divided into one- or
two-acre lots), allotment gardens for the use of the villagers (fifty-five
acres), an industrial loop (ten acres) to provide light factory work for the
women of the town, and town parks (325 acres).[16] Such was the land-use
scheme for the foreseeable future.

In terms of immediate development, the settlement pattern was much
less extensive. All suburban homesites, for example, were delayed indefi-
nitely, as were all recreation areas except for 180 acres of village parkland
and fifteen acres of resident gardens. The first town site consisted of only
155 acres with a gross housing density of approximately five units per acre
and a much higher net density within the actual housing sections. The con-
figuration of the pre-existing county highway system effectively determined the situation of the village. The town was centered within a crude
parallelogram of major traffic outfalls, county roads, and the proposed
parkway drive. These "regional" arteries fed into village streets approximately ninety feet wide which skirted the residential area.[17]

Excluding the surface area of the county roads, the first town plan called
for a permanent greenbelt of approximately 2,000 acres. The designations
and extent of land-use categories included 170 acres along the Root River
for a shelter belt of 500 willow trees (contributed by the Wisconsin State
Forestry Department), 560 acres to be deeded to the county park system
for the parkway, and 1,370 acres in farms.[18] Greendale was unique among
the greenbelt towns, because, in the opinion of Peets and Crane, "the
greenbelt area comprises first class agricultural land," divided among sev-
enteen dairy farms totaling 1,000 acres plus twenty-three small truck and
poultry farms.[19] In order to maintain agricultural productivity and to co-

ordinate the rural plan with the rest of the resettlement program, the planners conceived a range of options. The one most favored by the planners was the consolidation of all agricultural lands into a single cooperative society where individual farmers and farm families could participate on a salary basis. The "least advanced program" consisted of leasing the lands to tenant families. This most expedient measure was the one selected. A third intermediate program would have leased the land to individuals with opportunities to form a cooperative association for purchasing supplies and equipment. Farm produce then could have been sold to a consumers'

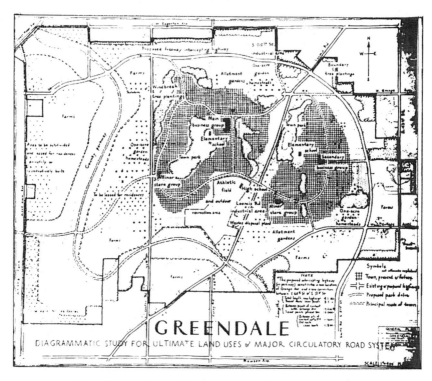

According to the original plans, farmsteads and copious parkland were to encompass three town units of Greendale. *Source: J.S. Lansill Papers.*

cooperative within the village. The planners also contemplated some exchanges of services, such as feeding the village's garbage to hogs in the rural area. To accommodate single farm laborers or bachelors holding jobs in the city, one of the farmhouses was to be converted into a boardinghouse.[20]

When considering physical design, the planners were concerned that they link the rural area to the village center by a network of pathways similar to the public rights-of-way that bisected the English countryside. Peets foresaw a natural history museum located in the middle of a recreation area replete with hiking and cross-country ski trails. "In the planting

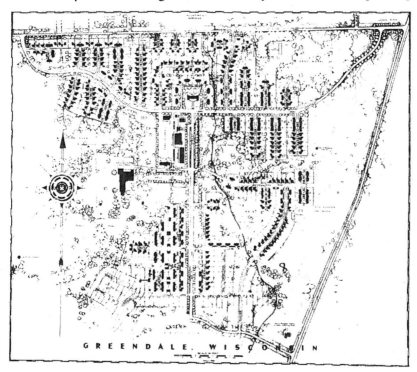

GREENDALE. WISCONSIN

In his residential site planning for Greendale (1938), Elbert Peets sought to combine the rusticity of the natural landscape with the formality of public groupings. *Source: J.S. Lansill Papers.*

of outlying parks and wildlife reservations," reported Peets, "we shall do whatever we can to preserve and create communities of native plants and we are planning a boundary-line walk, with other lanes running between the farms of the greenbelt so that our people may have close contact with the land and its plants and also with farm life and work." First, however, the planners wanted to bring the rural homes up to project standards of sanitation, convenience, and attractiveness. Rural planting and painting schemes were not to be phased into the esthetics of the village plan until electricity and running water had been installed in every farmhouse. Regional coordinator R. I. Nowell was a solitary voice in his concern for the preservation of indigenous farming practices, which, through diversification of animal husbandry and cropping cycles, reportedly had maintained a high level of soil fertility.[21]

In their rural program, Peets and Crane also hoped to restore and maintain historic buildings in the rural area. These included several lime kilns and the natal homestead of Jeremiah Curtin (c. 1840–1906), a noted Harvard University professor of linguistics and Abraham Lincoln's ambassador to Russia. With the assistance of a local chapter of the Daughters of the American Revolution, the Resettlement Administration restored the Curtin House, and in 1951, prior to the sale of the greenbelt lands by the government, the Curtin House was deeded to the Milwaukee County Historical Society. As early as 1935 the planners displayed a keen sensitivity to what they perceived as the pioneer heritage of the region: "Coming to Wisconsin, as we do, from outside the state, and claiming to be solicitous as to cultural values and the amenities of life, . . . we are particularly anxious not to do anything, in our modernization of the old farm houses and buildings, for which the future will blame us."[22]

Jacob Crane, together with John Lansill, believed that Greendale was the long-awaited opportunity to create a metropolitan land reserve, such as Stockholm, Sweden, already enjoyed. Crane suggested that the mayors of New York, Detroit, and Chicago might be persuaded to participate in greenbelt town projects at the borders of their own cities in order to control "wildcat subdividing" and to achieve a more equitable mix of social classes in the suburbs.[23] With few exceptions, planners of the 1930's had settled upon this concentric notion of the future metropolis—a thinly settled industrial core city ringed by compact communities and parkways. Implementing such a plan, however, proved to be far more difficult than writing about it, even in the heady days of the New Deal.

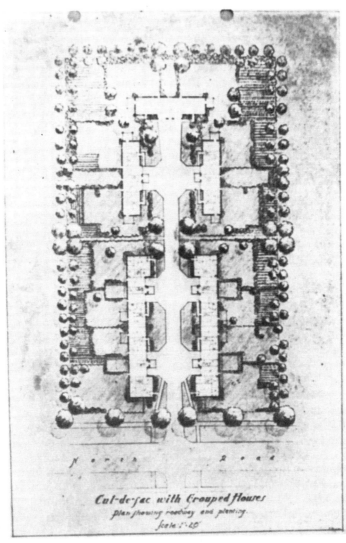

Cut-de-sac with Grouped Houses
plan showing roadway and planting.
scale 1" : 20'

In this early scheme for a section of Greendale, the entry lane and housing arrangement closely approximated that of Radburn, New Jersey. *Source: Greendale Historical Society.*

In the mid-1930's, the planned community in America that was most widely discussed and copied was Radburn, New Jersey, a project of the City Housing Corporation of New York.[24] Eugenie Ladner Birch has summarized the influence of this community, begun in 1928, on planners of that generation: "Although planners did not always practice according to the full Radburn ideal in this period, they believed they should aim for its objectiveness: decentralization, self-contained settlements, organized to promote environmental considerations by conserving open space, harnessing the automobile, and promoting community life."[25]

Already in 1930, for example, Milwaukee County planners had prepared a plan for a Radburn-type community on the off-chance that a large-scale developer might show interest. The Radburn ideal managed to incorporate principles from nearly every corner of the housing and community planning movement. These included sociologist Clarence Perry's neighborhood unit concept of housing blocks around a hub of public buildings, schools, and stores; a street plan that separated vehicular and pedestrian traffic by means of cul-de-sac residential groupings and underpasses; and most characteristically, superblocks of row houses connected by an integral park and pathway system.[26] The dominant paradigm, in other words, was the multi-cellular city that Peets described as "a new texture for this dispersion of the urban population, a texture that preserves much of the countryside, conforms to the best principles of regional traffic circulation, keeps land open for the gradual movement of industry, and groups the people into neighborhoods having a stimulating autonomy in many social ways, without giving up the sound foundation of participation in the industrial and economic life of the urban region."[27]

Here, then, was a means of controlling the city's growth without denying its right to grow, and a means of reaping the benefits of family living in the countryside without forgoing the cultural and economic advantages of the city.

The debt of Greendale to Radburn was especially apparent in the pedestrian scale of Greendale, in the central grouping of its public buildings and, most directly, in its street plan. At Greendale the main streets tapered off, first, into narrow, fifty- or forty-feet-wide collector streets, and finally into residential lanes, most of which terminated on cul-de-sacs (or "courts" as they were termed locally).

But while the Radburn idiom figured importantly in the overall plan, many of its aspects were rejected as inappropriate to Greendale. The land at Greendale offered a few level sites for the placement of a Radburn-type quadrangle or superblock of row houses, but the planners assumed that their midwestern public would prefer instead houses on "a definitely bounded and privately controlled lot." As architect Bentley stated, "The town will not be modernistic in the accepted sense. We want the people who live there to be happy and don't want to force upon them anything they don't want." In addition, the expansive town parks and pedestrian underpasses of Radburn were deemed too costly to replicate at Greendale, although careful street planning for the Wisconsin community was thought to have eliminated the necessity of frequent crosswalks. (To this day, Greendale has not suffered a pedestrian traffic fatality.)[28]

Rather than another Radburn, Greendale, according to Peets, "was to be a workingmen's town; in actuality and in appearance it must be direct, simple, and practical, free of snobbishness, not afraid of standardization."[29] The Greendale planning staff paid close, almost obsessive attention to costs and continuously rationed materials and manpower. Esthetics and services had to dovetail with costs. Cinder block, stucco, whitewash, and paints of drab hue, for example, were applied because they could be purchased locally and cheaply, but once in place such ordinary materials suggested "a gracious functionalism."[30] Peets once conceded that parsimony occasionally led to monotony in design, but, to compensate, he and Bentley worked tirelessly to utilize the natural complexities of the site profile. Failing that, the planners took comfort in the thought that even Henry James had once claimed a certain amount of uniformity could contribute to "a decent monotony."[31]

The Greendale plan was, in certain respects, vintage Peets. Displeased by the popular trend toward sinuous suburban streets, rolling lawns, and other anemic landscape designs, the landscape architect set out to prove that "rationality, lucidity, appropriateness of form, a clear simple rhythm ... appeal to human satisfactions that lie deeper than the cultural surface of our personalities."[32]

As in many European Renaissance cities and American colonial villages, Greendale was "built around a line instead of a point"—its street pattern articulated by a central boulevard, Broad Street, laid along a north-south lineal depression in a valley floor. Taking a lesson from the late Viennese architect-planner Camillo Sitte's *Der Stadtbau* (1899), Peets constricted the southern half of this street and several of the residential throughways in order to accentuate their vistas.[33] An administrative building, a multi-purpose community and school building, the town commons, and five shops comprised the apex of the street plan. A path and

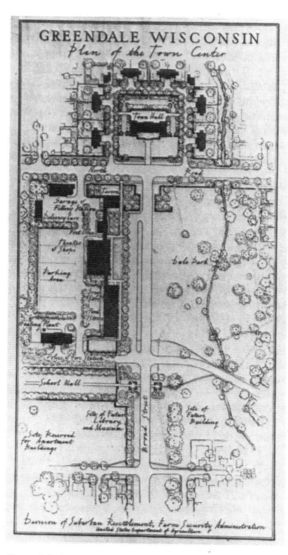

Greendale homes were situated within a half mile of an administrative and commercial center. *Source: J.S. Lansill Papers.*

park system followed the course of Dale Creek as it transected the village area. All homes were situated within a short walk that was ten or fifteen minutes from parks and the commercial and administrative complex. Residents, according to the planners, were to enjoy the best of city and country: "Living in Greendale will be as healthful, safe, and pleasant as modern knowledge can make it. The convenience of town life has been combined with many benefits of life on the land. Stores, community buildings, post office, and playgrounds will be within easy walking distances of every home. Children can find parks and open countryside within a few steps of their front doors."[34]

The sources of the Greendale plan were eclectic and indicated a lack of sympathy with contemporary high styles of architecture and town planning. Peets admitted that in preparing the Greendale plan he drew upon the layouts of midwestern county seats, European Renaissance marketplaces, and the reconstruction of Williamsburg, Virginia.[35] His colleague, architect Walter Thomas, borrowed unabashedly from Virginia's colonial buildings for Greendale's village hall and other public structures. Indeed, the architectural character of the incipient community moved Jens Jensen, a nationally recognized landscape architect who resided in Door County, Wisconsin, to remark in 1937: "The buildings are lost. Frank Lloyd Wright, a true son of Wisconsin, should have been the guiding hand, but a profit [sic] is always stoned in his own country."[36]

Jensen expressed even greater dismay over the planting plan proposed by Peets for Greendale. Peets's plan, which called for the introduction of some non-native plants into the community (about one-fourth of the total), drew immediate opposition from Jensen. As one of the earliest and foremost proponents of the use of native vegetation in landscape design, the Danish-born Jensen had gained considerable attention as the designer of several major landscape projects in the Midwest and as the former superintendent of Chicago's park system. Writing in 1937 from "The Clearing," his home and studio at Ellison Bay, Wisconsin, Jensen, who was then seventy-seven years old, directed his comments to Henry Wallace, U.S. Secretary of Agriculture. Jensen asked Wallace why foreign plants had to be used in American soil when the native flora of the Greendale area were so rich and varied. "To do this," claimed Jensen, "is really a tragedy." He continued that it was imperative to rescue the planting plan from utter mediocrity before it was too late. [37]

Peets, in responding to a query from the Department of Agriculture, acknowledged Jensen's mastery of "garden art," but claimed that the landscape architect's planting list was too limited. Stating that at least three-fourths of the selected plants were native to Wisconsin, Peets pointed out that he was being counseled by Franz Aust, a landscape architect who was a faculty member in the horticulture department at the University of Wisconsin, and by Stanley White, a staff landscape architect who was later affiliated with the University of Illinois. Peets then observed: "We are planting things that need little skilled care and we are leaving much of the planting in their own yards to be done by the Greendale people. We know that they will want to see the trees and shrubs that have been made dear to them by familiarity. The golden-twig willows that were planted by the pioneers to cheer the winter landscape, apple and cherry trees, lilacs and hollyhocks—all of these came from other continents, but we want the people who come out to their new homes in Greendale to find these old friends."[38] In this area, as in many others, Peets was guided by his vision of the suburbanite as settler: the new pioneer.

Despite Jensen's concern, Peets's planting list prevailed. From a design standpoint, Peets sought to use plant materials that would provide both beautification and screening. Calling for the placement of plantings at the front of each house, Peets also noted that the single-family dwellings were to have hedges or small trellises with vines to separate the street and entrance court. Vines, high-growing shrubs, and small trees were envisioned for the area between the garage drive and the neighboring structure; this, Peets and his colleagues claimed, would "better the appearance of the substantially blank wall which normally bounds the entrance court of a detached house at the southerly side." Peets believed that most of the backyards should have central open areas for recreation and the drying of clothes. Plants were to be used at the rear of the houses to create boundaries that would separate individual yards.[39]

The Greendale plan of 1936 was aimed at fostering a communal atmosphere where families could share their problems and their good times. Yet privacy also was important. While the streets and town center were meeting places, the residential lanes were set apart from the bustle and commotion of town life. Apart from these considerations, the lay of the land itself was critical in deciding many details of the site plan. Irregularities of terrain, for example, helped to account for the prevalence of single-family dwellings at Greendale, whereas the other two greenbelt towns were comprised mainly of group structures. Peets was adamant about the compositional flexibility of the single house on hilly sites, given the minimal grading program at Greendale.[40]

An apt illustration of site planning at Greendale was offered by the ubiquitous Greendale garage. Peets realized that the car-driveway-garage relationship was a potential stumbling block in his efforts to integrate the separate dwelling units and to avoid the impression of a scattering of isolated structures. To overcome such atomistic tendencies at the home-sites, all garages, except those at the end of blocks, were placed slightly to the rear and parallel to the windowless walls of neighboring houses. Access was by way of a private drive connected to the house by a side door. Thus, the Greendale plan secured for each individual unit a modicum of privacy and sunshine without sacrificing a sense of community. Greendale's "chain house" linkage of garages and dwellings and narrow and often constricted cul-de-sacs with generous plantings of trees and shrubs fused the monochromatic facades of the street into a unified yet varied visual experience. Furthermore, the houses were placed within a few feet of the street—a practice that had been employed at Williamsburg already in the 1600's. Peets felt so strongly about the importance of giving closure to a streetscape that he almost eliminated sidewalks altogether.[41]

Theories and practicalities of design were given equal weight by the town planner. A student of urban history, Peets once placed the origins of the Greendale street far in the Euro-American past—in the "old town plans" before the industrial age when the street was still "a defined channel of space." Yet Peets, ever the practical man, was not unmindful of the advantages to be gained by placing garages adjacent to homes in a northern climate of harsh winters.[42] Likewise, terrain, social survey, and rent formulae were juggled together before the planners hit upon a varied housing mix. They decided to build 350 single houses (46.7%), 250 row or group houses (33.3%), 100 twins or duplexes (13.3%), and fifty apartment dwellings (6.7%) divided among two buildings, one in the town center to accommodate shop clerks and teachers and the other at the southernmost end of the central Broad Street. In the final appointment of house types, the planners strayed in numbers but not in spirit from the questionnaire. Although nearly three-fourths of that sample had stated a preference for single-unit homes, the planners judged that Milwaukee citizens were not as familiar with duplexes and other row houses as they were with cottages and bungalows.[43]

The planners constantly sought the middle ground between thrift and attractiveness, between standardization and regimentation, and between the naturalism of the rural landscape and clarity of the urban form. Nonetheless, few decisions were made without careful consideration of possible long-term costs to the tenant family entailed either directly in monthly utility bills or indirectly in rents. This was true for relatively minor details such as the installation of coal-fired furnaces in every house, the use of fireproof construction materials, and the elimination of basements entirely from residential units (Greendale was the only greenbelt town without any basements). The same consideration was given to more complicated problems such as the construction of independent waste-disposal and water-treatment plants, the gift to Milwaukee County of land near the proposed parkway, and the switch from an overhead electrical distribution system to an underground system.[44] A few key recommendations by the Greendale staff followed closely on the heels of recommendations by the Greenhills staff, particularly those having to do with regional policy, such as utility systems and dedications to local parks commissions.[45]

In terms of land utilization within the village area, Peets and Crane worked diligently to increase the density of housing beyond local norms—so diligently, in fact, that the planners had to circumvent a 1935 Wisconsin planning statute that established a minimum lot size of 4,800 square feet.[46] What few concessions Peets did make to the code, such as slightly deeper lots than initially planned, reduced the "theoretical density" of a typical section of single-family homes from 7.5 dwelling units per acre to 6.5 units per acre—about half the density of an English garden city. If the space taken up by garages and driveways were deleted from the formula, then Greendale approached the garden city standard of a minimum density of twelve units per acre as specified by Sir Raymond Unwin, the English architect and town planner.[47] Regardless, Peets anticipated higher densities in future developments. As for the present, Peets wrote, "we feel that it [Greendale] is rather too much spread out . . . ."[48] The Greendale plan, then, signalled a halt to the typically American pattern of sprawling suburban housing.

Before designing Greendale's houses, Peets and his colleagues toured Milwaukee's residential areas. Following their sojourns, Peets reported: "We drove through square miles of workmen's homes on the outskirts of Milwaukee and West Allis—thousands of little cottages, too close together, often ugly, but neatly kept with liberally planted front lawns and rear yards. We saw the faults in this way of building, but the owners were proud of these houses. People who had dreamed of having one of these crowded cottages as their life's home, would live in our houses at Greendale. This was their folk-way, their pattern of building."[49]

Architectural planning at Greendale, as it evolved, accentuated the iconoclasm and the bare-bones functionalism of the town plan. Visual interest was maintained by a limited vocabulary of roof types and by interspersing fourteen basic house styles and minor variations on these. Nevertheless, all units approached a common style. As architect Bentley observed: "An outstanding visual characteristic of Greendale is its homogeneity." The planners disavowed any intention to mimic European villages, although Bentley noted that Greendale had attained "a degree of kinship to those pleasant towns across the water," first, because he and Peets had been limited in their choice of materials to the plain and the inexpensive, and second because considerable standardization had been enforced by restrictions of time and budgets. Bentley was bewildered at first by the comments of visitors to the effect that Greendale resembled the country villages of the Old World, but the designer came to understand that the illusion grew simply out of the practical solutions to the problem.[50]

In residential architecture, as in site planning, esthetic principles came after the arithmetic of living space. By doing away with the superfluous in home design, Bentley was able to improve upon the specifications of rival federal housing agencies, thereby producing sounder and larger homes that, the planners hoped, would encourage large families with "modest incomes" to move out of the city into "quarters sufficiently spacious to foster a complete and happy family life."[51] Typical Greendale houses had five or six rooms; these included two or three bedrooms on the second floor, and a kitchen and living room/dining room alcove at ground level. Eighteen four-bedroom houses also were constructed, as well as forty-two one-bedroom units that were nicknamed "honeymooners." Regardless of house styles—detached, row houses, or twins—all homes had equivalent amounts of floor space relative to the number of rooms per unit, and Peets modified the typical lot for row units so that most families could claim a distinct backyard. Somewhat to their own surprise, the planners found that the group dwellings actually were more expensive to build than single-family dwellings of similar dimensions. An average three-bedroom detached house, for example, cost $4,577 as compared to $4,654 for a similar unit in a group or row house. The marginal economy of multiple structures was due to the higher cost of garage construction. A rough comparison with private housing revealed that Greendale homes were not inexpensive to build, but neither were they exorbitant. The U.S. Bureau of Labor Statistics estimated that the average cost of a single-family house in

America in 1929 was $4,915—a cost that had declined by about 22 per cent in 1933.[52]

On February 9, 1937, the Special Skills Division opened a model house at Greendale; this house, according to Bentley, was complete with furnishings designed expressly to "radiate a degree of taste-forming influence." (Initially, all Greendale units were to be furnished, but the expense proved too great.) As with so much else in Greendale, the back-to-essentials artlessness of the government furniture gave only an illusion of affordability, since most of the provisions were beyond the pocketbooks of community residents. *House Beautiful* praised the plain beauty of the furniture: "not the self-conscious 'arty' type but functional and therefore living and real."[53]

The latest in kitchen appliances was installed in each dwelling unit of the town, and all kitchens were spacious: 10 feet by 12 feet in the largest units, and 9 feet by 7.5 feet in the smallest. This "female domain," however, was closed off from the living/dining area so that the family would not gather amidst "the dirt and confusion of food preparation" or dawdle after meals near the warmth of the kitchen range "with resultant excess consumption of unmetered electricity."[54] (Bentley, it might be noted, was married but childless, and Peets was a bachelor.)

The greenbelt towns, John Lansill once wrote, "look forward to new patterns, away from old confusions." But the Greendale plan looked back to a time in America before cities were a way of life, and before governments, corporations, and collusions took away the prerogatives of average citizens. The comment of Jacob Crane to the American City Planning Institute was typical in this respect: "Finally, the deepest significance of this kind of project may lie in its wide reestablishment of confidence in democratic processes . . . ."[55] Such historical allusions had only a slim basis in fact, and indeed the contradictions were all too apparent; the greenbelt towns actually represented clear signs of an increasingly centralized planning function. In the face of pressing environmental and societal problems, the planners of Greendale conjured up memories of Main Street and even fainter recollections of the pre-industrial village.

CHAPTER SIX
Dollars and Dreams

DRAWN amidst the rococo splendor of the Walsh mansion, the Greendale plan was only partially realized at the site.[1] The mixed public reaction to the resettlement idea in Milwaukee (and throughout America) did not bode well for the planners. When it became clear that Congress was not likely to appropriate additional funds, the Resettlement Administration decided to rush its three suburban projects to completion. Greendale's collective farmsteads and recreation center were scrapped, as were proposals for an industrial loop and a section of parkway estates scheduled to be leased to private builders. Money was diverted into home construction while the planners banged heads with consultants from other federal agencies and the University of Wisconsin. For months they squabbled with veterans of the subsistence homesteads program over whether Wisconsin farmers would tolerate "socialistic" schemes and modern conveniences such as electricity and indoor toilets.[2]

In the heat of this controversy, Peets and Crane scarcely listened as a fish and game specialist presented plans for the preservation of wildlife habitats at Greendale. Meanwhile the rural planning staff waited on the sidelines until, in April, 1937, Crane asked the Management Division to assume responsibility for the farms. During the summer months, the Division repaired the existing rural structures, sprayed the fruit trees, and then offered annual farm leases to tenants on a first-come, first-serve basis. In February, 1938, Peets wrote of the rural program: "There is little evidence of progress toward the fine ideal. . . ."[3]

Deserted farmhouses and desolate pastures surrounded a beehive of town-building in the center of the tract. In April, 1936, construction at Greendale began in earnest with a crew of 332 men. By October the number of laborers had peaked at about 2,000, most of whom were paid on a force account of the Works Progress Administration (WPA).[4] Although the relief army never approached earlier predictions of 3,600 or 5,000 men, the total number of manhours climbed to disastrous heights as the project lagged far behind schedule.[5] Moreover, the Resettlement Administration hired a disproportionate number of skilled workmen at Greendale, primarily union tradesmen and journeymen from the Milwaukee area. Such workers were hired partly because the planners wanted to ensure that the homes would be well constructed. Also, relief workers were in short supply during the summer months of 1936 and 1937 when the local economy, on its own, was able to absorb many of the unemployed men. According to the final report of project costs, 55 per cent of a $5.5 million payroll went to non-relief workers who earned as much as two dollars an hour; their wages were significantly higher than the fifty cents an hour earned by some unskilled laborers. Furthermore, 20 per cent of all non-relief payrolls went to appointed, salaried positions—the best paid of whom were the four planning principals, who each earned $5,000 a year.[6]

The budgetary burden of non-relief labor at Greendale consisted not solely of large payrolls, but also of incidental funds spent to support a skilled crew. The WPA, for example, regularly asked hirees to provide their own transportation to and from work sites, but the Resettlement Administration at Greendale, relying so heavily on Milwaukee tradesmen, decided to spend $140,000 on 15,000 feet of spur line connecting Greendale with an urban electric rail line. Besides the initial expense of laying the track, the Resettlement Administration agreed to pay a surcharge on all men and materials hauled by rail.[7] Though Lansill and others blamed the inefficiency of WPA workers for the delays and cost overruns at each greenbelt town site, it must be added, in fairness to the WPA and its laborers, that the Suburban Resettlement Division generally traveled first class.

Foul weather and a balky Milwaukee city government exacerbated an already difficult situation. On July 7, 1936, for instance, the temperature climbed to 110° F. The workers persisted, but twelve of them collapsed on the job. During the next winter (1936–1937), a spell of sub-zero temperatures made work difficult and, on some days, impossible. Heavy rains the following April once again halted work, but this time the planners took comfort in knowing that the paint was adhering to the cinder blocks and that the roofs were not leaking. However, trouble was brewing on the local political front. A public utilities commission declined to extend metropolitan water lines to Greendale, and the cost estimates of a metropolitan sewer commission were so high that already in July, 1936, the planners had opted to install an independent sewage treatment plant. Unfortunately, this decision came after the Resettlement Administration had incited the residents in the neighboring community of Hales Corners to petition for metropolitan services.[8]

The dual purpose of the new town program—to demonstrate efficiency and conservation in housing and land use and to create jobs—brought the Resettlement Administration into conflict with the Works Progress Administration, the labor relief agency run by Harry Hopkins. The Resettle-

ment Administration was obsessively concerned with the swift and economical implementation of the greenbelt town plans. The WPA
manifested a wholly different attitude towards worker productivity. The
WPA's mission was to generate employment, and it regularly provided its
employees with the most rudimentary, labor-intensive equipment (horse-
drawn road graders, wagons, and shovels)—in essence, a planned ineffi-
ciency devised to keep workmen occupied. By sheer dint of numbers, however, the Construction Division at Greendale often outdistanced the planners in the Suburban Division. During August of the first summer, 343
housing units were under roof, and already Peets and Bentley were hard-
pressed to deliver plans and specifications on schedule. Architect Walter
Thomas had slightly more time to spare on his plans for public buildings,
since housing construction came first. Nevertheless, preliminary plans for
the community building had no sooner arrived from Washington than the
foundations were dug during a bitterly cold week of December, 1936.[9]

The Construction Division was in charge of nearly all on-site activities,
but the planners were able to float a few of their own projects. Responding
to a suggestion made by Peets, the National Youth Administration trained
thirty young men in landscaping techniques, but not before the objections
of Construction Division engineers had delayed the program until April,
1939—nearly a year after the first tenants had moved in to Greendale.[10]

As in other New Deal programs, artists were hired to capture the spirit
of this "new beginning" for America. Since the WPA sought to employ
professional artists on various projects throughout America, Lansill had a
particular interest in giving sculptors and painters greenbelt town commissions. To this end, he corresponded frequently with Adrian Dornbush,
Director of the Special Skills Division of the Resettlement Administration.
A series of watercolors was completed in 1936 at Greenbelt, Maryland, by
Richard Jansen; another series was done at Greenhills, Ohio, by Richard
Sargent. Still another was contemplated for Greendale early in 1937, but
while Dornbush was beating the bushes (of Michigan's Upper Peninsula)
for an artist, the commission was cancelled. Eventually all of the Green-
belt and Greenhills paintings (with such forbidding titles as "Shovel at
Work," "Concrete Mixer," and "Dusting Cement Bags") were offered to
Fortune magazine, whose editor showed no interest whatsoever. Finally,
they were hung on the office walls of Dornbush, Lansill, and Tugwell.[11]
Although the director of the Special Skills Division gave up on WPA watercolors, he persevered with another medium: sculpture. In 1938
Dornbush commissioned Alonzo Hauser to execute a flagpole grouping

for Greendale. (Hauser, from 1926 to 1931, had studied at the Wisconsin State College of La Crosse, the Layton School of Art in Milwaukee, the University of Wisconsin at Madison, and the Art Student's League of New York.) His work, which still stands, memorialized in a direct, representational manner the mothers, youths, mechanics, and farmers who would participate in forming a new suburban order.[12]

Soon after the novel patterns of streets and homes became apparent at Greendale, the project area was awash with visitors, particularly on Sunday afternoons. After June 23, 1936, guided tours were conducted by members of the National Youth Administration, and the crowds of visitors seemed "almost unbelievable" to the guides and their supervisors. Nearly 650,000 people were reported to have visited Greendale between September 1, 1936, and August 31, 1937; about one of every five or six of these onlookers was reported to be from outside the Milwaukee area. On one particularly pleasant Sunday afternoon in October, for example, it was estimated that some 21,000 people walked the fresh streets and sidewalks of the new community; later, thousands of individuals toured a model house which had opened in February, 1937.[13] Among the visiting hordes were numerous city planners, architects, builders, realtors, and housing officials from across America and from as far away as Moscow. (The two Soviet officials, stating that large apartment buildings were superior to any other form of housing, could not fathom the reason for so many single-family dwellings.)[14]

Throughout the period of construction, and for a year after the town was opened for occupancy, the visitors continued to come and the guides continued to send encouraging reports to Washington about the favorable impression that the Greendale plan was making upon visitors. One such report commented on the various reactions that the guides noticed on the faces of visitors who inspected the model home. "Some are awed by the beauty of the furniture," stated one of the guides; "others skeptical at the outset undergo a subtle change in their feelings and leave with a feeling that it isn't so bad after all." Walter Wyrick, real estate editor for the *Milwaukee Journal*, was not so much captivated by the design of the town as by the spirit of the workers: "I have been at Greendale frequently and never have seen any boondoggling or shovel leaning. There is something about building homes which changes a man's outlook."[15] On February 16, 1937, Mayor Hoan, with some 200 members of the Milwaukee Real Estate Board in tow, was taken through the half-finished town and the newly appointed model home; afterwards the guide service treated the group to a lunch of sandwiches and coffee. In addressing the assembled group, Hoan observed of government housing: "If private capital is able to build low cost housing, it will have my support as against the government in the housing business. But if private capital is unable, the government must do it. I am not as much interested in who is providing the housing as I am in seeing that much housing is provided."[16]

As imposing as this entourage must have been, undoubtedly the visitor who caused the greatest stir was the First Lady of the nation, Eleanor Roosevelt. During a whirlwind thirty-six hours in Milwaukee after her husband's 1936 election victory, Mrs. Roosevelt paced reporters and aides around the suburban project. Noting that Greendale was "laid out beautifully," Mrs. Roosevelt also observed that since the village was "absolutely wonderful," she would tell the people in Washington what a fine job was being done in Wisconsin. Perhaps half-jokingly, the First Lady did chide the architects for placing the coal bins and laundry tubs in the same room. "It simply proves what I always say," reported the president's wife, "that a man should always have a woman at his elbow when he's planning these things." (Half-joking or not, Mrs. Roosevelt's suggestion was quickly heeded; three months after her visit it was noted that the coal bins had been enclosed in tight doors.) Turning more serious, the visitor from the White House voiced, with characteristic circuitry, her disappointment in the lack of housing for blacks. "If we are to have racial good feeling and fairness," commented the distinguished observer, "we must not permit discrimination to creep in."[17]

The exclusion of blacks from Greendale and the other greenbelt towns may or may not be attributable to a conscious color bar. Fundamentally, the all-white racial complexion of each town was a consequence of income restrictions. Yet the objective of integrated housing never became part of greenbelt town planning. One recent account of Greenbelt, Maryland, for example, has pointed out that quotas existed for Protestants, Catholics, and Jews, but not for blacks; this approach reportedly was adopted since officials did not want to aggravate the already controversial issue of a planned community by including black residents.[18]

During the time that the greenbelt communities were underway, blacks had already been or were being housed in a dozen all-black resettlement projects, most of which were rural. In Macon, Georgia, for example, a black project manager was put in charge of a land reclamation and farm resettlement scheme, and as early as April, 1936, plans were underway for a suburban resettlement project near Newport News, Virginia, where black participation was expected, but quotas were not specified. As far as employment and race were concerned, the Resettlement Administration was somewhat ahead of its time in fair hiring practices. In 1938 approximately 150 blacks were employed by the agency in administrative, technical, clerical, and menial capacities.[19] When considering Greendale and the entire greenbelt towns program, however, it appears that outside of comments by Eleanor Roosevelt and a few other individuals, the racial issue simply was not mentioned directly. (It might be noted in passing that in 1930 only 7,500 of Milwaukee's 570,000 residents were black.)

Before the first summer construction season drew to a close, Greendale's planners realized that the work was far behind schedule and that costs were far above the original $7,050,000 allocation. While the project was scheduled for completion in February, 1937, only 343 houses were under construction by August 11, 1936, and roofing work was not begun until the middle of September. Plans for a second town unit were summarily tabled. On October 8, 1936, with great reluctance, the project planners recommended deferring construction of 158 dwelling units in the southernmost part of the town tract, including the thirty multi-family dwellings planned for that section. A week later they weighed a further decrease in the size of the project to 500 units. Although a calculation showed that reduction much below 750 units would mean either a dramatic rise in rents or a cut in community services, no additional houses were attempted after October 15, 1936.[20] On that date there were 572 units started (366 structures). Of this total, 274 were detached one-family units (48.0%), 208 were row houses (36.3%), and ninety were twins (15.7%).[21] Plans for two apartment buildings never reached the drawing board.

The project principals tried, during the winter and spring of 1936–1937, to widen the scope of their project beyond the primary objective of providing middle-income family housing. In January, 1937, they proposed a loop of 600 low-cost dwelling units for needy families that otherwise would be unable to afford the homes already underway. In justifying this expansion of the town, the planners cited social as well as economic reasons. "To achieve a representative and more complete community life," they reported, "it is important to include among the families a wider variety of occupations, incomes and attitudes. . . ." Although Lansill and Bigger approved of the plan, they regretted that such an addition would have to be delayed until more funds became available.[22] In February, 1937, a special "deficiency allotment" of $1,000,000 was appropriated, but a month later, Secretary of Agriculture Henry Wallace, beseiged by Congressional budget-cutters, was compelled to require a 50 per cent reduction in the construction costs of Resettlement Administration communities. In May, 1937, Lansill approved a budget of $10,026,000 as requested by the Greendale planners, but this amount, too, proved insufficient. Before major construction activities had ended, Greendale cost the government nearly $10,418,000. Of this amount, $8,247,000 had been spent on construction and land development.[23]

Over the summer, the entire Suburban Division was reduced to a skeletal staff of planners and, in the middle of August, 1937, all remaining personnel were moved onto the sites of Greenhills and Greendale. Bigger resigned at the end of August, and two days later the Washington offices of the Suburban Division closed. Shortly thereafter the entire Resettlement Administration was absorbed into a new omnibus agency of the U.S. Department of Agriculture, the Farm Security Administration (FSA), under the direction of W. E. Alexander. Lansill stayed active in the Suburban Division until June 30, 1938.[24]

The elusive goal of parity between costs and rents at Greendale was now impossible to meet. None of the careful projections of expenses and revenues had taken into account the fact that fewer than 750 homes would be built. Still, Peets hoped that Greendale might be "liked by its people, envied by the people of other towns, and admired by the relevant experts."[25] The community planner correctly recognized that only by retaining the attention and support of the public would Greendale ever realize its full potential as a garden suburb.

CHAPTER SEVEN
Years of Pride and Protest, 1938–1944

JOHN Lansill wrote glowingly in 1937 of the New Deal era greenbelt communities: "The Towns of Greenbelt, Greenhills and Greendale are as well planned as the best technical talent could make them—pleasant, permanent, safe. They are starting life as self-governing communities, paying taxes, owning their own land and controlling their own destinies in a way that no community in the United States has done or has been able to do since the first little towns were founded in Virginia, Massachusetts and Connecticut. They are a return to the first American way of life."[1] But, as Lansill and his colleagues would find, the era of the Great Depression was far different than that of the Founding Fathers, and the birth of the greenbelt towns was not accomplished without struggle and controversy.

Henry Churchill, architect and greenbelt town consultant, once reflected that the Suburban Division was the only government agency to consider housing "not merely a matter of shelter, but of the whole socioeconomic-political complex."[2] In fact, the physical planning of the projects had scarcely begun before various political and legal problems were broached. An early plan to turn Greendale over to the City of Milwaukee was dropped when it was decided that the greenbelt project would not qualify as a low-income project under pending state requirements for housing authorities. When, in 1937, it became apparent that Greendale would not, in the near future, have a local industrial base and thus no chance for self-sufficiency, the planners suggested—without elaborating the concept—the merger of surrounding village and township governments into "one metropolitan city."[3] Vinton, often the one to supply a new idea, came up with a more direct course of action. In April, 1936, he recommended the speedy formation of a quasi-public land-holding corporation followed by the incorporation of the project area as a village. By establishing a legal entity before the relocation of urban tenants, Vinton assumed that the politically naive rural folk already on the land could be easily persuaded to adopt a village-manager form of government, thereby giving indirect steerage to federal projects in Greendale.[4]

All of these options were effectively closed when the project was ready to receive a tenant population. Greendale with 572 homes was far too small, by the planners' own calculations, to survive as a tax-supported jurisdictional entity. Greenbelt with 885 homes and Greenhills with 676 homes (exclusive of the farms) were no better off.[5] The Farm Security Administration, the new parent organization of the Suburban Division after September, 1937, thus had no choice but to retain all three projects.

At Greenbelt, Greenhills, and Greendale, resident managers were appointed by the Resettlement Administration. (Though not a federal project, Radburn, New Jersey, had adopted a policy of appointing managers in the late 1920's; this same procedure was used for the greenbelt towns.)[6] Sherwood Reeder, Greendale's first manager, was a graduate of the School of Public Administration at Syracuse University, and before leaving Greendale in 1941 for a job in defense housing, he had the advantage of learning from the mistakes and successes of Greenbelt, Maryland, which had opened on September 30, 1937.[7]

In 1937 a standard procedure was implemented to select families for the greenbelt communities and for the rural homestead communities within the Resettlement Administration. Each case was reviewed by a panel of social workers from the Family Selection Section of the Management Division, following a series of home investigations of the applicant's present housing and habits of cleanliness. Starting in February, 1938, over 2,000 families in the Milwaukee area were screened for admission to Greendale.[8]

In Milwaukee, the selection officers looked for "people who have in the past taken care of the property in which they have lived, persons of good moral character, who have been able to get along with their neighbors."[9] Despite the number of those interviewed, family selection proceeded slowly. By July 19, 1938, only one-half of the anticipated 2,500 tenants had moved into the village, and as late as January, 1939, it was reported that 68 per cent of Greendale's houses stood empty. One reason for the lag was the blanket disqualification of many families whose income had declined during a severe local recession in Milwaukee.[10] Nor were Greendale houses a bargain at an average monthly rate of $28. Actually Greendale's rents (from $19 to $32 a month) were in the same range as 60 per cent of all rents in the Milwaukee urban area for 1940.[11] For the first year of occupancy, Greendale's rental rate had an upper limit of $36 per month; however, in March, 1939, the FSA lowered the limit to $32.50 and permitted small families to occupy the eighteen four-bedroom units, most of which had stood empty through the winter.[12]

The long-awaited opening of the village on April 30 and May 1, 1938, was somewhat anticlimactic. The Ernest Knutson family, the first residents to settle into a new house, were so anxious to move that they and their packed trailer arrived in Greendale at 3:00 A. M. Unable to secure a key for their house until government officials arrived several hours later, the Knutsons simply unloaded the items onto the curb and went back to their former residence on West Walker Street in Milwaukee to fill the trailer once again. The Knutsons, and four other families who moved in during that first day, reportedly were not concerned about losing any "beauty sleep" since they foresaw that in Greendale "the kids would have a real place to play, that there were no vermin scuttling back of old mopboards, [and] that there would be fresh carrots and rutabagas from the garden before long."[13]

Complicating the exodus to the new town was a city-wide teamsters' strike that forced many new tenants to call upon friends and relatives with automobiles. Yet adversity only contributed to a sense of adventure. Among the early tenants in Greendale an activist element took charge almost from the beginning and began to cultivate attitudes of self-help and interdependence. At Greendale, as at Greenbelt and Greenhills, the tenants came to view themselves as "pioneers," a perception enhanced by managerial rhetoric and the slant of local newspaper coverage. For example, John P. Schroeter, an official with the Suburban Division who later became a Greendale resident, wrote voluminously about the positive attributes of living in an enclave that was based upon new modes of community planning and organization. The virtues associated with proximity to land and soil were especially lauded by Schroeter: "We are living close to nature and shall adjust ourselves to her for our benefit; we are able to recover our lost affinity to the soil." Similar sentiments were expressed by the *Milwaukee Sentinel* as the first families arrived in Greendale during the spring of 1938. Such people, proclaimed the *Sentinel*, would raise "radishes and roses and children" in a community replete with "fresh air, grass and black dirt." The report also described the vehicles that delivered personal belongings and food to the community during its early days of pioneer existence as "uncovered wagons" and "traveling caravans." At the same time, the *Milwaukee Journal* sought to compare the comments of Greendale's residents with those of other people who had chosen not to move to the new town. Acknowledging that Greendale's settlers appeared "glad to be out in the country," several people in Milwaukee, West Allis, and elsewhere expressed their dislikes about such a distant location: "How are those fellows out there going to get to work," asked one stay-at-homer, "when the snow is deep?"[14]

The mere novelty of Greendale was enough to lure idealists. As the editor of the *Greendale Review* (the community weekly) wrote in 1939, the settlement was working "because a fellow named Tugwell wrote a book, and the people of Greendale are living up to it!" Other people were attracted to Greendale for more pragmatic reasons. One recently married couple which moved into a new home said they were especially attracted by the electric stove and refrigerator supplied in each house, while another husband and wife were confident a "new home would make their sick baby grow strong." When twenty-five original pioneers were asked, in 1978, why they had moved to Greendale forty years earlier, five stated that the community appeared to be an ideal place to raise a family; four noted that the low-cost housing was attractive to them; four said the design, including open-space provisions, was especially appealing; two said that they hoped their children's health would improve in the "country air"; and two wanted to leave the city to reside in a more rural environment: "We wanted country life without being in the country." (The remaining eight could give no specific reason for their decision.)[15]

The garden city paradigm supplied a code of living for many of these first families. Greendale gave more than deliverance from the city: it filled a lacuna of identity during those difficult years. To people trapped in workaday routines, it offered a chance to dabble in the political currents of their time. This was especially true of two civil engineers, both from Milwaukee and formerly with the Suburban Division, who chose to live in Greendale after the project ended. One was Walter E. Kroening, who later served as community manager. The other was John P. Schroeter, who became an ardent spokesman on behalf of resident causes. (Schroeter had headed a mayoral commission report on public ownership of Milwaukee's sewer system in 1932.) The resident population included many others who, like Schroeter, were active members of the Farmer-Labor-Progressive movement in Wisconsin. Schroeter, in fact, personified Milwaukee's down-to-earth (literally "sewer") socialism and the practical optimism of the New Deal.[16]

Other less-well-known residents of Greendale found themselves involved in community affairs to an extent that they previously would have deemed unimaginable. One woman, reflecting on her forty-five years as a Greendale resident, recalled that her late husband tended to "join everything" with great enthusiasm after they moved to the community. It was her belief that he never would have had an opportunity to be so involved had they remained in their former home, situated in the nearby community of West Allis.[17]

The government did all it could to attract such people. Families with incomes slightly above or below the official limits were allowed to slip through the screening process if they seemed likely to contribute to community social life. Greendale was perhaps more inclined to idealism than communities of comparable size because of the relative youth of its population. Tenants were primarily couples between twenty-five and thirty-four years of age. (Table 1.) They also were somewhat better educated than the general population of Milwaukee proper. College attendees, for instance, were twice as numerous in Greendale as in Milwaukee. (Table 2.) [NOTE: Tables begin on page 146.]

By 1939, Greendale was a town of young families, most of which were headed by blue-collar wage earners. Only sixty-six residents were classified as professional or semi-professional workers; these individuals represented about 9 per cent of Greendale's 723-person work force, a figure not much above urban Milwaukee's white-collar total of 8.4 per cent (out of a work force of 260,000). The Greendale figure, however, was far above the 2.2 per cent white-collar population projected by the Research Section in 1936.[18] Nevertheless, the white-collar minority in Greendale added a cosmopolitan dimension to community affairs, for the life styles of the first tenant populations—a cross section (albeit a thin one) of Milwaukee's ethnic and class structures—introduced many of the poorer residents to the other side of the tracks. A few of the more well-informed residents were supportive of radical causes. Fund-raising drives, for example, were held on behalf of Republican Spain during the late 1930's.[19]

If, as historians contend, the state and national elections of 1938 indicated an embrace of liberal politics by both urban professionals and labor groups, then the working-person's town of Greendale was a microcosm of the New Deal's diverse constituency. In the gubernatorial primary held during the summer of 1938, Greendale gave ninety votes to the Progressive incumbent, Philip La Follette, two Democratic candidates split 136 votes between them, and a Republican picked up forty-four votes.[20] In the presidential elections of 1940, President Roosevelt clearly was Greendale's choice as he received 871 votes to the 196 cast for Wendell Willkie. Candidates to the left of the President—Norman Thomas, the Socialist Party candidate, and Earl Browder, the Communist Party candidate—received only thirty-three and three votes respectively.[21] Greendale typifies one effect that the New Deal had upon the industrial class: it provided alternatives to confrontational unionism, and as a consequence of mild reforms, worker politics was centered between the extremes of Left and Right.

The common conviction that Greendale counted in the world was one of the threads—perhaps the most enduring—that pulled the village together, but there also were practical reasons for acting in unison. The families had to depend upon new neighbors and their "congenial" community manager, Sherwood Reeder, who was himself a young husband and, in October, 1938, a father for the second time.[22] A host of trivial but daily problems faced the settlers. Some conveniences proved more troublesome than helpful. In the summer months, for example, the coal-fired water heaters turned utility rooms into ovens, and the rugs on downstairs floors mildewed since there were no full basements beneath. The coal furnaces (chosen by the planners after they decided that cheap coal was the "workingman's fuel" in Milwaukee) were so sooty that all were converted to clean-burning gas or oil devices once the residents purchased their homes in 1952. Even hair washing was an unpleasant chore for those who moved to Greendale before a water-softening plant was completed. Yet management did its best to make amends and lend a helping hand. One woman remembered that "the government was always fixing something in the sub-area in the beginning, causing an inconvenience." The installation of ventilators and insulation in this sub-basement, for example, eliminated the mildew problem. A farm wagon also stood ready to facilitate frequent swaps of homes as babies were born and larger quarters were required by the new parents.[23] Some observers from throughout the Milwaukee area were both curious and cruel in the questions they raised about Greendale and its new residents. Calling the inhabitants "guinea pigs" and the community a "boxlike modernistic project," the critics asked how people could find their houses since all appeared so similar. Other gibes were directed against the paint colors: "Those pink houses. How can you stand them?"[24]

Despite the inconveniences and criticisms, a sizable number of residents considered their new Greendale houses a marked improvement over former dwellings. One early inhabitant, whose family formerly had looked out onto a brick wall from their Milwaukee apartment, stated that close inspection revealed noticeable variations among Greendale's houses: "a gable, a porch or an angle that distinguishes a place from its neighbors." After praising the "cheerful" pink color, the "squeakless" floor built over a concrete base, and the cinder-and-block construction which displayed the "beauty of the strictly functional," the contented resident continued by noting that Greendale was the "nearest thing to perfection that a man with a wife and two children and moderate income is likely to find anywhere."

A Norwegian architect voiced similar comments in 1939 when observing the quality of construction in Greendale. "This is fine, fine," he reportedly exclaimed, ". . . it is excellently done."[25]

A Greendale woman, when asked in 1978 what especially pleased her about a house that had served as home for forty years, noted the attractive arrangement of rooms and the beamed ceilings in the living room. Indeed, seven of the twenty-five original residents who were interviewed in 1978 commented on the beauty or quaintness of the beamed ceilings. Another long-time resident recalled, in 1984, that Greendale in 1938 looked similar to an army camp with barracks, but that once he and his wife saw how nice the interior of their house appeared, they forgot about the exterior. "Greendale was 'a wilderness of provided facilities'," recalled another inhabitant, "which the new residents made into a community." Perhaps the attitudes of many long-term residents were best summarized by one of the original pioneers who replied in 1978: "I like every little bit about our house."[26]

Weightier matters called for more than good will and administerial tinkering. The size of the project and its remoteness from the central city made it difficult to attract basic services, such as telephones and public transportation, at reasonable prices. The women were greatly affected by the isolation, since it was they who were confined to the village, miles away from relatives and friends, while their husbands were at work. As one woman recalled in 1978, loneliness led her to cry for three months after she and her family moved into Greendale in the summer of 1938. Women were expected, by the greenbelt town planners, to assume traditional roles as homemakers when residing in any of the three communities. One recent critic of the greenbelt towns program has stated that "the planners were unable to imagine women outside the social and spatial context of suburban home and community." Income restrictions, in fact, allowed few two-income families to qualify for housing in the towns; as observed by one male resident of Greendale, it was only after his wife became pregnant and resigned from her job in Milwaukee that they were able to qualify for a home in the 1930's.[27]

Of course, the dismal economics of the depression demanded stoicism and stiff upper lips of everyone. The first of many social events in the village was a "hard-time" party complete with nickel cider and donuts. A Labor Relations Committee in Greendale tried to find jobs for the unemployed and under-employed village men, and in 1940 the committee established its own relief fund.[28] During the summer of 1939, a total of 136

families paid a nominal fee of one dollar for garden space and the horticul-
tural advice of a state extension worker. Every summer, members of the
garden club and others gathered in the early evening hours to till and chat.
During the war years, their plots became victory gardens.[29]

On July 14, 1938, a delegation of Greendale citizens formed a General
Committee to resolve some of their common difficulties and to act as a
clearinghouse for resident activities. The demands upon the waking hours
of the twelve committee members, five women and seven men, proved to
be so unrelenting that families, as one commentator later recalled, frequently were ignored: "Some of the wives were complaining and stated
that they would leave their husbands if they continued to go out to meetings. Some of the husbands complained because they had to be child's
nurse while mama went out."[30]

During the first year, a bureaucracy of subcommittees tackled many
problems—the most pressing of which was transportation. Beginning in
April and continuing into July, 1938, Sherwood Reeder had petitioned the
Public Service Commission of Wisconsin for regular bus service between
Milwaukee and Greendale. As resident manager, Reeder was anxious to
improve a mornings-only service offered by the Midlands Coach Lines and
to eliminate a resident-run station wagon shuttle which, though free, took
up to an hour for the round trip between Greendale and the closest city
bus stop. Negotiations with the Milwaukee Electric Railway and Light
Company (the same company that had hauled WPA workers to Greendale) were complicated by the fact that Greendale men traveled to such
widely scattered work sites. Sixty-five per cent of the men commuted three
to five miles within a zone around the village, while some worked as far
away as ten miles.[31]

Under order of the Public Service Commission, the Milwaukee Electric
Railway and Light Company began bus service on October 10, 1938, but
after a six-month trial period, the company abandoned the line amidst a
round of complaints from residents about poor service and overcharging.
For the next five years, both Midlands and the Milwaukee Electric experimented with lines from Greendale to Milwaukee or to the end of the Milwaukee transit system. None of the operations, however, proved successful, either as a business venture or as a public service. It still took up to two
hours to return to Greendale from some factories in Milwaukee. The
pending expiration of a bus service contract in 1942 and the growing exas-
peration of resident commuters forced reconsideration of a resident-oper-
ated jitney shuttle.[32] Requests to the government for better bus service in

order to save gasoline went unheeded. Instead, the residents looked to car pooling. A committee was able to enlist the cooperation of over 500 car owners in Greendale who were willing to share their vehicles. The deficiencies of public transportation annoyed users throughout the 1940's and even into the 1950's. Early resident demands to have the Greendale telephone exchange included within the urban service area met with even less success. Every time Greendale residents dialed mothers and friends in Milwaukee, they had to pay for a long-distance call.[33]

The remoteness of Greendale from the central city and its marginal role in the life of the metropolis were made painfully clear by the rows of empty shops along the central village mall. During the first summer, the tenants could neither buy pharmaceuticals in Greendale nor have their hair cut or coiffed. In order to shop for food, bank their paychecks, or fuel their autos, Greendale's inhabitants had to drive to Milwaukee. After a few weeks of such inconveniences, the residents began to explore alternatives. During a meeting of the Yard Equipment Purchase Committee, Sherwood Reeder, reminded no doubt by what had been done at Greenbelt and Greenhills, suggested that Greendale start its own cooperative businesses. Within a month, between late July and August, 1938, the Greendale Cooperative Association was formed, and during succeeding months a food store, a service station, and a barber shop were leased from the Farm Security Administration. The drug store and movie theater were leased to private individuals.[34]

Although residents traded on a regular basis with outside merchants and itinerant vendors, the various consumers' cooperatives achieved moderate financial success. The food store, for example, during its peak year of 1943, grossed nearly $25,000 from January through August and reported an annual profit of almost $7,000.[35] The versatile and viable Greendale Cooperative Association (GCA) was chartered initially under the famous Rochdale Plan and operated as an affiliate of Midland Cooperative of Minneapolis.[36] (The Rochdale Plan takes its name from a textile manufacturing center in southeastern Lancashire, England—the birthplace of the British cooperative movement, dating to the activities of the Rochdale Pioneers Equitable Society in 1844.) A prelude to broader resident participation in village life, the association served as a vehicle for principles of pacificism, international collectivism in economics, and diplomacy. During the early years of the association's existence, the flag of the International Cooperative Alliance, "a blend of all flags containing all the colors of the spectrum and the rainbow," hung from the ceiling of the food store.[37]

The residents were conscious of outside interest in their cooperative endeavors—though perhaps some of their claims to fame were a bit extravagant (such as the one which attested that "all socially minded people of Milwaukee and Wisconsin are eagerly and critically watching the progress of Greendale and its resident-owned enterprises"). In an effort to broadcast its message, the association hosted national experts on the cooperative experience, including Professor J. R. Cotton from the Milwaukee Normal School who addressed Greendalers on the beginnings of the Rochdale movement in England. In none of its activities, however, did the GCA solicit the aid of the farm tenants, although a large dairy and pasteurization plant in the rural area delivered the milk from four or five local dairy herds to the cooperative and later provided door-to-door service throughout the village.[38] None of the other rural families showed any interest in the town, and the management did nothing to bridge the gap between the two populations in the village. In 1943 Douglas Marshall, a graduate student in sociology at the University of Wisconsin, termed the Greendale farmers a "forgotten people" most of whom took "practically no part in the formal group participation of the community." Only one had ever visited in the village, and none, according to Marshall, had ever traded farm goods, nor had any been encouraged to do so by management.[39]

Other than an agricultural extension service run by state agents and consultants from the University of Wisconsin, the thrust of the management's community education program was the village, although rural children from the locale were permitted to attend the school on a tuition-free basis. Teachers and social workers from local WPA units conducted evening classes and helped organize innumerable clubs. Greendale residents could choose from among such diverse pastimes as bowling, gardening, birdwatching, dancing, astronomy, and philately.

Two popular organizations, however, were most relevant to local and national politics. One group was formed by fifteen to twenty residents who studied the refinements of Robert's Rules of Order and learned the complexities of labor economics. The second group of three men and nine women volunteers, with the help of a WPA journalism teacher and the talents of a local technical writer, published the first issue of a community newspaper on August 24, 1938. This was the *Greendale Bulletin* which, in a month, became the *Greendale Review*. The production soon established itself as an indispensable guide to the many "goings on" in the village.[40] At a cost to the government of six to twelve dollars a month (advertising space also was sold), the *Review* tried to fulfill its stated purpose of expressing "the best sentiment of the people on matters of public policy and public welfare. . . ." Its first Thanksgiving Day edition printed the greeting sent earlier to President Roosevelt conveying the "deep feeling of gratitude for the courageous leadership, the deep, human understanding that created our beautiful community."[41]

An informed discussion of world and national events was aided by a community library stocked with 3,000 volumes. A periodical collection spanned both popular and erudite tastes, but it was the more solid fare that seemed to attract the most readers, at least in the first years. Among the most popular items, the *Greendale Review* enumerated *Current History, Century, Forum, Hygeia, The Nation, New Republic, Scholastic, Survey Graphic,* and *Forecast,* as well as *Harper's,* the Sunday edition of the *New York Times,* and several other publications.[42]

The school curriculum in Greendale, too, reflected the pedagogical ends of management that found expression in the pragmatic philosophy of education espoused by John Dewey. Nearly the entire teaching staff had been educated at the University of Chicago, and along with the personnel came social science notions about the importance of interpersonal relations in the classroom, especially within the context of the arts and unstructured play. The experiential methodology of the school was summed up by its superintendent, J. R. Ambruster, who felt that each child, like his or her parents, ought to learn every day "the lesson of adapting himself to the social group of which he is a part."[43] In September, 1938, school began for 432 pupils. By the following March, nearly 100 more were enrolled. This student group constituted, in all, about four out of every ten Greendale residents. Greendale's few high school students were bused to Milwaukee's West High School where they were subjected to more traditional methods of instruction.[44]

Incoming residents were presented with a whirl of parties, amateur shows, coffee hours, German polka bands, galas, and other sorts of get-togethers. The community calendar in July, 1938, was cluttered with a Fourth of July celebration, a gentlemen's smoker, a "Get Acquainted" social, the first church meetings, and plenary sessions of the young cooperative movement. There were "loads of clubs," according to one pioneer, with "too many things going on"—especially for people who chose to plunge into everything. The physical compactness of the village encouraged and sometimes necessitated an ecumenical sharing of space. During the early federal years, for example, Lutherans and Catholics held

Easter services, one after the other, in the movie theater, with portable altars affixed to pushcarts. Wedding invitations were simply broadcast over backyard fences.[45]

A Greendale Recreation Committee, after meeting with WPA officials from Milwaukee and Washington, approved a Recreation Unit for Greendale to supervise outdoor and indoor games. The Recreation Unit also screened free films in the community building until the movie theater was opened in April, 1939. The *Greendale Review* smugly asserted that the new theater conformed to the "Williamsburg Colonial" style: "It does not incorporate the gaudy modern architecture of so many of the present-day theatres."[46]

Carloads and busloads of visitors continued to wind down Loomis Road from Milwaukee. A few of the guests were renowned, such as Goran Sidenbladh, the Swedish planner, or Ernest Bohn, former president of the National Association of Housing Officials. Catherine Bauer, one of the Suburban Division's housing consultants, and Sir Raymond Unwin, the architect and site planner of Letchworth (England's first garden city), along with his wife, walked through Greendale. On June 17, 1939, Henry A. Wallace, Secretary of Agriculture and presidential hopeful, stopped briefly for a Saturday morning chat with residents.[47] The many individuals, groups, associations, and conventions which toured Greendale represented a broad economic and political spectrum. A delegation from the Soviet Union was followed by twenty busloads of delegates from a National Park Service Convention, and soon thereafter by forty people who drove from the Lathrop Housing Project in Chicago with signs on their cars proclaiming: "Greendale, Wisconsin or Bust." During fall 1938, the Greendale management reported that over seventy-five people per day had toured the model home and many more came on weekends. The exhibition continued to attract curious crowds until a family rented the house in April, 1939.[48]

The weekly surrender of the town to tourists was not without some inconvenience to the resident families, particularly those who lived near the administration building. But gradually they became accustomed to strangers peering through the windows or asking if they could go through the homes. No one complained to management, and on October 9, 1938, Greendale staged its first Guest Day, drawing a crowd of over 4,000 people.[49]

Photographs of Greendale and the other greenbelt towns, supplied by the Farm Security Administration, also began to appear during the late

1930's and early 1940's and drew local and national attention to the communities. Most images of Greendale were made by Russell Lee and John Vachon, two of several acclaimed photographers employed by Roy Emerson Stryker, Chief of the Historical Section of the FSA. Stryker, who was Tugwell's former student and assistant at Columbia University, oversaw the production of 270,000 images from 1935 to 1943, and created what has been termed "the greatest [collection] ever assembled in the history of America." The pictures of destitute migrant workers, impoverished Appalachian families, and Dust Bowl farms and farmers served to justify the New Deal, and they survive today as the most poignant and enduring images from the entire collection. A large portion of the FSA photographs, however, were more prosaic and sought merely to demonstrate the good job that New Deal agencies were performing in the field—especially when contrasted with the illustrations of slum housing taken in 1935. Therefore, what better impression of the Resettlement Administration could have been offered than to portray the healthy children, happy families, thriving gardens, and sturdy houses that were to be found in Greendale and other greenbelt towns?[50]

Despite the number of clubs, organizations, and meetings already evident in Greendale, Manager Reeder suggested to the new residents the need for yet another committee to coordinate non-political events. In mid-October of 1938, seven Greendalers found the time to organize what later became the Greendale Citizens' Association, which was to be limited to the encouragement of community pride and responsibility. Vowing never to interfere with local government, the association pledged itself to "civic improvements that don't require ordinances." On October 16, just two days after the committee first convened, its members briefly considered a joint tenants' association with the residents of Parklawn, the PWA project in Milwaukee. The Greendale group, however, decided that local issues might become "more confused by calling in outside opinion . . . ."[51]

When the residents gathered in January, 1939, to formulate the bylaws of the association and to elect its officers, the association's mandate was broadened to encompass "efficiency in the Greendale Government" and the "general welfare of residents of Greendale."[52] Along with the *Greendale Review*, the association persevered throughout the years of federal ownership—its membership contracting and expanding around a loyal core as the times and the tempo of village life changed.

The planners might have envisioned a village where women would spend most of their time as homemakers, but both males and females shared the responsibilities of community leadership in the early days. Besides the scores of day and evening classes and clubs, women filled key posts in the Greendale Citizens' Association, and all three of the first co-editors of the *Greendale Review* were women. There obviously was some male displeasure over such feminine leadership, at least as perceived by one of the female editors of the *Review*; she claimed that the men in the village were the "severest critics" of the women involved in community affairs, and would "gossip about the manner in which we manage our households and families." The editor concluded by stating that it was "unfortunate when many intelligent women take no part in community activities because they fear this censure, and therefore their services are lost to the community." Males, however, dominated the Greendale Cooperative Association (deemed the "meetingest" organization in town), and, as it took shape, the local government.[53]

The Farm Security Administration permitted the residents to decide first, whether or not to incorporate Greendale and second, what form of local government they preferred. The first question was easily settled. On October 22, 1938, the residents voted 312 to 142 against incorporation, and on December 10, public officials were elected.[54] The choice between a village manager or a mayoral form or government gave rise to the first real factionalism in the village. A government committee sided with Reeder and advised the election of a village manager. On the opposite side of the question, a majority of the Greendale Citizens' Association held that such a centralized system was wholly inappropriate for a community based in principle upon cooperation. It voted that its referendum committee withdraw an invitation to Charles A. Dykstra, president of the University of Wisconsin, who was to speak in Greendale on city-manager governments and other municipal reforms. Finally the trustees agreed, with some reluctance, to let the residents vote on the matter.[55]

On the eve of the referendum, and coincidentally, on the day before the first annual Cooperative Association meeting, the *Greendale Review* reminded its readers that municipalities across the country were waiting for the decision of Greendale. By approximately the same margin as approved incorporation, the residents voted 238 to 110 for a village manager-town council government.[56] In April the Board named Sherwood Reeder village manager by acclamation, and in July Walter Kroening was named his assistant. Since Reeder was a federal employee, he received no remuneration.[57]

The excitement of settling in faded with the formalization of local government. In January, 1939, the *Greendale Review* registered its alarm at the growing indifference of a "majority of the residents." Dissatisfaction had already caused many to leave. Agency reports show that during the 1938–1942 interim, 236 families had vacated after occupancy. Marshall's study of Greendale society in 1943 concluded that out-migrants were

Management's subtle invasion of their privacy, exemplified by the title of this booklet, affronted many Greendale residents. *Source: Greendale Historical Society.*

"malcontents" who could not tolerate the demands of social life or of condescending management practices.[58]

Apparently even some of those who stayed and adjusted were nettled by intrusions of management into all aspects of life. The town was efficiently maintained—garbage was collected several times each week and home repairs and paint jobs were done promptly—but the implicit trade-off was a small measure of self-respect. The village regulations, recalled one husband and wife in 1984, could be bothersome at times.[59] Every incoming family, for instance, was handed a pamphlet of "Helpful Suggestions for Greendale Residents"—actually a compilation of rules on everything from proper disposal of garbage to yard care, accompanied by the stern warning: "Neglect in the observance of the suggestions herein set forth will result in increased management costs." Failure to report damage to the homes brought an official reprimand, and, if the tenants wished the walls painted some color other than a recommended hue, they had to do it themselves. In 1941, Kroening announced that he would hire men to paint the exteriors of houses once again to "eliminate some of the vivid colors"; the new hues were to be in six ranges of buff, ranging from deep buff "to white in six gradations of colors."[60]

The leasing of the Village Hall, rather than simply lending it to the Greendale Village Board, was another perennial vexation. From the first, the arrangement inspired much grumbling about the "paternalistic and unfair" contract, even though the village's attorney assured the board that the lease "had more leeway than a great many other contracts of a similar nature."[61]

What deeply bothered the pioneers was not so much any overt mistreatment, but rather the refusals by a succession of alphabetical housing bureaucracies to concede a special status to the greenbelt towns. When the popular Reeder left in 1941 for a job in defense housing, his place was taken by assistant manager Walter Kroening, who worked tirelessly for the community welfare, first as assistant manager and later as purchasing agent and village engineer. But for all his efforts, he was no politician, and while punctilious in the execution of his duties, Kroening had little rapport with Greendale's residents and was never able to stop the swift deterioration of relations between town and management.[62]

Furthermore, certain editorials in the *Milwaukee Journal* aroused the converted. When the *Journal* claimed, for example, that a typical home in Greendale had cost the government an exorbitant sum that exceeded $16,000, the editor of the *Greendale Review* protested that the prices were not out of line: "Now, we have had a taste of that 'new home' independence. Now we are *more than ever* determined to own and live in our own homes if and when we can accumulate enough or when for one reason or another we leave Greendale." Indeed, Marshall reported in his 1943 study that a reason frequently given for renting in Greendale was to set aside enough money for a home in Milwaukee.[63] Beginning in 1940, John P. Schroeter, Kroening's former colleague on the Engineering Section of the Suburban Resettlement Division, chaired a small mutual housing committee of the Greendale Citizens' Association, and along with others, he spent much of the next decade studying ways for his neighbors to join together and purchase Greendale (the first of several ad hoc cooperative purchase committees.)[64]

Signs of an international conflagration in 1940 rekindled a Rooseveltian verve within the village. Greendale's mood prior to America's entry into World War II had been stridently pacifistic, but once the United States committed its forces in 1941, civil defense became the watchword. Greendalers claimed that theirs was the first community in America to initiate donation drives for scrap metal, waste paper, and blood. In September, 1941, the Board resolved to promote the "ideals of all-out Americanism" and, in that same month, invited a national convention of the American Legion to inspect "a government designed and built housing project."[65]

While the war intensified patriotic feelings in Greendale, it also accelerated the drift of national housing policies away from satellite models of urban decentralization. According to Jacob Crane, then Director of Urban Studies for the new National Housing Agency, "the migration of single workers and married workers who leave their families at home is encouraged."[66] The need to limit domestic use of fuel and construction materials of all sorts forced the location of defense housing as close as possible to major industrial sites. Meanwhile, rising wartime incomes in Greendale and the other greenbelt towns made rent subsidies highly suspect in the eyes of the general public. In January, 1943, for instance, the *Milwaukee Journal* published a careful accounting of Greendale's operating costs and its rent revenues (the former, of course, were shown to be far in excess of the latter), and the paper concluded that Greendale harkened back to an era of fiscal irresponsibility: "It was an era of free and easy federal funds and noble experiments, but all this is water over the dam."[67]

In October, 1942, as if to underscore this new attitude towards rent subsidies, the federal government undertook a full re-evaluation of its forty-two non-farm and three greenbelt communities before they were transferred to the Federal Public Housing Authority (FPHA) within the National Housing Agency. In April, 1943, the FPHA announced a revised rental policy on all units effective June 1.[68] Under a new schedule, rents were raised an average of five dollars per month. While families living in the smallest units paid only a few dollars additional rent each month, families living in the four-bedroom units saw their monthly rental payments increase from thirty-five to forty-five dollars. On the other hand, families with incomes far in excess of the maximum limit (up to $3,600) were permitted to remain in the village. Kroening blithely predicted that "this pol-

Front-page cartoon by R.A. Lewis in the *Milwaukee Journal*, June 3, 1943, satirized wartime "hardships" that beset Greendale residents.

icy will be readily and sympathetically understood by residents of the community."[69]

Instead, it was mainly Milwaukee realtors who received the news "readily" and "sympathetically." The Milwaukee Real Estate Board pronounced the increases "perfectly logical," albeit poorly timed, since city landlords were being penalized by the Office of Price Administration's nation-wide rent freeze. The *Milwaukee Journal* fired a two-barreled salvo: "The rent situation at Greendale was a scandal, as the whole enterprise—and Parklawn—were examples of broken faith and misrepresentation to this [Milwaukee] community."[70] Needless to say, Greendalers were indignant. The Citizens' Association and the Village Board immediately sent telegrams to Wisconsin's senators and congressmen in Washington. Blaming "pressure groups and bureaucrats," the trustees and citizens' association members consoled each other and vented their collective anger "at the dictatorial and un-American attitude" of management. Groups and individuals urged their elected representatives to help repeal "this autocratic manifesto which encourages inflation rather than controls it." The condition in the new lease arrangement that particularly irked the residents was a compulsory twice-yearly interview with Kroening to verify family earnings. Trustees complained that while most residents had anticipated higher rents, they did not expect the hike to be "such a stiff one" and certainly not one handled in a manner that struck many as "communistic."[71]

Yet the village trustees and others found most official doors closed. Wisconsin's senators and congressmen went through the motions of investigating the constitutionality of the hike but, to a person, they washed their hands of the affair. Senator Alexander Wiley, for example, simply forwarded the answer he had received from Herbert Emmerich, Commissioner of the FPHA. John Schroeter, speaking on behalf of the Greendale Citizens' Association, wrote to a friend in Milwaukee that he was "somewhat disgusted" by the diffidence of Wisconsin's progressive Senator Robert La Follette. An official delegation dispatched from Greendale to Washington in early June was virtually ignored, and when Kroening urgently requested an interview with a highly placed official in the FPHA, an assistant wired back that Kroening could come ahead but that such a waste of train travel seemed inexcusable in wartime.[72] Greendale had few sympathizers except in Greenhills and Greenbelt, where residents were trying to mount resistance movements of their own.[73] There was a war on, and Greendale's problems seemed trivial in Washington.

Initially, the Greendale C...zens' Association was able to unite enough of the village behind it to make the whole affair unpleasant for the FPHA. One three-hour meeting of the residents, for example, unleashed a barrage of complaints from 200 residents about the inconveniences of living in Greendale and about home construction flaws. Afterwards, a lengthy manifesto of resident rights was mailed to President Roosevelt.[74] Kroening, of course, was a man in the middle. The Citizens' Association tended to blame the messenger for the bad news, and a few town leaders, including two trustees, wanted to abolish the manager position. As the fight continued through the summer of 1943, residents turned out in large numbers of 200 to 400 people to air grievances.[75] Kroening stayed aloof from the public commotion, and on May 11, 1943, the beleaguered community manager reported to the board that of about 350 families contacted, none had refused to renew their leases under the revised schedule. At this, three of the trustees raised the question of duress; and the entire board recommended that residents refuse to pay their rents.[76]

Duress or not, all but nine residents signed leases as they came up for renewal in June and in succeeding months. Of the rebels, all but two moved out of the village or buckled under and signed during the ten-day grace period. The hold-outs (one of them a trustee) found themselves at the center of a year-long legal battle financed by resident donations. After losing in Federal Court, the Greendale Citizens' Association regrouped, and in February, 1944, the association took the two rent strike cases to the Seventh District Court in Chicago where, once again, the decision went against the residents.[77]

Village officials publicly acknowledged the deleterious effect of the rent turmoil upon both the conduct of affairs and community spirit. While the adults were acting against management, the young people of the village were indulging in a spree of destructive mischief. Twenty-eight cases of vandalism and disturbance of the peace were logged by the village police in the first ten days of August, and the rate did not decline as the temperature cooled. In October, 1943, spokespersons for the town youths complained before an open meeting of the Village Board about the regimented summer youth program. As reported in the *Greendale Review*: "They stressed their desire to do something for themselves, they do not like sports or dancing, they got everything ready-made without being consulted . . . ."[78] The parallels between adolescent and adult politics seem to have eluded the *Review* or else the lesson was left unsaid. In any event, that summer's youth revolt showed as much staying power as its adult counterpart. One resident, feeling that the lawless deeds of the children reflected the disrespect of their parents for management, urged the Village Board to follow the example of Greenbelt, Maryland, by making parents responsible for any damages done to town property. A newspaper respondent, identifying herself as a "Greendale Mother," urged a more outreaching approach, but stated that the wartime atmosphere of the early 1940's contributed to "emotionally speeded up" youths, some of whom were becoming delinquents who experimented with sex and attended unsupervised parties that seemed to have "no end." Furthermore, the mother contended, such immorality included Greendale girls who spent weekend evenings in Milwaukee.[79]

Naturally, the rent strike left a residue of ill-will towards the management. On the heels of courtroom deliberations, resident leaders stepped up the sporadic campaign to oust Walter Kroening. In June, 1944, the Village Board briefly suspended the federal/village manager's salary until the legality of dual appointment could be determined. Finally, in March, 1945, the board was able to convince a state assemblyman to introduce a bill (Bill 467-A) before the state legislature enabling the trustees of a community to remove their manager by a majority vote and to prohibit a federal employee from holding such a position.[80] Only the village nurse, Merrill (Ma) Burke, spoke out on behalf of the much-criticized manager, but her protests against the dump-Kroening maneuver were futile. That same summer, the procedural bill passed into state law, and in January, 1947, the board appointed Richard Eppley to the separate position of Village Manager.[81] Afterwards, and almost as long as the federal government remained the owner, Greendale, a village of 2,500 people, was served by two full-time managers, a dual government that prefigured the coming transition from welfare town to private suburb.

CHAPTER EIGHT

A Greater Greendale for Postwar Milwaukee

In the face of mounting difficulties with management, and despite increasing apathy among most of the residents, several old-timers—perhaps a score of the original families—attempted to preserve links with the past. When the village entered a float in Milwaukee's 1946 Metrorama Parade (and won first prize), the design was a familiar one: a garden city queen surrounded by an arbor of roses and children dressed as flowers. Later that summer, Tugwell Day was proclaimed by the Greendale Village Board to honor the founder of the greenbelt towns program.[1]

Professional planners who visited Greendale in those days also perceived the village through rose-colored lenses. From Chile came a housing official who was struck by the "simple straight-forward architecture" and the "large open park area." Richard Dewey, a city planner from Milwaukee, described Greendale "as the closest approach to the ideal rural-urban fringe community." What impressed him most was the enthusiasm of the residents with whom he talked.[2] Visiting Greendale in 1948, Clarence Stein, architect of Radburn and greenbelt town consultant, concurred with this sunny assessment and remarked upon the "restful and gracious unity" of Greendale; the overall success of the plan was due, Stein claimed, not only to the skill and ability of Peets and Crane, but also to "the love that they put into the work." Stein anticipated a "constellation" of neighborhood villages within Greendale that would be "dynamically designed and spaciously arranged, so that they may grow, develop, and change to reflect the expressed interests and desires of the people of the neighborhood." Implicit was the pilotage of planners, such as those members of the original planning staff who returned to Greendale (with Elbert Peets prominent among them) to celebrate the decennial anniversary of Greendale.[3]

But tranquil appearances belied a deep division within the town between backsliders and boosters. The *Greendale Review* often bemoaned the waning of community spirit and atmosphere: "The affairs and problems are still besieging its occupants, but the interest and spirit [are] gone." Following the fiasco of the rent strike, community leaders took it upon themselves to lecture their less civic-minded neighbors on the necessity of cooperation. One candidate for the village board pledged "to re-establish the true community spirit which prevailed in the early days of Greendale," while another wished to extend "the spirit of cooperation" throughout the community. Meanwhile several of the pioneer residents joined together to form the Greendale Civic Group with the aim of reviving "the husking bee and ice cream social spirit" such as prevailed before "the village assumed a more cosmopolitan way of living."[4]

Residents tended to blame the demise of interdependence upon negligent management, but, in truth, rising incomes and the stigma of subsidized housing were in large part to blame. As industrial wages climbed during and after World War II, the upper income limit at Greendale was raised from $3,200 in 1947 to $3,500 in 1948.[5] Residents interviewed by Douglas Marshall, a University of Wisconsin doctoral student in sociology, confided that a common incentive for moving to Greendale was a savings in rent that later could be used as a down payment on a home in Milwaukee. Instead of families bustling to and from the cinema, adult classes, and nightly meetings, Greendale's streets were deserted at dusk and the glow of television sets lighted living rooms throughout the town.[6]

Rarely did the federal government come to the aid of faltering village organizations. The Greendale Cooperative Association received the coup de grace in 1948 when the government declined to renew leases on the cooperatively run food store. The last meeting of the GCA was a pitiful affair attended by only thirty-five die-hards. While volunteerism was on the decline, the federal management refused to provide any but the most basic services, and even on this count Uncle Sam played the miser. When, for example, the Greendale School Board requested more money in 1947, the deputy director of the FPHA responded by reciting a list of ways to trim wages and waste. The *Greendale Review* was itself forced to close temporarily in September, 1946, by shortages of both money and staff.[7]

Two incompatible views on federal housing surfaced in greenbelt town planning and management. From the presidency of Herbert Hoover and increasingly on into the New Deal, the government claimed a moral obligation to aid families directly in securing shelter. After World War II the opposing argument gained credence: that the government had a constitutional responsibility to respect private interests in the housing market since the plight of the homeless was attributable to a sluggish free economy.

The upshot of this dispute over policy marked an end to the greenbelt town program. In 1944, with the end of the war in sight, the National Housing Agency, through its subunit, the Federal Public Housing Authority (FPHA), tried to find a means of increasing the resident populations to levels of self-sufficiency; this was done in order that the community projects might be sold to private concerns. Although the general goal was clear enough, the exact course of action was long a matter of debate and indecision. Various parties clamored to be heard. In March, 1944, the community managers of Greendale, Greenbelt, and Greenhills formed the American Communities Corporation, hoping to lease the greenbelt housing stock and lands on behalf of the tenants in the three communities. This plan was devised, according to the managers, "as a supplement to, but not a part of, the subsidized housing program designed for the benefit of the lowest income group."[8]

Within the FPHA, Oliver Winston, director of the General Field Office, led a one-man crusade to sell the greenbelt towns to enlightened syndicates. Concentrating his efforts upon Greendale, and anxious to keep old promises to Milwaukee, Winston conferred with Warren Vinton, Walter Kroening, and a group of labor leaders and city officials from Milwaukee. Winston also engaged Elbert Peets to prepare a series of planning studies for the addition of 3,000 homes at Greendale. Peets's plan, virtually in final form by March, 1945, became the model for all subsequent public and private planning in the village. For the sake of attracting a private builder or consortium of realtors and developers, Peets forsook the more unusual aspects of the 1936 plan. He also took into account Federal Housing Administration mortgage guidelines for lot lines and home sitings. The cul-de-sacs of the original plan gave way to "a polygonal" arrangement of streets in which pairs of parallel streets terminated upon an apical connector loop. The block was then joined to others by main thoroughfares. But such innovations merely underscored Peets's old wish to preserve the small-town character of the project. The additional 3,000 homes were to be clustered into three or four discrete neighborhoods—each with its own complement of shops and parks. An unbroken greenbelt of 1,330 acres included the 510 acres dedicated ten years before to the Milwaukee County Parks Board, as well as 820 acres of working farms.[9]

On the basis of an in-house real estate study, it was decided to provide "a relatively small number of acreage plots," one-half to five acres in size, adjacent to the county parkway.[10] Peets and Winston discounted the objections of experts that Greendale was ill-situated to attract upper-income families and light industry. The FPHA, largely on the force of Peets's intuition, pushed a policy of diversification at Greendale—a mix of income classes and a blend of urban and rural land uses. A permanent greenbelt reserve, claimed Peets and Winston, was the critical element in setting the style of Greendale's future growth. "The close proximity," wrote Winston

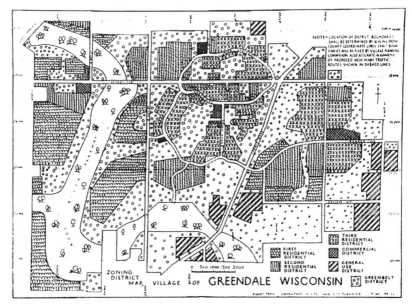

The first zoning map of Greendale (above) was drawn by Elbert Peets in 1948 and reflected his concern to preserve the original greenbelt. *Source: Greendale Historical Society.* Between 1945 and 1958, Peets prepared similar versions of his 1950 plan for the private development of Greendale (detail, below). *Source: Paul Spreiregen, ed., On the Art of Designing Cities: Selected Writings of Elbert Peets (MIT Press, 1968).*

and Peets in 1945, "of Greendale housing to genuine farm land is one of its greatest aesthetic advantages and is of some social and economic value . . . a protection to health and safety . . . a valuable demonstration of good planning."[11]

For months after the 1945 plan was drawn, Winston talked in vain to potential buyers of Greendale. A series of negotiations with Alexander Bing, the financier-builder of Radburn, New Jersey, proved fruitless. The only earnest offer to buy Greendale came from Arthur Marcus, a resident of Greendale. After a medical discharge from the U.S. Merchant Marine during World War II, Marcus became a seasoned spokesman for veterans' housing. It was in his capacity as a member of the National Housing Committee of the American Legion that he queried the FPHA in 1947 about land prices in Greendale. Winston and his superiors briefly considered the offer and even quoted a tentative price of $500 per acre for approximately 2,300 acres of undeveloped land. Lacking adequate funds, however, Marcus and his committee momentarily sank from sight of the federal agency, only to resurface the following year with a bolder plan and fuller purse. In the meantime, the government refused to deal directly with local resident cooperatives such as the Greendale Tenants Committee on Mutual Housing. From 1945 to 1948, the committee (chaired by the president of the village board), agitated for an amendment to the proposed Wagner-Ellender Act, which would have permitted mutual housing organizations to purchase public housing projects.[12]

Ignoring the criticism directed at his Greater Greendale idea, Winston decided to test the scheme in a sluggish postwar housing market. Winston's field office designated the Clover Lane section south of the existing village for subdivision into sixty-four lots. Winston had several ends in mind for this scheme. First, no one in Washington was quite sure of the market value of land in Greendale, and a limited sale of lots would, in Winston's opinion, at least indicate an appropriate price range for the remaining outlying lands. Second, reports from Milwaukee citizens to Winston told of a latent demand for cheap suburban lots from veterans in the area. Finally, Winston believed that, in order to safeguard the credibility of federal housing programs in Milwaukee, the FPHA would soon have to initiate a project in Greendale.[13]

Unfortunately for Winston's plans, the demand for Greendale lots was not so great as has been reported. Priced at $800 each, the lots in the new Clover Lane division averaged about 9,700 square feet in area (over twice the size of lots in the original village). Only thirty-one lots out of the sixty-four-lot parcel were sold in 1945 and 1946. A second subdivision, Dahlia Hills, was left untouched at this time. An arrangement between the FPHA and the Greendale Village Board, whereby the village would be reimbursed for preparing the lots for sale, soon led to bickering among federal and village officials over the propriety of a reserve fund of excess revenues in the village coffers.[14]

When, in 1946, Congress made a special appropriation "to expedite liquidation" of the greenbelt towns, the Greendale Village Board began to clamor for guarantees that the government would play a role in the expansion of its former ward.[15] Elbert Peets was asked to help formulate a village zoning ordinance along the lines of his 1945 Greater Greendale plan. In his 1948 report to the village, the town planner recommended a zoning category that he labeled the "greenbelt district," that is, a reserve of farms and parks to ensure in perpetuity Greendale's essential "semi-rural character." Peets urged the village board to retain one-third of the village area as "a kind of partially public park—an area which is indeed fenced against public access, yet affords to the public the valuable privileges of sweeping landscape views, an atmosphere freshened by fields and woods, and relief from many of the dangers and irritations of a crowded urban environment."[16]

Clarence Stein especially applauded the proposals to protect and maintain the greenbelt. Stating that just as medieval towns had been shielded from external dangers and encroachments, Greendale also enjoyed a similar advantage. The major difference, Stein quickly pointed out, was that the communities of the Middle Ages were fortified, while Greendale was ". . . secured by a belt of natural green." The most significant advantages of the greenbelt, Stein claimed, were the limitations that could be placed upon the size and growth of the community, and the ability to sustain the "neighborly character" of the village.[17]

Although Peets and Stein were anxious that the village hold onto its surviving greenbelt, the residents were more heartened by the government's continuing interest in the enlargement of the resident population and the diversification of its economic base to include limited nonresidential building. Kroening pointed out that while 1944 tax figures for all suburban municipalities in Milwaukee County showed 48.8 per cent of combined tax revenues came from commercial and industrial sources, only 2 per cent of Greendale's public revenues were derived from such nonresidential taxes.[18]

The bright outlook of Greendale quickly faded during another reshuf-
fling of federal housing agencies. Winston's field office, scheduled to expire
in 1948, lost control over the greenbelt towns. In May, 1947, the duties of
the FPHA and its branches were assumed by the Public Housing Administration (PHA), a unit of the Home and Housing Finance Administration
(HHFA).[19] The new commissioner of the PHA was John Taylor Egan,
once a senior architect on the original planning staff at Greendale. Egan
was under orders to dispose of its greenbelt properties in all due haste, and
as so often was the case, the futures of the greenbelt towns were left to
middle-echelon bureaucrats such as Egan; they were well-meaning and
hard-working, even ingenious, but they lacked the necessary authority or
inclination to revive federal participation in the communities. Egan's superior, Raymond Foley, the new administrator of the HHFA, entrusted
Egan to devise a formula for the sale of the towns that would be fair to all
parties: tenants, developers, and the federal government. In August, 1948,
Congress passed Public Law 901, thereby making federal FHA loans
available to purchasers of greenbelt housing, and at Egan's request Foley
exempted the greenbelt towns from a general ruling that federal community housing projects would have to be sold to the highest bidder regardless of mitigating deed restrictions on future development.[20]

While Congress was clearing the way for a sale of federally sponsored
communities on very uncertain terms, two citizens' groups in Greendale
came forward with their own divergent plans. Representing an older cooperative tradition within the village, a Mutual Housing Corporation (a rein-
carnation of the 1945 Committee on Mutual Housing) requested of the
government that it be permitted to purchase the housing in Greendale at
cost.[21] On another front, the veterans' housing movement, still led by
Arthur Marcus, was gaining momentum. Marcus, now supported by the
popular president of the Greendale Village Board and by a number of city
and state officials, offered the PHA $2 million for the entire Greendale
property. Although this initial bid was too low for Egan to accept, it did
identify the veterans' housing group as a serious contender. In the following weeks and months, this veterans' group reorganized and refinanced
itself into the American Legion Community Development Corporation
(ALCDC). In October, 1948, the national convention of the American Legion, meeting in Miami, Florida, roundly endorsed the purchase plan of
the Greendale veterans' corporation.[22]

While the view of Greendale from Egan's office in Washington was
sunny, clouds were gathering over the village. To begin, a growing number

of residents were beginning to wonder whether Marcus had ulterior motives for wanting to purchase Greendale. Moreover, the residents were beginning to question the growing involvement of the Milwaukee Common Council in the American Legion scheme. Marcus' reputation in the village had been deteriorating ever since he testified in 1947 before a congressional small-business subcommittee that the leases of the Greendale Cooperative Association ought not be renewed the following year because they represented a "monopolistic" challenge to free enterprise in his hometown. All signs seemed to indicate that Marcus was out to end Greendale's effort at cooperativism. In hindsight, his purchase of a lot in Clover Lane (the first private land purchase in that village) fell into a pattern of misdirected patriotism, at least according to many Greendale pioneers. But the ALCDC issue was anything but clear-cut. The plan at least allowed the residents to remain in their homes, and the membership of the ALCDC was representative of local interests. The Board of Directors included an official of the American Legion, three veteran residents of Greendale (Marcus was elected president), two city attorneys, the city comptroller, three aldermen, and Frank Zeidler, Milwaukee's socialist mayor. On December 7, 1948, the city council, during an extra session, unanimously approved the entire purchase of ALCDC preferred stock for a sum of $300,000.[23]

At first, few residents displayed concern. The village board followed its president in supporting the Legion plan, and Kroening even prepared a confidential report for the Legion Corporation concerning the economic prospects of land development and the serious tax problems the village would face if there were an end to federal participation. The first person within Greendale to sound the alarm was Richard Eppley, the village manager. Three days after the stock purchase by the city, Eppley asked the village attorney if the city could annex Greendale without annexing the intervening territory.[24]

The Legion group, trying to shore up its credibility within the village, printed brochures and a newspaper, the *Greendale Reporter* ("The Voice of Greater Greendale"), to publicize its intentions.[25] Most of Marcus' energies, however, were directed outside the village and over the heads of the residents. Between September and December, 1948, Marcus, sometimes in the company of Kroening and Milwaukee city officials, met to discuss the means necessary for the Legion group to enter into direct negotiations with the PHA and to exclude other bidders.[26]

In the spring of 1949, Marcus again was in Washington seeking support for enabling legislation permitting the PHA, in the case of the greenbelt towns, to skirt the bidding procedures required by Public Law 901. Marcus acquired a strong ally in the person of U.S. Senator Joseph McCarthy of Wisconsin, who on March 18, 1949, told a House subcommittee that the ALCDC was "a good legitimate veterans' organization" with a sound plan to sell homes to veterans "at the lowest possible figures." The subcommittee also heard testimony from a somewhat surprised Congressman Clement Zablocki, within whose Wisconsin district Greendale was located. At that first hearing, Zablocki, clearly caught off guard, was prepared to do little more than register his displeasure that neither he nor his constituents had been told of the hearings in advance. A few days later, Zablocki submitted several resolutions and letters from members of a Greendale Home Purchase Committee, another resident group committed to winning ownership of the village. Marcus, however, minimized the importance of this factor. His testimony represented the committee as a small and well-to-do elite with annual incomes "over the $4,500 mark." The Marcus-McCarthy no-bid resolution sailed easily through the House and Senate, where Illinois Senator Paul Douglas (also a veteran) amended it to protect the rights of the residents to buy or rent their present homes. President Harry S. Truman signed the bill on May 19, 1949.[27]

Assured that tenants would not be displaced for at least a year after the sale, the PHA Subjected the Legion plan to close scrutiny and tried its best to discourage home-owners' cooperatives which, the PHA suspected, lacked sufficient grasp of high finances. As early as the fall of 1947 Peets had been at work on a tentative plan to expand the village—this time for the immediate addition of 1,000 units by the Legion Corporation.[28] Meanwhile a Chicago-based research firm set a figure of $3,285,000 as the highest price that the government could ask for if a plan for middle-income veterans' housing were part of the bargain.[29]

The tenants of Greendale did not intend to be steamrollered by another government order. Rather than risk annexation or, worse, eviction, the members of various citizens' groups—the Home Purchase Committee, the Greendale Citizens' Association, and the *Greendale Review*—joined forces behind a local Greendale Veterans' Cooperative Home Association (GVCHA). In July, 1949, the Greendale Mutual Housing Association was dissolved and all its funds were transferred to the GVCHA.[30]

Battle lines were drawn through the resident community as both groups promised to help the "average income man" own a home in Greendale.

Supporters of both the ALCDC and the GVCHA canvassed the village during the summer of 1949 trying to sway uncommitted residents. The tide of public opinion was just beginning to turn in favor of the Legion plan when the ALCDC made the tactical mistake of announcing that annexation of Greendale by Milwaukee was the only way to avoid exorbitant property taxes.[31] The residents were in a quandary: they did not want to be part of Milwaukee, nor did they want to move. The firm hired by the PHA to assess the Greendale property had reported that 360 out of 469 (77 per cent) Greendale families contacted wished to purchase the homes they inhabited. It was this dual desire for home ownership and self-determination that welled up in resistance to the ALCDC. The editor of the *Greendale Review* went so far as to accuse Milwaukee's Common Council of metropolitan imperialism. "Do you think," asked the editor, "that for one moment the City of Milwaukee will colonize [annex] Greendale using the same despotic methods employed by the British of the Revolutionary War days?"[32]

Finally on August 23, 1949, the Greendale management held a referendum on the various sales options the residents had been demanding all summer. To the surprise of the city and the PHA, the residents soundly rejected the Legion plan (621 to 98) in favor of the local veterans' association. Mayor Zeidler explained to the press that Milwaukee was solely concerned with saving "the lower income groups of the village from the heavy burden of this new debt."[33] Under the harsh glare of public scrutiny, the implausible partnership of urban socialists and legionnaires fell apart. Seeing that the Greendalers were united on the question of annexation, the city withdrew its financial support from the ALCDC. Virgil Hurless, the city comptroller, now contended: "It is my conviction that the City of Milwaukee has no legal or moral right to directly subsidize this project or any other private or public project located outside the corporate limits of the city of Milwaukee." So ended the federal government's effort to link Greendale more closely to the metropolitan center or, as Peets was fond of saying, the "mother-city."[33] Although the village board and most prominent people in Greendale endorsed the local veterans' association and the GVCHA plan, the federal government refused to enter into negotiations.[35]

As Milwaukee city officials tendered their resignations to the ALCDC board of directors, the Milwaukee Common Council began a two-year legal fight to recover its $300,000 investment in the ill-fated corporation. In the midst of a well-publicized scandal over the expense accounts of

ALCDC members, Arthur Marcus died and left the city responsible for wages paid to his private nurse. Back in Washington, Marcus' old ally, Senator Joseph McCarthy, initiated his own vendetta against the cooperativists in Greendale. Acting independently of the PHA, McCarthy contacted several parties who had expressed to him an interest in purchasing the greenbelt town. But McCarthy had no more luck in selling Greendale than did anyone else, and in February, 1950, the PHA rescinded the special negotiating status of the Legion group—even while last-minute merger talks were proceeding between the ALCDC and GVCHA.[36]

In the wake of the referendum, the village remained bitterly divided between pro-ALCDC and pro-GVCHA groups. The longtime president of the Greendale Village Board, as well as those trustees who had supported the ALCDC, were ousted in the next village election and replaced by members of the local veterans' group. Meanwhile, the perennial cry went out to get rid of Walter Kroening. The PHA's handling of the Legion proposal had done further damage to its credibility in Greendale, and worse still, any esprit de corps in Greendale had all but disappeared. These certainly were not the best circumstances in which to work out the terms of a sale, nor did they form the best circumstances in which to reside in the community. The editor of the *Greendale Review* wrote a poignant line on village life: "We would like to go down every street in Greendale and greet everyone as a friend."[37]

The outbreak of the Korean War in June, 1950, slowed but did not halt the government's effort to sell the greenbelt towns. President Harry S. Truman froze all negotiations for federal community properties, given the off-chance that they might prove useful as defense housing—a possibility that Senator Paul Douglas angrily discounted in the case of the "greentowns."[38] Behind the public controversy, preparations for the sale of Greendale continued quietly in the office of Roy M. Little, an assistant commissioner of the Division of War Emergency Housing. During the war interlude, the government displayed a renewed determination to turn over the greenbelt properties to private home buyers and builders. In earnest about straightening up its books in Greendale, the government demanded compensation for budget surpluses cached in the reserve fund of the village board, a sum of $15,000. The government reacted by ordering federal marshals to seize municipal equipment—the snow plow, fire engine, garbage truck, and police car—much of which was so sorely in need of repair that it had to be pushed out of the village garage by Kroening and the marshals. After months of haggling, the board reluctantly agreed to ser-

ABOVE: *In the original plan for Greendale, about one-third of the 2,000-acre greenbelt was to revert to a natural state, while the remainder would be retained in farms.* BELOW: *By 1938, the initial town plan of Greendale was plainly discernible from the air.*

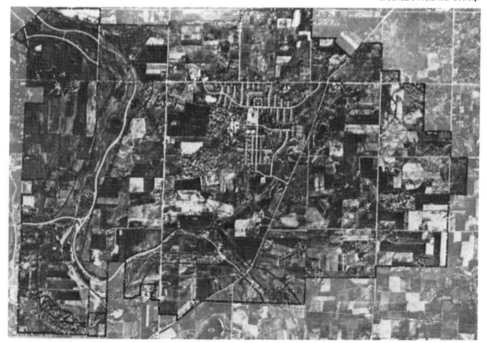

ABOVE: *Farm Security Administration photographers in 1936 documented slum conditions in cities such as Milwaukee, providing New Deal officials with visual evidence to justify their housing and planning programs.* BELOW: *Landscape architect Elbert Peets (1886–1968) designed the initial layout of Greendale in 1936, and in the 1940's and 1950's he prepared a series of plans that guided subsequent community development.*

ABOVE: *Members of the Greendale planning staff in front of their workplace, the Washington mansion of Lady Evalyn Walsh McLean, 1936.* BELOW: *The designers of Greendale sketched this aerial overview of the Village Center with its vision of the street pattern, buildings, open spaces, and plantings.*

Scale models (here indicated by two views of the same dwelling unit) were used by Elbert Peets to determine how the house, garage, and driveway for each lot could be sited to provide privacy and sunlight for prospective residents.

ABOVE: *Rendering of a typical court in Greendale, showing the visual relationship that Peets and architect Harry Bentley sought to develop between single and multiple family housing units.* BELOW: *The central pathway and park system crossed Dale Creek near the Village Center of Greendale.*

J.S. Lansill Papers.

ABOVE: *The objectives of the New Deal Resettlement Administration—to implement the Green-dale plan swiftly and economically—conflicted at times with the labor-intensive approach of the Works Progress Administration (WPA).* BELOW: *The multiple housing units of Greendale were considered novelties by the planners of the community since most low-income residents of Mil-waukee lived in tenements or bungalows.*

J.S. Lansill Papers.

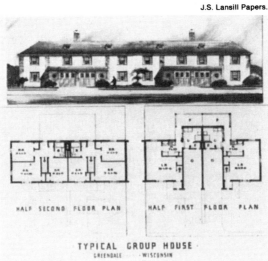

HALF SECOND FLOOR PLAN   HALF FIRST FLOOR PLAN

TYPICAL GROUP HOUSE
GREENDALE · WISCONSIN

ABOVE: *Versatile and more strictly institutional in style than Greendale's other public buildings, the community center served as a school and meeting hall.* BELOW: *While unskilled WPA workers were employed in the building of Greendale, over half the relief funds went to skilled construction laborers.*

Architect Walter Thomas prepared several designs for Greendale's village hall; all versions, including the final proposal and the completed structure, indicated a contemporary colonial vogue in architecture that was reminiscent of Williamsburg, Virginia.

J.S. Lansill Papers.

ABOVE: *Although the planners of Greendale disdained ornamental frills, they insisted upon safety and soundness in home and utility construction.* BELOW: *From September, 1936, through August, 1937, while Greendale was under construction, some 650,000 people reportedly visited the community and the model home at 5503 Acorn Court.*

J.S. Lansill Papers. (*Milwaukee Journal* photo.)

Milwaukee Journal photo.

ABOVE: *On November 11, 1936, Eleanor Roosevelt (right) accompanied Florence Kerr, a regional director of federally sponsored women's programs, on a tour of Greendale.* BELOW: *The National Youth Administration (NYA) trained guides to conduct tours of Greendale and the model home.*

J.S. Lansill Papers.

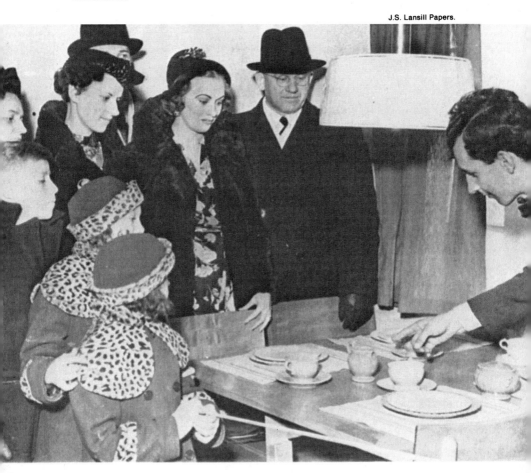

J.S. Lansill Papers.

ABOVE: *Nowhere in Greendale was a clinical economy of design enforced more severely than in the kitchen, where each unit was furnished with a new electric range and refrigerator.* BELOW: *Oak flooring and pine beams softened the stark atmosphere of the living room/dining area in the Greendale home.*

J.S. Lansill Papers. (*Milwaukee Journal* photo.)

ABOVE: *The detached houses and pedestrian pathway system used at Greendale were especially well suited to the rolling terrain.* BELOW: *For several years after Greendale was settled, the agricultural character of the greenbelt continued to be reflected in the dairy barns and fields surrounding the village.*

Photographers for the Farm Security Administration often featured the sturdy houses, well-tended lawns, and abundant gardens that were to be found in Greendale.

Shortly after Greendale opened in early May, 1938, the Milwaukee Sentinel *proclaimed that the community was replete with fresh air, black dirt, and grass, and that residents would soon be raising radishes, roses, and children. Early photographs especially stressed the opportunities available for healthy outdoor activities and family interaction.*

J.S. Lansill Papers.

Some of the proposed architectural details and the variety of materials exhibited in an early version of a proposal for the Greendale movie theater were eliminated before the building was constructed.

J.S. Lansill Papers.

ABOVE: *By the late 1930's, the structures along Greendale's Broad Street included (from right to left) a tavern, the post office, and a building that housed several small shops. The theater entrance was situated to the far left of the latter structure, while the heating plant chimney may be seen in the background.* BELOW: *The cooperative food store was the most visible of several communitarian ventures established during the early years of Greendale's existence.*

ABOVE: *By 1939, an economical arrangement of unpretentious homes within a park-like setting was evident at Greendale.* BELOW: *Sculptor Alonzo Hauser was commissioned in 1938 by New Deal officials to create a flagpole grouping that featured the ordinary citizens who would settle in Greendale.*

ABOVE: *From the early days of construction to the present, visitors and observers have commented on the architectural and planning similarities between Greendale's residential area and that of European towns and villages.* BELOW: *Elbert Peets laid out ample backyard space to accommodate such domestic chores as clothes drying.*

Arnold R. Alanen (1986).

ABOVE: *The Greendale village hall continues to serve as the focal point for Broad Street. During the 1960's, the row of shops to the right was built on a portion of the original village park.* BELOW: *By the 1980's, over half the original homes in the Village Center had been covered with aluminum siding and/or structurally altered to suit contemporary tastes.*

Arnold R. Alanen (1981).

Arnold R. Alanen (1986).

ABOVE: *The high-priced houses of the Overlook neighborhoods, which had a median value of $120,000 in 1980, are in striking contrast to the original moderate income orientation of Green-dale.* BELOW: *The authentic facade and form of this 1930's home, still evident in the mid-1980's, attest to a nascent architectural preservation movement in the original Village Center.*

Arnold R. Alanen (1981).

vice the village and to remit the disputed reserve funds.[39] Richard Eppley, Kroening's village-appointed counterpart, thought the government action was clearly beyond the bounds of reason, and claimed that "they were seeking to destroy local government here by attempting to usurp all the village's legal and moral duties under the guise of preserving the general welfare of the community by emergency action."[40]

The confrontation over the village budget had no sooner ended before another piece of dirty laundry was aired in public. A year earlier, in November, 1949, when it became clear that the PHA intended to ignore the concern of cooperative housing committees, the village board created its own housing authority under state law. The move was made in the hope that the PHA would consent to sell the village to such an entity. A Pittsburgh contractor had even agreed to invest $3 million in the Greendale Housing Authority to enable it to purchase the entire village. The Greendale Veterans' Cooperative Homes Association had also expressed a willingness to work with the Housing Authority on a "pooled purchase" plan.[41]

Unfortunately, none of the proponents of the housing authority scheme did the requisite homework on legalities. Nor, it appears, was the State of Wisconsin very clear about the definition and scope of such an authority. At any rate, one resident decided to foil the sale of Greendale by challenging in court the right of the village to establish a housing authority. The trustees were red-faced, since only by a stretch of the imagination could Greendale be said to be suffering a housing shortage. Although a circuit court rejected the plaintiff's claim, this decision was later overturned and a trial ordered by the Wisconsin State Supreme Court in August, 1951. While the Greendale case was being heard in the state courts, all fifteen of Wisconsin's municipal housing authorities were thrown into a legal limbo, and a $10 million housing construction project in Milwaukee was jeopardized. Needless to say, city and federal officials were losing patience.[42] The bad publicity spurred the PHA to sell the project; the housing was to go first and the underdeveloped land at some future date. Acting on a suggestion by Congressman Clement Zablocki, the government chose to give the occupants first chance at their own residences at prices fixed by an independent assessor. Following this, the unsold homes were to be offered to veterans, and finally, the general public would be permitted to purchase any remaining units.[43]

Since little in Greendale seemed to go smoothly for the federal government, the problems surrounding the home sales came as no surprise. The residents continued to find fault with offical policy. There was, for example, the obvious matter of the row houses: how were they to be divided? Kroening came up with a solution that suited the PHA but scarcely anyone else. The plan was to hold a lottery for those buildings in which the tenants could not agree upon the terms of a group purchase. As a result, some of the 208 families living in row houses were displaced and, even before the lottery was held, the residents were denouncing it as a mockery of justice.[44]

The row house problem was only one of several complications. Residents were adamant in their opposition to another appraisal of home values and to a replat of the village that separated single-family units from their customary garages and centered all such units on lots with attached garages.[45] But the most heated debate was sparked by the decision of the PHA to sell the Greendale village hall along with the greenbelt land and the rest of the municipal buildings. Little, himself, had urged other PHA officials to delay the sale of the village hall—still a focal point of village pride—at least until the Greendale Village Board had an opportunity to assess its new tax situation and perhaps purchase the building.[46] In the midst of these and similar stand-offs, the sputtering veterans' cooperative association rallied more than three hundred residents on one evening in June, 1951, to protest PHA policies. The *Greendale Review* served as another forum for resident discontent; scarcely an issue went to press without some indictment of the PHA on its front page. The village board, so as not to appear too pliable to the will of a future developer, asked its new Plan Commission to complete a village zoning ordinance as soon as possible.[47]

The PHA, meanwhile, went ahead with the sale despite adverse weather conditions and widespread resident discontent. The survey of the central village area was completed during the bitterly cold January of 1952 with the help of Dale Johnson, a member of the Plan Commission and, until 1949, an architect and city planner in Milwaukee.[48] By the end of the month, all forty-four vacant lots scattered throughout the Village Center had been sold to residents, and in March, Kroening's office began to accept offers made earlier on the homes. Within a few weeks after the completion of the center plat, all of the detached and duplex units and most of the row houses were in the possession of resident owners.[49]

Prices on the homes ranged from just under $2,500 per unit in the six-family row houses to as much as $9,500 for the detached units. Overall, the government estimated it would realize, at most, $4,296,550 from the sale of its property at Greendale.[50] This amount can be compared with the original federal outlay of $10,417,490 to build the community (1936–1938 dollars). The federal government gave all utilities to the village at no cost.[51]

The sale of homes on fair terms for all resident families and in such a manner that they would be eligible for federal home loans (hence the replat of the village) were among John Taylor Egan's main concerns at Greendale. Next on the PHA administrator's list was the sale of the green-belt land to a conscientious developer. Egan reviewed numerous applications from Washington, Milwaukee, and New York, just as Diogenes had searched for an honest man (and one with enough capital to pursue a comprehensive development plan). The parcel of 2,236 acres was offered in October, 1952, ostensibly to the highest bidder, but with a discretionary review of bids to guarantee good planning. Shops, municipal buildings, and scattered lots were to be sold separately.[52] The rural tenants hastily formed a Rural Tenants Association in order to negotiate with the PHA, but a PHA spokesman ineloquently told the village board: "The primary concern of Greendale was for residence and the farmers are here on an industrial basis."[53] It was becoming increasingly obvious that despite the pleas of Elbert Peets and Clarence Stein to protect the size and inherent integrity of the greenbelt, the natural buffer was coming under increasing threat.

The danger that Greendale might fall into the hands of real estate speculators deeply concerned Milwaukee's Mayor Zeidler, who took it upon himself to forestall such a sorry end to the greenbelt town project. Joined by Walter Kroening, Zeidler met in mid-October of 1952 with two prominent businessmen: Richard Herzfeld, scion of a Milwaukee department store magnate, and W. A. Roberts, president of the Allis-Chalmers manufacturing firm. Zeidler suggested to these two leaders of the Milwaukee business community that they approach Warren Vinton, still an official in the Public Housing Authority, to discuss "coordinating the new growth of Greendale with the City of Milwaukee." The upshot of Zeidler's idea was the organization of the Milwaukee Community Development Corporation (MCDC) under the directorship of Herzfeld, Roberts, Francis J. Trecker, another Milwaukee manufacturer, and Louis Quarles, a Milwaukee lawyer and president of the new corporation.[54]

Although the initial bid of the MCDC ($738,600) was lower than the PHA could accept, the credentials and the concerns of the MCDC directors for sound planning principles won the attention of Egan. Besides, the closest rival bid ($612,681) had come from a Chicago realty firm which Kroening described as "fast operators" with a long record of bankruptcies.[55] Quarles assured Egan that the expansion of Greendale would be undertaken in such a way as to relieve a chronic housing shortage among Milwaukee's industrial workers.[56] In January, 1953, the MCDC and the PHA agreed upon a price of $825,000 for 2,228 acres of greenbelt land, along with fourteen other parcels and the shops and public buildings in the village center.[57]

Within Greendale, news of the sale to the MCDC generally was welcomed with relief. From all appearances, Greendale would enter the Eisenhower era in responsible hands. Alfred Lenz, president of the Greendale Village Board and a frequent critic of governmental tactics, pledged full cooperation with the new owners, while the *Milwaukee Sentinel* called the deal an exercise in "civic leadership" which would result in "a model community of workingmen's homes." Ex-federal manager Kroening, no doubt eager for a respite, took a job as manager of a new Milwaukee shopping center.[58]

Rid at last of a fumbling and intransigent federal housing bureaucracy, the traditional Milwaukee partnership of "sewer socialism" and big business brought Greendale into the metropolitan fold on far different terms than its New Deal founders had envisioned. Housing was still the aim— housing sited with respect for the land and designed for the urban worker—but now the motives echoed the traditional company town mix of noblesse oblige and self-interest.

CHAPTER NINE

Old Visitors, New Tastes: 1955–1985

DURING its eleven-year existence, the Milwaukee Community Development Corporation (MCDC) adhered to most of the original principles of greenbelt planning: a neighborhood cluster of housing blocks with centralized commercial and public functions, a generous provision of open space around homes, and (a new wrinkle) an industrial park on the edge of the community. Compared to other land developers in Wisconsin, the MCDC was exceptional in its reliance upon professional site planners and its commitment to sound environmental practices. During the early 1950's, for example, only one Wisconsin developer in five hired professional consultants to prepare subdivision plans.[1] The concern of the MCDC for the future of Greendale was partly an expression of a stewardship mentality among the directors and planners. There also was more than a modicum of shrewd business involved: the corporation had settled into Greendale for a long period of time. With 2,200 acres of vacant land and a physical plant ready to absorb thousands of new families, Greendale possessed clear investment advantages over other sites in the growing metropolis.

The MCDC quickly assembled a professional staff under the supervision of two Milwaukee architects who also served as spokespersons for MCDC policy within the community. Elbert Peets was immediately engaged as a consultant and put to work on a master plan for residential development. Completed in 1957, the plan contained a familiar mix of garden city motifs. Streets and lots were planned to minimize disruption of natural contours, while each neighborhood was left with 10 to 20 per cent of its area in parks. Housing types ranged from $50,000 estates along the parkway to $10,000 pre-fabs in the vicinity of the original 1936 village. Finally, the master plan for Greendale called for the development of a more diverse tax base by providing for additional commercial facilities and limited industrialization. The corporation worked closely with the Greendale Village Board and carefully timed the implementation of its development plans with the construction of schools and utilities by the community.[2]

For nearly a decade, from 1955 when the first plat was filed until the early 1960's when the physical and psychological limits of growth were beginning to be reached, the MCDC and the village were caught up in a building boom. As before, young families began to move from Milwaukee, and Greendale was again making news as a planned community. Press releases from the corporation portrayed the familial atmosphere of churches and safe streets, the natural solace of a remnant greenbelt, and, last but not least, low taxes. An activist faction of old-timers and newcomers alike pushed aside more conservative members of the town council and, led by architect and former Milwaukee city planner Dale Johnson, rubber-stamped the new plats proposed by developers and dutifully rezoned planned development units.

Hoping to preserve the neighborhood character of Greendale and thus to stabilize property values throughout the village, the MCDC created homeowner's associations by mandatory deed covenants.[3] Under these agreements, any person who purchased a new home in Greendale automatically became a member of such an association. A local newspaper was published after a ten-year hiatus, and city planners once more flocked to see the old greenbelt town bloom after so many years of dormancy.[4] The MCDC encouraged the citizen effort to restore the community to its former level of visibility in the region and nation. The chief planner for the MCDC tried (but failed) to initiate a discussion between the Greendale Village Board and the Board of Regents of the University of Wisconsin concerning the advantages of locating a branch campus in Greendale.[5] There also were suggestions for a golf course and recreation club, and Dale Johnson, as president of the village board, corresponded with the heads of research-oriented firms in the hope of bringing clean industries, white-collar families, and new sources of tax revenues into the town. In the early 1960's the village board even operated an Industrial Development Commission that launched a brief promotional campaign replete with glossy brochures on the industrial suitability of Greendale.[6] This effort, however, failed to lure any developers or firms to the community.

Stimulated by generous federal home loan policies and a much-improved county highway system, Greendale's population more than doubled from its federal-era level of 2,752 persons in 1950 to 6,843 persons by 1960. The corporation divested itself of the downtown shopping center, and a new investor from Milwaukee came up with a set of ambitious plans (never carried out) to revamp the street pattern in the town center, to carve a V-shaped intersection, and to line the forked artery with shops to serve the growing population. In a magnanimous gesture, the MCDC gave the village hall to the village board in 1958.[7]

Beneath the public show of goodwill, however, the honeymoon between developers and residents was turning sour. Older residents were alarmed at the changes taking place in Greendale. New faces were appearing in the campaigns for local office. School children, equally unfamiliar, trooped along the pathways in ever-growing numbers from the apartment buildings and fine homes on the outskirts of the Village. Whether justified or not, it became common wisdom among many townspeople that they would have to pay a heavy price for such a rapid expansion of their community. Over 250 families a year were moving into Greendale by the early 1960's, and the burden of taxation threatened to swell accordingly. Unfortunately to many, the bright hope of industry in Greendale proved a chimera. Though the industrial loop has rather slowly increased in size, tax revenues from nonresidential sources remained relatively insignificant budgetary items. Furthermore, the new research laboratories and office buildings generated few jobs for the men and women of the community, and Greendale has had problems holding onto firms. In fact, the first facility in the industrial loop, an Allis-Chalmers laboratory, was vacated in 1979. The idea of giving tax breaks to firms that would relocate in Greendale met a lukewarm reception from a jaded village board in 1965.[8]

On other fronts, too, the MCDC and its plans for economic and social diversity in Greendale were losing ground. By the 1960's, the issue of multi-family housing was becoming a political liability for the supporters of the corporation. A clique of the original residents, most of whom were still living in the Village Center, formed the Greendale Residents Committee in 1958 and warned that the MCDC would pull out of the village once the classrooms were full and the physical plants were strained to capacity.[9] As had happened in the 1940's, the community was split between factions with different outlooks on the town's future and with different levels of tolerance for change. At this juncture the conservatives prevailed. Village elections were carried repeatedly by anti-development candidates after 1958, and the village board slowly weaned itself from its customary reliance upon MCDC planners. In 1958, and regularly thereafter, the board hired its own planning consultants to prepare master plans for development and to suggest ways for Greendale to improve its tax situation.

The MCDC, for its part, argued that the board ought to get on with its business of zoning new additions and forget about assuming a "straitjacket" of long-range growth plans. This advice fell on deaf ears. In the early 1960's the board undid many of the MCDC reforms. It assumed control of the park areas then in the hands of idle homeowners' associations, and in 1966, fearing an overload on its sewage disposal works, it threatened to suspend all home construction until a metropolitan sewer interceptor line reached Greendale, sometime in 1968 or 1969.[10] Patience on both sides wore thin. Finally, development issues drowned out all others in local elections. After a particularly strident electoral clash between pro- and no-development forces in 1964, the MCDC decided to sell its remaining greenbelt properties, about 1,100 acres, to a Milwaukee realtor for $1 million.[11]

The new owner, the Greendale Land Company, promised to abide by the same priorities in planning that had guided the MCDC—a mix of housing types, a balance of commercial and residential development, and generous reserves of open space. During the coming years, metropolitan water (1964) and sewer (1969) services sustained residential construction while escalating land prices justified greater outlays for conversion of marginal lands from agricultural to residential uses. Given the inexorable land market forces that were at work on the periphery of Greendale in the 1960's, the original idea of maintaining a permanent agricultural greenbelt around the village was shelved. Provisions were made, however, to offer an "approximation" of a greenbelt via the inclusion of Milwaukee County parklands along the Root River.[12] In the absence of the MCDC planning staff, the Greendale Land Company also instigated some dramatic departures from former practices by calling for condominiums, subsidized housing for the elderly, and extensive commercial investments.

During the 1970's, the largest undeveloped areas of Greendale were subdivided and many new houses emerged throughout the community. By the 1980's, following the platting of two small subdivisions along the parkway, land development was virtually completed. (There also were a few condominium complexes scattered throughout the village.)

The current land-use map of Greendale, therefore, serves to illustrate the various changes in subdivision platting that have occurred from 1935 to the 1980's. (See map on back endpapers.) The eastern half of Greendale, which includes the original Village Center and several subdivisions built during the 1950's (East Town), has a net density of some eleven housing units per acre. However, the more recent developments in the western area of the community (Overlook Farms and Overlook West) allowed a net density of about 1.5 dwellings per acre only. Overall, the extensive area of estates that altogether covers several hundred acres along the county parkway in the western section is in striking contrast to the small houses and lots in the older Village Center.

By using data from the federal censuses of 1970 and 1980, it is possible not only to compare the two areas (Village Center-East Town and Overlook) of Greendale, but also to contrast the entire community with the Milwaukee Standard Metropolitan Statistical Area (SMSA). The latter figures especially illustrate the progressive maturation of Greendale's population, and the relative affluence of the community's current residents. (Tables 3 and 4.) It is indeed ironic that much of Greendale, originally created as an enclave for persons of moderate means, is now populated by large numbers of rather high-income people.

When considering age groups, it is clear that Greendale, to date, has served as the home for relatively large numbers of families with children. The percentage of the population under nineteen years of age in Greendale, for example, exceeded the Milwaukee SMSA figure by about 5 per cent in both 1970 and 1980. Nevertheless, the aging of Greendale's overall population is especially noticeable when tracing changes in the relative distribution of residents who ranged from twenty-five to forty-four and forty-five to sixty-four years of age. In 1970, just over 30 per cent of Greendale's residents were in the twenty-five to forty-four-year-old age group, while some 24 per cent of the Milwaukee metropolitan population was in the same category. By 1980, however, the relative proportion was the same in both Greendale and the SMSA. The group ranging in age from forty-five to sixty-four years constituted about 15 per cent of Greendale's population in 1970, while the figure for the SMSA exceeded 20 percent. Ten years later, in 1980, the figure for Greendale had increased to some 22 percent, while that of the metropolitan area remained at about 20 per cent. When considering the entire population, the median age for Greendale in 1980 (32.2 years) was higher than that for the metropolitan area (29.8 years).[14]

About 70 percent of Greendale's work force was employed in white collar occupations in 1980, while the figure for the SMSA approached 54 percent (Table 4.) In a similar vein, by 1980 close to 50 percent of the adults 25 years of age or older in Greendale had completed at least one year of college, whereas the SMSA figure was 33 percent. The 50 percent figure for Greendale, it should be noted, had increased from about 16 percent in 1940 to just over 40 per cent by 1970.[15]

Following the lifting of artificial income ceilings after Greendale was sold in 1952, median family incomes increased from $4,000 in 1950 to $7,700 in 1960; to $13,700 in 1970; and to $26,300 in 1980. (Table 4.) The latter figure exceeded the amount for metropolitan Milwaukee by some

$3,000. Only 1.3 per cent of Greendale's residents were below the poverty line in 1980, contrasted with 6.3 per cent of the population in the SMSA. A similar pattern was evident in housing values. The median value of a Greendale house in 1980 was $78,000, while the overall figure for metropolitan Milwaukee was $60,200. The Greendale house also was larger than its counterpart in the metropolis. Likewise, in Greendale the median number of rooms was 6.1, while the Milwaukee SMSA figure was 5.2 rooms.[16]

Differences of a similar magnitude were revealed when comparing the two census tracts that comprise Greendale (Tables 5 and 6.) The easternmost tract, formed by the original Village Center and the East Town subdivisions built primarily in the 1950's, has rather parsimonious lots, small houses, and a 1980 population of 13,800 residents. The western tract (identified as Overlook) has much larger lots and houses and a population of some 3,100 residents in 1980. As might be expected, the median value of a house in Overlook in 1980 ($119,800) was considerably greater than that of the Village Center and eastern Greendale area ($73,400).[17]

The Overlook census tract also is more white-collar-oriented than the Village Center-East Town area, although the difference between the two lessened from 1970 to 1980. In 1970, slightly more than 60 per cent of all employed residents in the former tract were working in managerial, professional, technical, and administrative occupations, while 38 per cent of the residents in the latter tract were similarly employed. By 1980, the respective figures were 78 per cent and 69 per cent. Similar differences were reflected in median family income figures. In 1970, the median figure was $19,350 for Overlook and $13,385 for the Village Center tract; by 1980, the totals were $33,600 and $25,900 respectively.[18]

A decline in the birth rate and a normal out-migration of young adults from the aging suburb have contributed to a slowing of Greendale's population growth rate. The community's population, for example, increased to 16,928 persons by 1980, and although this represented more than a fivefold increase since 1955, the population grew by only 1,830 residents during the 1970's; this, in sum, represented a relative increase of 12.2 per cent from 1970 to 1980. Meanwhile the number of dwellings grew from 4,075 to 5,412 units, a growth of 32.8 per cent during the period.[19]

While the number of dwelling units grew at a faster rate than did the total population from 1970 to 1980, an increase in commercial development also contributed to a sharp rise in assessed property values. The total value of property in Greendale rose from $6 million in 1955 to $168 million in 1972, and during the following eight years, the amount nearly tripled—to $333 million in 1978 and then to $480 million in 1980. Residential property accounted for about 73 per cent of the latter figure; only 3 per cent was in personal property. Of the remaining property tax sources, only 1 per cent was industrial and 1 per cent agricultural. Commercial properties, therefore, provided 22 per cent of Greendale's tax base, and about one-fourth of this amount was for an enclosed shopping mall (Southridge), still the largest such facility in Wisconsin, that was built along the northwestern edge of the original village in 1970. Not surprisingly, many Greendale residents, particularly the aging pioneers, saw the commercial intrusion of the shopping mall into the village environs as a sad and ill-conceived development.[20]

The emphasis upon homes and parks in development planning was quite apparent in the land-use schedule that had evolved by the late 1970's. Approximately one-third of the 5.4 square miles of village area was in parkland (this converts to about 1,150 acres, 780 of which were owned by Milwaukee County), about 40 per cent of the village area was in housing, and the remainder was divided among commercial, industrial, and residual agricultural lands.[21]

As in suburban towns elsewhere in America, the amenities of Greendale's open space and services have been enjoyed by a largely white, solidly middle-class segment of the metropolitan population. Between 1970 and 1980, for example, Greendale's black population increased from but six to twenty-three people; this latter figure represented less than two-tenths of 1 per cent of the total village population. The color line seems all the more sharply drawn between city and suburb when it is noted that the City of Milwaukee was 23 per cent black in 1980, and that about 11 per cent of the SMSA population could be similarly classified. Despite sporadic attempts since the late 1960's by a church-affiliated Greendale Integration Committee, the village still lacks the subsidized housing base upon which to build a truly "multi-cultural" Greendale.[22]

From its beginning, Greendale has been planned on the basis of new town assumptions concerning relationships between people and environment and with a sentimental attachment to small-town ambiance and imagery. According to an MCDC publicity brochure issued around 1960, Greendale was an ideal community in several respects. The brochure illustrated, both verbally and pictorially, such attractions as planned roads, streets, churches, parks, residential sites, and commercial areas; the image of a garden community; safe and quiet streets; a friendly and child-centered social life; and a responsible village administration.[23]

All of these features, of course, have long been the stock-in-trade of new town planners, not to mention townsite promoters for an even longer time. Professional planners over the years have remarked upon similar site relationships—the skillful modulation of the street pattern to accommodate natural contours, comprehensive planning of discrete residential areas, and the close proximity of parks and homes. Although residential planning at Greendale had adhered to these general principles, the recent attraction of the village to affluent families and individuals is especially apparent in the extensive estate developments that altogether cover several hundred acres along the county parkway. The overall result has been a close juxtaposition of the 1936 village plan, reflecting a regionalist-ecological model, and a garden suburb in the modern sense with generously parked and extensively platted neighborhoods of curvaceous streets and distinctive homes. These two suburban textures span fifty years of change in middle-class tastes and approaches to planning.

A question that presents itself, then, is this: Have the more land-profligate developments of post-1950 Greendale produced a higher level of resident satisfaction than was attained by the New Deal planners? To provide some insight to this question, a resident preference survey was conducted in 1978 in two neighborhoods of Greendale—the original Village Center neighborhood of the 1930's, and the Overlook neighborhoods, the latter primarily products of the 1960's. The survey focused on several aspects of life in Greendale, most of which were connected to features of the town plan.[24]

It was evident that the Village Center and Overlook differed widely in such matters as occupation, age, and family size. In some instances such differences translated into different housing preferences. A typical Overlook household consisted of between four and five persons, with the principal wage earner most likely employed in a white-collar position. (Table 7.) Adults in Overlook generally were middle-aged, that is, between the ages of thirty-five and fifty-four, while the Center was much less homogeneous with regard to these characteristics. Retirees in the Center were as numerous as respondents below the age of thirty-five years. Households with two persons and even one person were common, while both workers and retirees in the Center held or had held predominantly blue-collar jobs. Since the Overlook area had been developed within the last thirty years, most respondents had moved to Greendale after 1958. In the Center, on the other hand, old-timers (those dating back to the 1930's and 1940's) and newcomers were present in nearly equal numbers.

When interviewees were asked why they had moved to Greendale, the responses fell primarily into one of four categories: social (in anticipation of friendships of family atmosphere); economic (reasonable housing costs or good investment); image (the village's reputation as a planned garden community); and the town plan itself. (Table 7.) Social considerations were most often given by Centerites as the most important reasons for moving to Greendale (40.0%), followed by economic factors (29%). Overlookers, on the other hand, moved primarily because of the community image (35%), and secondarily because of economic considerations (28%).

The two sample groups were in close agreement on whether life in Greendale was satisfactory. Nearly all respondents—87 per cent in the Center and 80 percent in Overlook—replied in the affirmative. However, the prospect of remaining in the same neighborhood was met with varying degrees of favor by the two groups. Nearly all of the Overlook respondents stated that they would wish to remain in Overlook rather than move to the Center or elsewhere. On the other hand, just over one-half the Center respondents indicated a desire to continue living in the Center if money were not an issue.

The two sample populations were in close agreement when asked: "What do you like most about Greendale?" Approximately 30 per cent in each neighborhood cited village esthetics and nearly as many cited friendliness or community spirit. (Table 8.) Convenience (proximity to shopping, schools, and so forth) and traffic safety also elicited favorable responses, although not as often as other factors. Despite Greendale's historic commitment to open-space planning, open space per se was not often singled as a "most liked" feature. Other responses, however, suggested that Greendale's parks and pathways do add much to the perceived beauty and planned image of old and new areas.

An entire series of questions dealt with resident use of parks and with the values assigned by residents to open space in their vicinities. As for the latter, about one-third of the respondents in both neighborhoods stated that they valued the parks primarily as play areas for children or for the esthetic character of the open space. (Table 9.) Perhaps because the pathway system transects the Village Center, over one-fifth of the respondents there valued the open space as a place to walk—a sharp contrast with the few in Overlook, only 6.4 per cent, who expressed similar sentiments. Center respondents also reported a higher level of park use in general. Over one-half of them stated that they used the parks daily or several times per week, as opposed to one-third of the Overlook sample. The two types of parks in Greendale, one with an internal pathway system and the other with an adjacent parkway, varied significantly for the kinds of activities pursued within them, although the differences may have been partly a function of the relative age of the residents in the two areas (a higher proportion of retirees in the Center). Thus the Center's open-space areas were used more frequently for reflective pastimes (nature study, birdwatching, looking, etc.), whereas more active pastimes (sports, games, and so forth) tended to predominate in Overlook. (Table 10.)

When asked which type of open space was preferred—town parks and pathways in the Village Center and parkways in Overlook—respondents in both areas voiced relatively similar attitudes. (Table 11.) However, just over one-fourth of the residents (27 per cent) in Overlook preferred the open space areas provided in the Village Center over those found in their own neighborhood, while under one-fifth (19 per cent) of the respondents in the Village Center voiced a preference for the open space features of Overlook. The overall layout and planning of each neighborhood was evaluated somewhat differently: a clear majority of Village Center residents (62 per cent) believed their area to be superior to or equivalent to the other neighborhood, but an even larger total (90 per cent) of Overlook residents considered their neighborhood either better than or equal to the Village Center.

In sum, the salient and historically important features of the original Greendale plan seem to have served many of the purposes that Elbert Peets originally intended. Where the traditional neighborhood unit principles have been applied most rigorously (i.e., the Village Center), the consequent design generally has met with resident approval. This lends support to the original garden city hypothesis that at least certain suburban dwellers will adapt to, and may even come to prefer, high-density living if site and architectural relationships are compatible to human scale and if population densities are compensated for by accessible open space.[25]

Nevertheless, while the attractions of safe streets and good neighbors seem to have produced high levels of resident satisfaction in the Center, the differences in family sizes and the social status between Center and Overlook indicate that housing in the former area has been chosen by many simply because of economics. Hence, many Center residents seem to attach less importance to community image or planning esthetics than do their Overlook counterparts.

Clearly, important generalizations cut across the sample population: many respondents consider Greendale an exclusive place with special social and environmental benefits. Yet residents and planners alike have been mistaken in their supposition that Greendale's suburban location would permit selective contact with the central city. Loss of open space, concern about crime in the parks and along the attractive village pathways, drastic renovations to Village Center housing, and traffic around old and new shopping facilities continue to raise doubts about separating Greendale from the people and the problems of the metropolis.[26]

Perhaps the most lasting elements of the greenbelt town program were not those of earth and concrete, but those of dreams and visions unfulfilled. Some of the very innovative aspects of the original 1935 plan for Greendale—the merger of farm and town, the metropolitan-management agency, and the early inclusion of very low-income families—were not even implemented. Some were tried and found wanting—for example the federal village manager arrangement, the economic cooperatives, the industrial park, and the permanent rental status of the residents. Still other innovations must be judged successful—among them the village open spaces of parks and pathways, the neighborhood cluster plan, and the diverse mix of housing that included small units but with many more larger homes to accommodate growing families. More important than these disparate elements, however, was the overall concept of a self-contained and self-governing public housing project designed in a familiar style and laid out in a manner that fostered feelings of privacy and belonging.

To be sure, real problems frequently intruded upon the village idyll of Greendale. The goals of ecological balance, functional design, and maintenance of the agricultural greenbelt often conflicted with a perceived need to expand the village tax base through residential development. Though Clarence Stein had assured Greendale's residents in 1948 that the greenbelt would protect them and would continue to do so as long as they chose to preserve it, Carol A. Christiansen, in a recent critique of several garden city experiments in America, states that Greendalers actually had no choice in this issue. Noting that the greenbelt could have been maintained only by offering a system of land values that resisted local market economies, Christiansen observes that multiple ownership and the nearness of Greendale to the expanding metropolis meant that the land eventually would fall to the pressures of speculation and increasing taxes: "Greendale lost its greenbelt and its village character because change could not be so easily restrained."[27]

Racial integration also was retarded by the desire to enhance property values through strict land planning and architectural controls, combined with the distance from the city's industrial areas and social services. As a result, low-income black families were virtually excluded from Greendale. Yet, even though the New Deal vision of metropolitanism and co-operation was nearly forgotten after World War II, the historical images and values of the 1930's village nonetheless do occasionally emerge when current development activities are discussed.

Greendale of the 1930's grew out of a plain and common vision of how factory workers and shopkeepers might live and of how future cities might grow. Greendale's planners returned to bygone townscapes for inspiration—to the colonial village and the midwestern small town—and in memory of those places they hoped to create a simpler, more orderly environment where families would live in harmony with each other and with the land. To be sure, Greendale soon began to grow in more pragmatic directions, fitting new notions to old patterns; and yet the metaphorical landscape at the center of the suburb has remained a vital influence upon town politics and self-perception.[28]

In 1973, Jacob Crane looked back at the communities he helped to create in the 1930's and stated that even though Greendale and the greenbelt towns had experienced problems, they displayed the "hunger" people had for suburban environments. The issues of environmental design and social change that have been engendered by Greendale, however, bring to light a certain ambivalence toward urban living in America, and the prevalence of these conflicting attitudes goes far towards explaining the cultural dynamics of suburbanization. The question that can be asked, historian Kenneth Jackson has recently pointed out, is: "Why have we neglected our cities and concentrated so much of our energy, our creativity, and our vitality in the suburbs?" He responds that there have been two conditions necessary for the deconcentration of residential activity in America—the suburban ideal and population growth—and two essential causes—racial prejudice and inexpensive housing.[29]

Greendalers, like Americans elsewhere, have been ambivalent about commitment to "community." They have sought neighborliness even while trying to guard their privacy. They have been receptive to and concerned with social welfare, but they have taken care to protect property values. Greendale became, then, what the people themselves have wanted—not a utopia, but a town where changes could be carefully planned and where the problems of the city seldom intruded. Indeed, planning was used not so much as a directive for change, but as a restraint.[30]

Yet it is easy to overstate the abruptness of this transition from communitarianism and regionalism to a more parochial form of advocacy. It is tempting, too, to search the historical record for signs of a socialistic arcadia as evidence of a nascent radicalism among American working people in the 1930's. The truth is far less dramatic. Seldom did Greendalers look beyond the green borders of their town to a locus of civic belonging and responsibility, and while the metropolis, per se, came to play an important part in the physical development of Greendale through its provision of basic services and the out-migration of its business firms, political affairs within the suburb often were conducted in opposition to the aims of metropolitan commissions and city governments. In fact, much of the chauvinism exhibited by Greendale's leaders in the past stemmed largely from fears about annexation by Milwaukee, which was perceived as threatening the loss of local control and returning to the colonial status of the federal years.

A recent renaissance of the "new towns" idea began in the early 1960's and continued into the mid-1970's.[31] That movement culminated in scores of new community projects and in some highly innovative federal enabling legislation, notably the Urban Growth and New Community Act of 1970 (Title VII), which provided direct and indirect federal assistance for new town construction until 1975 when the program was terminated.[32] Critics of the new communities, however, were quick to point out that planners possessed scant understanding of, or empathy for, the city's cultural and esthetic nuances. The diversion of federal housing funds into middle-income suburbs was denounced, as was the implicit consignment of the poor to decaying inner cities.[33] Given the experiences of the greenbelt towns, all of these results could have been predicted.

While federal and city planners saw Greendale as a key to sound regional policies, residents (and later the corporate owners of the greenbelt lands) acted regardless of regional concerns and ends—despite the realtors' professed belief that what was good for Greendale was good for Milwaukee. The vital economic, administrative, and sentimental ties that New Deal planners had hoped to forge between city and suburb failed to emerge. This occurred partly because an adequate statutory basis upon which to build intra-metropolitan cooperation was always lacking, and partly because the townspeople had little incentive or inclination to seek a closer affiliation with the central city. Their bonds of affection extended to village hall and, at first, to the nation's capital; but they skipped entirely the construct of a Greater Milwaukee.

Naturally, the existence of so many self-willed communities complicates the rational development and conservation of land-based resources. So, too, this municipal atomism frustrates the equitable apportionment of the region's wealth and amenities. This fragmentation of metropolitan America has resulted, in large part, from "the inability of cities to extend their boundaries through annexation and consolidation."[34] Controlled decentralization remains an elusive goal, at least in the American context where metropolitan, state, and federal governments have refrained from any long-term commitment to the design, planning, and development process.

The Greendale of the New Deal era still exists today—in its pedestrian pathways and clustered housing, and in its pleasing vistas and harmonious setting. Undoubtedly the most enduring legacy of the original Greendale is to be found in the physical layout and planning of the community, although even here much of the rural greenbelt was carved into high-priced housing estates that began to spring up in the 1960's. What Greendale clearly lacks, however, is the realization of the collective plans and visions that brought the community into existence: whether due to expediency, self-interest, haste, or short-sightedness, obvious gaps exist between original ideology and actual practice. Here, as elsewhere in America, there has yet to be instilled a perception of the metropolis as a community of individuals who possess mutual needs, mutual interests, and mutual dependencies. Unfortunately, the privatization of suburban society and space throughout America has led to reduced levels of concern for other social, economic, and racial groups—especially when "other" refers to inner-city residents.

Given the differences between the real and the ideal at Greendale, what does the experience of this one enclave have to say about the planning and development of other communities in America—especially since so many of the proud expectations of the greenbelt town fell short of fulfillment? The record of social reform is as mediocre at Greendale as it is elsewhere in suburban America. What Greendale does clearly show, however, is that the ecology of the earliest town plan—which called for a plenitude of parks, peaceful streets and walkways, and an intimacy between nature and townscape—generally has been maintained and perpetuated to the present. Just as some architectural theorists such as Leon Krier view the early eighteenth-century plan of Williamsburg, Virginia (and its twentieth-century reconstruction), as a desirable and perhaps even radical alternative to current modernist planning, the layout of the original village area of Greendale—Williamsburg's twentieth-century counterpart—might be evaluated in a similar light. Both, for example, are pedestrian-oriented. Whereas automobiles are eliminated entirely from historic Williamsburg, the Village Center of Greendale was designed to accommodate the automobile without being dominated by it. In addition to pedestrian access, both provide ample open space—"green lungs"—to complement their compact axial plans.[35] Emphasizing their pleasing physical form, of course, begs the question of social responsibility.

As important as the natural and cultural amenities are, the promise of a humane urbanism that the Greendale plan embodied was not realized. Its premise that the metropolis is a community of interdependent places and intersecting lives was not fulfilled. Still, practical design succeeded even as utopian planning failed. The Greendale experience thus suggests both the limitations and the continuing allure of urban design and planning in modern American society.

NOTES TO THE TEXT

Preface

[1]Hal Prey, ed., Greendale: The Little Village That Could . . . and Did (Greendale: Reiman Media Group, Inc., 2004), 163-64, 166-67.

[2]Ibid., 166-67.

[3]Ibid.; Linda McClellan, Elizabeth Miller, and Daina Penkiunas, "National Historic Landmark Nomination, Greendale Historic District" (Washington, D.C.: National Park Service, 2011); Roy Reiman, "Tidbits of Tomatoes and Daffodil Bulbs," Country (June/July 1997): 32.

[4]U.S. Census of Population, 1980-2010. Dan Veroff of the Applied Population Laboratory, UW-Madison Extension, assisted in gaining access to the 2010 data.

[5]U.S. Census of Population, 1980 and 2010.

[6]Ibid.

[7]Besides Main Street Ready-Made these books include the following: Joseph L. Arnold, The New Deal in the Suburbs: A History of the Greenbelt Town Program, 1934-1954 (Columbus: Ohio State University Press, 1971); Zane L. Miller, Suburb: Neighborhood and Community in Forest Park, Ohio, 1935-1976 (Knoxville: University of Tennessee Press, 1981); and Cathy D. Knepper, Greenbelt, Maryland: A Living Legacy of the New Deal (Baltimore: Johns Hopkins University Press, 2001).

[8]David L. Ames and Linda Flint McClelland, Historic Residential Suburbs: Guidelines for Evaluation and Documentation for the National Register of Historic Places—National Register Bulletin (Washington, D.C.: National Park Service, 2002).

[9]"United States National Register of Historic Places," Wikipedia (accessed 26 January 2012); National Park Service, "National Historic Landmarks Program," www.nps.gov/history/nhl/ (accessed 26 January 2012).

[10]Elizabeth Miller, "Greendale Historic District," National Register of Historic Places Nomination (Madison: Preservation Division, Wisconsin Historical Society, 2005); Linda McClelland, Daina Penkiunas, and Elizabeth Miller, "Greendale Historic District," National Historic Landmark nomination (Washington, D.C.: National Park Service, 2011).

[11]McClelland, et al., "Greendale Historic District," NHL nomination; communications from Kathleen Hart (Greendale Historical Society) to author, 8 February, 10 February, and 15 February 2012.

[12]Tracy Rohzon, "New Deal Architecture Faces Bulldozer," New York Times, 8 February 2009, citing Robert Karo. See Robert Karo, The Power Broker: Robert Moses and the Fall of New York (New York: Knopf, 1974).

[13]The fiftieth anniversary was marked by a symposium held in Greendale's high school on 10 September 1988. The hundreds of Greendalers and other interested people who attended the event heard Prof. Joseph J. Arnold of the University of Maryland, Baltimore, begin with an overview of the government's Greenbelt Town program; he was followed by Prof. Stanley K. Schultz of the Department of History at the University of Wisconsin-Madison, who spoke about conditions in Milwaukee County during the 1930s. The morning sessions concluded with two offerings that dealt with the planning and building of Greendale: one, a presentation that I made, focused on the community's physical planning, landscape design, and buildings; the other, by former New Deal administrator Tilford Dudley, offered an account of his experiences as the Chief of Land Acquisition for the Suburban Division of the Resettlement Administration. The afternoon sessions began with an overview of the community's transition from public to private ownership, given by former village manager Robert Eppley, Jr.; and appearances by three Greendale "pioneers" who discussed their experiences during the 1930s and 1940s. The symposium concluded with future planning and preservation options for Greendale, made by Ernest Alexander, a professor of urban planning at the University of Wisconsin-Milwaukee; Kurt Bauer, executive director of the Southeastern Wisconsin

Regional Planning Commission; John Jahnke, Greendale's planner; and James Stahlman, vice-president of the Greendale Land Company. A tour of Greendale followed the symposium. See Village of Greendale, et al., "Greendale 50 Years, 1938-1988: A Symposium on Greendale's 50th Anniversary," 10 September 1988.

Chapter One

[1]A penetrating analysis of anti-urbanism among American intellectuals is Park Dixon Goist, *From Main Street to State Street: Town, City, and Community in America* (Port Washington, New York: Kennikat Press Corporation, 1977). See especially Goist's discussion of Lewis Mumford's notion of the garden city, 151–157. Another presentation along these lines is the chapter by Jeffrey K. Hadden and Josef J. Barton, "An Image That Will Not Die: Thoughts on the History of Anti-Urban Ideology," in *New Towns and the Suburban Dream: Ideology and Utopia in Planning and Development*, Irving Lewis Allen, ed. (Port Washington, New York: Kennikat Press Corporation, 1977), 23–60. In this same volume, sociologist Bennet M. Berger takes exception to the academic stereotype of a monolithic suburban culture. See his "Suburbia and the American Dream," 229–240.

[2]The most extensive history of American town and city planning, especially for the early colonial and antebellum eras, continues to be John W. Reps, *The Making of Urban America: A History of City Planning in the United States* (Princeton, New Jersey: Princeton University Press, 1965). Also see John W. Reps, *Cities of the American West: A History of Frontier Urban Planning* (Princeton, New Jersey: Princeton University Press, 1979).

[3]A thorough summary of company-town planning in America through the late 1930's is contained in Arthur C. Comey and Max S. Wehrly, *Planned Communities, Part 1 of Urban Planning and Land Policies; Volume 2 of the Supplementary Report of the Urbanism Committee to the National Resources Committee* (Washington, D.C.: U.S. Government Printing Office, 1939). Greendale's chief landscape architect and town planner, Elbert Peets, assisted for a time in the design of Kohler, a company town in Sheboygan County, Wisconsin. See Arnold R. Alanen and Thomas J. Peltin, "Kohler, Wisconsin: Planning and Paternalism in a Model Industrial Village," in the *Journal of the American Institute of Planners*, 44 (April, 1978), 145–159.

[4]Ebenezer Howard, *Garden Cities of Tomorrow* (London: Faber and Faber, 1898, reprinted by the M.I.T. Press, 1965). English planners brought the lessons of Letchworth directly to the pages of American journals; see, for example, C. B. Purdom, "New Towns for Old: I. Garden Cities—What They Are and How They Work," in *Survey*, 54 (May, 1925), 169–172. A thoughtful examination of the garden city in history is in William Petersen, "The Ideological Origins of Britain's New Towns," in the *Journal of the American Institute of Planners*, 34 (May, 1968), 160–170; also see Walter L. Creese, *The Search for Environment— The Garden City: Before and After* (New Haven, Connecticut: Yale University Press, 1966). Finally, Carol A. Christiansen, in *The American Garden City and the New Towns Movement* (Ann Arbor, Michigan: UMI Research Press, 1985), argues that during the twentieth century "the garden city idea has been an enduring theme in [American] urban planning" (quotation on p. 2).

[5]For a summary of Odum's thoughts, see Howard W. Odum, *The Regional Approach to National Social Planning* (New York and Chapel Hill, North Carolina: Foreign Policy Association and the University of North Carolina Press, 1935). The Southern regionalists, particularly Odum and his intellectual debts to Mumford and to German historiography and geography, are treated in a review essay by David R. Goldfield, "The New Regionalism," in *Journal of Urban History*, 10 (February, 1984), 171–186.

[6]Originally published in 1917, Geddes' organismic philosophy applied to urban growth is set forth in Patrick Geddes, *Cities in Evolution: An Introduction to the Planning Movement and to the Study of Civics* (New York: Howard Fertig, Inc., 1968).

[7]A brief history of the Regional Planning Association of America is presented in Roy S. Lubove, *Community Planning in the 1920's: The Contribution of the Regional Planning Association of America* (Pittsburgh: University of Pittsburgh Press, 1963). See also Roy Lubove, "Housing Reform and City Planning in Progressive America," in *Cities in American History*, Kenneth T. Jackson and Stanley K. Schultz, eds. (New York: Alfred A. Knopf, 1972), 344–355; and Lubove's "New Cities for Old: The Urban Reconstruction Program of the Thirties," in *Social Studies*, 53 (November, 1962), 201–213. Writings by the regionalists have been collected by Carl Sussman, ed., as *Planning the Fourth Migration: The Neglected Vision of the Regional Planning Association of America* (Cambridge, Massachusetts: The M.I.T. Press, 1976). The title of the latter is taken from Lewis Mumford, "The Fourth Migration," in *Survey*, 54 (May, 1925), 130–133.

[8]A theoretical discussion of regional planning in America is offered by John Friedmann and Clyde Weaver, *Territory and Function: The Evolution of Regional Planning* (Berkeley and Los Angeles: University of California Press, 1979), 22–86. For a history of populist aspects of regionalism during the Great Depression, see Michael C. Stern, "Regionalism in the Great Depression," in *Geographical Review*, 73 (October, 1983), 430–446.

[9]A discussion of Radburn and other garden communities, including the greenbelt towns, is in Clarence Stein, *Toward New Towns for America* (Cambridge, Massachusetts: The M.I.T. Press, 1957). A more recent book-length appraisal of Radburn is in Daniel Schaffer, *Garden Cities for America: The Radburn Experience* (Philadelphia: Temple University Press, 1982).

[10]Lilienthal's most famous defense of the TVA is contained in David Lilienthal, *TVA: Democracy on the March* (New York: Harpers, 1944). The TVA's doctrinal roots have been traced by Philip Selznick, *TVA and the Grassroots: A Study in the Sociology of Formal Organization* (Berkeley: University of California Press, 1949), while Rexford Tugwell and the urban historian Edward C. Banfield have offered a sobering view. See their article "Grassroots Democracy—Myth or Reality?" in *Public Administration Review*, 10 (Winter, 1950), 47–59. Some of Tugwell's early writings are in Rexford G. Tugwell, *The Battle for Democracy* (New York: Columbia University Press, 1935). For a recent overview of the TVA and associated regional planning refer to Daniel Schaffer, "Ideal and Reality in 1930s Regional Planning: The Case of the Tennessee Valley Authority," in *Planning Perspectives*, 1 (January, 1986), 27–44.

[11]A short synopsis and analysis of institutionalist political and economic thought are to be found in David Seckler, *Thorstein Veblen and the Institutionalists: A Study in the Social Philosophy of Economics* (Boulder, Colorado: Associated University Press, 1975).

[12]Howard C. Hill and Rexford Guy Tugwell, *Our Economic Society and Its Problems: A Study of American Levels of Living and How to Improve Them* (New York: Harcourt, Brace, and Company, 1934), 91.

[13]Tugwell, *The Battle for Democracy*, 66. Greenbelt planning is discussed from an international perspective in Paul and Percival Goodman, *Communitas: Means of Livelihood and Ways of Life* (New York: Vintage Books, 1947), 25–42.

[14]The term "greenbelt" or "green belt" was originally used in England by Raymond Unwin, the planner of Letchworth. It is not clear whether Tugwell actually coined the term "greenbelt towns" to describe the American planning program, but he has claimed credit for the Resettlement Agency that developed the communities. "The idea for this agency was my

own," stated Tugwell, "and I was named its administrator." Tugwell's colleague, John S. Lansill, director of the Land Utilization Division of the Federal Emergency Relief Administration, noted that the "greenbelt towns" were so named because of "the encircling belt of farm and woodland that protect them from encroachment." For background on the origins of the term "green belt," see F.J. Osborn, Preface to Ebenezer Howard, *Garden Cities of Tomorrow* (1965), 27. The quotation by Tugwell is found in his article, "The Resettlement Idea," in *Agricultural History*, 33 (October, 1959), 159; Lansill's comment is in his letter of transmittal to W. W. Alexander, Vol. 1, Sec. 1 of the *Final Report of the Greenbelt Project of the Greenbelt Town Program*, 1938, p. 1, Box 1, John S. Lansill Papers, Special Collections, University of Kentucky Library, Lexington (hereinafter cited as the Lansill Papers). The Lansill Papers represent the most complete record of the activities of the Suburban Resettlement Division.

Chapter Two

[1]This formative period of the greenbelt towns program is recounted by Wallace Richards, "Summary Chronological History of Greenbelt Project, Greenbelt, Maryland," Vol. 2, Sec. 8 of *Final Report of the Greenbelt Project of the Greenbelt Town Program*, 1938, Box 1, Lansill Papers. For a published account of the early months of the program, see David Myhra, "Rexford Guy Tugwell: Initiator of America's Greenbelt New Towns, 1935–1936," in the *Journal of the American Institute of Planners*, 40 (May, 1974), 176–188. For a contemporary newspaper account of Tugwell's land relief empire, see "Tugwell to Head $950,000,000 Plan for Land Relief," in the *New York Times*, March 26, 1935.

[2]Henry S. Churchill, *Greenbelt Towns: A Study of the Background and Planning of Four Communities for the Division of Suburban Resettlement of the Resettlement Administration, John S. Lansill, Director, Prepared and Edited from Official Records by Henry S. Churchill, A.I.A.*, Ch. 3, "Organization," p. 2, Box 2, Lansill Papers. Churchill's study is a book-length manuscript prepared at the behest of John Lansill. Though it contained a wealth of information, the manuscript was never published, perhaps because of the criticisms it generated among staff members of the Resettlement Administration. The planners of Greenhills, Ohio, for example, stated that the manuscript was "ill-suited to use as an historical document for a permanent record. It is entirely too personal, too emotional, and perhaps conducive to arousing undesirable prejudices." See memorandum from Project Principals, Greenhills Project to J. S. Lansill, "Proposed Project Book—The 'Greenbelt Towns'," Lansill Papers, Box 2.

[3]That Tugwell was already thinking of satellite communities prior to the New Deal experiment is evidenced by references in published works. See Hill and Tugwell, *Our Economic Society and Its Problems*, 228; and Rexford G. Tugwell, *The Battle for Democracy* (New York: Columbia University Press, 1935), 65. For a thorough presentation of Tugwell's political successes and shortcomings in Roosevelt's Washington, see Bernard Sternsher, *Rexford Tugwell and the New Deal* (New Brunswick, New Jersey: Rutgers University Press, 1964); the Resettlement Administration is discussed on pages 262–306 of this work.

[4]The rural bent of Roosevelt's personality and political style is discussed in Gertrude Almy Slichter, "Franklin D. Roosevelt's Farm Policy as Governor of New York State, 1928–1932," in *Agricultural History*, 33 (October, 1959), 167–176.

[5]Richards, "Summary Chronological History of Greenbelt Project, Greenbelt, Maryland," p. 1; and the U.S. Resettlement Administration, *What the Resettlement Administration Has Done* (Washington, D.C.: U.S. Government Printing Office, 1936).

[6]For the views of the program's administrator on the unfair reception of the greenbelt towns, see Tugwell, "The Resettlement Idea," 159–164. The gamut of federal resettlement programs undertaken during the 1930's is the large topic of Conkin, *Tomorrow a New World*. For brief information on rural resettlement in Wisconsin, see W. A. Rowlands, "Possibilities of Rural Resettlement in Wisconsin," in *Agricultural Engineering*, 17 (June 1936), 251–253; and G. L. Sorden, "The Northern Wisconsin Settler Relocation Project, 1934–1940," in *Transactions of the Wisconsin Academy of Sciences, Arts and Letters*, 53 (1964), 135–138.

[7]Executive Order No. 7027, April 30, 1935, reprinted in U.S. Resettlement Administration, *First Annual Report, 1936* (Washington, D.C.: U.S. Government Printing Office, 1936), 1–2, quotation on 1.

[8]"Tugwell Names Aides," *New York Times*, June 22, 1935; "Social Planners Advise Tugwell," *New York Times*, July 1, 1935.

[9]Churchill, *Greenbelt Towns*, Ch. 3, "Organization," 1–2, and Ch. 4, "Planning the Town," 2. The accomplishments of the Regional Planning Association of America are reviewed in Roy S. Lubove, *Community Planning in the 1920's: The Contribution of the Regional Planning Association of America* (Pittsburgh: University of Pittsburgh Press, 1963).

[10]Arnold, *The New Deal in the Suburbs*, 41–49; J. R. Wadsworth, "Summary Description of the Greenbelt Project at Prince Georges County, Maryland," Vol. 1, Sec. 1 of *Final Report of the Greenbelt Project of the Greenbelt Town Program*, pp. 2–9; Inez Manderson, "Planning Organization, Greenbelt Project," Vol. 1, Sec. 2 of same report, pp. 1–5; and Warren Vinton, "Appointment Diary, 1938 to 1952," Record Group 196, Records of the Public Housing Administration, National Archives and Records Administration, Washington, D.C.

[11]U.S. Resettlement Administration, *Greenbelt Towns: A Demonstration in Suburban Planning* (Washington, D.C.: U.S. Government Printing Office, 1936); quotation from U.S. Resettlement Administration, Suburban Resettlement Division, "Homes for Workingmen" (pamphlet), Box 2, Lansill Papers.

[12]Letter of transmittal from John S. Lansill to W. W. Alexander, Vol. 1, Sec. 1 of the *Final Report of the Greenbelt Project of the Greenbelt Town Program*, p. 1.

[13]Manderson, "Planning Organization," p. 1; and John Nolen to Roy N. Hendrickson, May 11, 1934, Box 1, Lansill Papers. Nolen deemed the landscape architect the key figure in a regional planning team of experts. See also John Nolen, "The Landscape Architect in Regional and State Planning," in *Landscape Architecture*, 25 (June, 1935), 199–202. In addition, refer to Earle S. Draper, "Shall We Plan the Future?" in *Landscape Architecture*, 25 (July, 1935), 183–186.

[14]Phoebe Cutler, *The Public Landscape of the New Deal* (New Haven, Connecticut: Yale University Press, 1985), 5.

[15]Elbert Peets to Doris Ann Krupinski, November 29, 1960, Greendale Village Collection, Greendale Historical Society, Greendale Village Library, Greendale, Wisconsin (hereinafter cited as Greendale Village Collection); *Greendale, Wisconsin: Project History*, Ch. 6, "Planning," Part D, "Planning Staff," pp. 1–7, Box 9, Lansill Papers.

[16]Alanen and Peltin, "Kohler, Wisconsin: Planning and Paternalism in a Model Industrial Village," 145–179; Werner Hegemann and Elbert Peets, *The American Vitruvius: An Architects' Handbook of Civic Art* (New York: The Architectural Book Publishing Company, 1922). A biographical resume of Peets's career and many of his seminal writings on the art of town planning are to be found in Paul Spreiregen, ed., *On the Art of Designing Cities: Selected Essays of Elbert Peets* (Cambridge, Massachusetts: The M.I.T. Press, 1968). Also see

Caroline Shillaber, "Elbert Peets, Champion of the Civic Form," in *Landscape Architecture*, 72 (November–December, 1982), 54–59, 100.

[17]*Greendale, Wisconsin: Project History*, Ch. 6, "Planning," Part D, "Planning Staff," p. 1; Jacob Crane, "Russian Planning Norms," in *City Planning*, 8 (July, 1931), 168–169; Eugenie Ladner Birch, "Advancing the Art and Science of Planning: Planners and Their Organizations," in the *Journal of the American Planning Association*, 46 (January, 1980), 28.

[18]Peets acquired a scholarly reputation as an expert on American colonial town planning. See Elbert Peets, "L'Enfant's Washington," in *Town Planning Review*, 15 (No. 3, 1933), 155–164.

[19]"Alphabets and Architects," in *American Architect*, 148 (January, 1936), 23; Henry Hubbard, "Annual Report of the President, American Society of Landscape Architects," in *Landscape Architecture*, 25 (April, 1935), 162.

[20]Churchill, *Greenbelt Towns*, Ch. 3, "Organization," p. 3. See also Albert Mayer, "Greenbelt Towns: What and Why," in *American City*, 51 (May, 1936), 59–61.

[21]U.S. Resettlement Administration, *Greenbelt Towns* (Washington, D.C.: U.S. Government Printing Office, 1936); Churchill, *Greenbelt Towns*, Ch. 3, "Organization," 1–5; Mel Scott, *American City Planning Since 1890* (Berkeley and Los Angeles: University of California Press, 1969), 337–338; Arnold, *The New Deal in the Suburbs*, 47–48.

[22]Several inter-agency memoranda sent between the offices of the Special Skills Division and the Suburban Resettlement Division of the Resettlement Administration are in Record Group 96, Records of the Farmers Home Administration, National Archives and Records Administration, Washington, D.C. (hereinafter referred to as Record Group 96, National Archives).

Chapter Three

[1]Richards, "Summary Chronological History of Greenbelt Project, Greenbelt, Maryland."

[2]See the comments in Tilford E. Dudley, "Suburban Resettlement Land Acquisition," Vol. 2, Sec. 9 of the *Final Report of the Greenbelt Project of the Greenbelt Town Program*, 1937, pp. 1–2, Box 1, Lansill Papers; also refer to Dudley's "Analysis of Milwuakee Land Acquisition," Vol. I of *Greendale Project History*, p. 4, Record Group 196, Records of the Legal Division, Public Housing Administration, Regarding Management and Disposition of Greentown Projects, 1935–64, National Archives and Records Administration, Washington, D.C. (hereinafter cited as Record Group 196, Records of the Legal Division, PHA, National Archives). In addition, see the comments in Fred Naumer, "Summary Chronological History of the Greendale Project," Vol. 1, Sec. 7 of *Final Report of the Greendale Project of the Greenbelt Town Program*, Box 8, Lansill Papers; another copy of Naumer's report may be found in Vol. I, *Greendale Project History*, cited above.

[3]Milton Lowenthal, "A Study of the Characteristics, Customs and Living Habits of Potential Tenants of the Resettlement Project in Cincinnati, and the Effect of Such Characteristics, Customs, and Habits on the Planning, Design, Construction, and Equipment of the Dwelling Units," February, 1936, p. 1, Box 10, Lansill Papers.

[4]Warren Jay Vinton, "Report on Milwaukee and the Selection of a Site for Suburban Resettlement," Vol. 1, Sec. 2 of *Final Report of the Greendale Project of the Greenbelt Town Program*, p. 50, Box 8, Lansill Papers. This report is also included in Ch. 3 of *Greendale, Wisconsin: Project History*, Box 9, Lansill Papers.

[5]This particular incident is mentioned by William E. Leuchtenberg, *Franklin D. Roosevelt and the New Deal, 1932–1940* (New York: Harper and Row, Publishers, 1963), 111. For a concise overview of the labor movement of the 1930's and its links to the New Deal, see Murray Edelman, "New Deal Sensitivity to Labor Interests," in *Labor and the New Deal*, Milton Derber and Edwin Young, eds. (Madison: University of Wisconsin Press, 1957), 159–191. For an account of Milwaukee's Socialist Democratic Party, see Frederick J. Olson, "The Milwaukee Socialists, 1897–1941" (unpublished Ph.D. dissertation, Harvard University, 1952).

[6]Vinton, "Report on Milwaukee and the Selection of a Site," 44–56. An intimate and understandably sympathetic view of Milwaukee's Garden Homes project has been given by Emil Seidel, Milwaukee's first socialist mayor (1910–1912); see Emil Seidel, "Garden Homes Steps Out," in the *Historical Messenger of the Milwaukee County Historical Society*, 28 (Summer, 1972), 73–78. The metropolitan zoning ordinance has been described by Milwaukee County Supervising Engineer A. E. Howard, "Milwaukee County Plan Successful," in *City Planning*, 8 (October, 1932), 237–238. A less readily accessible source is the Milwaukee County Park Commission and the Milwaukee County Regional Planning Department, *Annual Reports, 1924–1927* (Milwaukee: Court House, 1927); a copy is on file in the Milwaukee Public Library. The push by Hoan's city hall for a metropolitan land planning entity with county-wide jurisdiction was part of an uphill battle against a predominantly rural Wisconsin state legislature. See Bayrd Still, *Milwaukee: The History of a City* (Madison: State Historical Society of Wisconsin, 1948), 559–561. Also see Mel Scott, *American City Planning Since 1890* (Berkeley and Los Angeles: University of California Press, 1969), 213.

[7]"Minutes of Meeting of Visiting European and American Housing Experts Conference, Held in Milwaukee, Wis., September 10–11–12, 1934," p. 26, Box 19, Daniel W. Hoan Papers, Milwaukee County Historical Society Library, Milwaukee, (hereinafter cited as the Hoan Papers). The composition and itinerary of this international tour are given in "European Housing Experts Now Touring the United States," in *American City*, 49 (September, 1934), 99. See also "Housing Experts Arrive to Study Local Project," *Milwaukee Journal*, September 10, 1934; "U.S. Housing Plans Lauded by Europeans," *Milwaukee Sentinel*, September 12, 1934; and "Site of Housing Project is Debated by Experts," *Milwaukee Journal*, September 13, 1934.

[8]The correspondence that has survived between Glickman and an ad hoc Milwaukee County Committee on Subsistence Housing is found primarily in the C. B. Whitnall Papers, Milwaukee County Historical Society, Milwaukee. The county parkway plan, an outgrowth of the first comprehensive city plan for Milwaukee (1909), is outlined in William Schuchardt, "The Milwaukee County Highway and Park Plan," in *American City*, 28 (April, 1923), 363–364. C. B. Whitnall, one of the originators of Milwaukee's parkway plan, foresaw villages or workingmen's homes along the drive. See C. B. Whitnall, "By Regional Planning the Milwaukee of Tomorrow Conserves Nature's Attributes," in *Park and Recreation*, 6 (March–April, 1923), 278–286. The use of federal relief labor after 1933 is mentioned in Milwaukee County Park Commission and the Milwaukee County Regional Planning Department, *Quadrennial Report, 1933–1936* (Milwaukee: Court House, 1936), 63–64; a copy is on file in the Milwaukee Public Library.

[9]C. B. Whitnall to Glickman, July 12, 1935, Whitnall Papers.

[10]*Greendale, Wisconsin: Project History*, Ch. 17, "Public Relations," p. 1; Tilford E. Dudley, "Diary on the Milwaukee Project," December 21, 1936, pp. 1–2, in Vol. 1 of *Final Report of the Greendale Project of the Greenbelt Town Program*.

[11]Vinton later incorporated Gelnaw's material into his comprehensive overview, "Report on Milwaukee and the Selection of a Site," cited previously.

[12]Dudley, "Suburban Resettlement Land Acquisition," quotation on p. 18; Dudley "Diary on the Milwaukee Project," December 21, 1936, pp. 1–2; Tilford E. Dudley, "Analysis of Milwaukee Land Acquisition," Vol. 1, Sec. 3 of Final Report of the Greendale Project of the Greenbelt Town Program, pp. 1–2.

[13]Dudley, "Diary on the Milwaukee Project," December 21, 1936, pp. 10–11.

[14]Ibid., pp. 2–3; "Diary on the Milwaukee Project," December 14, 1936, attached to letter from Tilford E. Dudley to Harold C. Gelnaw, December 17, 1936, Record Group 196, Records of the Legal Division, PHA, National Archives.

[15]Vinton, "Report on Milwaukee and the Selection of a Site," 58–61; "Diary on the Milwaukee Project," December 14, 1936, p. 2; and Dudley, "Diary on the Milwaukee Project," December 21, 1936, pp. 2–3.

[16]Dudley, "Analysis of Milwaukee Land Acquisition," 2; Dudley, "Diary on the Milwaukee Project; December 21, 1936, p. 1.

[17]Dudley, "Analysis of Milwaukee Land Acquisition," 1–9; Dudley, "Diary on the Milwaukee Project," December 21, 1936, p. 4; Harold Gelnaw, "Site Acquisition (History of Each Tract)," Record Group 196, Records of the Legal Division, PHA, National Archives.

[18]Gelnaw, "Site Acquisition" (see especially the acquisition history of Tract No. 202, Herman Bohn, owner).

[19]Dudley, "Suburban Resettlement Land Acquisition," preface and p. 6, quotations in preface; Dudley, "Diary on the Milwaukee Project," December 21, 1936, 8–9 and 25–26.

[20]Dudley, "Analysis of Milwaukee Land Acquisition," 2–4; Dudley, "Diary on the Milwaukee Project," December 21, 1936, pp. 11–19; Greendale, Wisconsin: Project History, Ch. 4, "Land Acquisition," 2.

[21]Dudley, "Diary on the Milwaukee Project," December 21, 1936, pp. 7–8; Frank H. Osterlind to Victor Rotnem, November 8, 1935, Box 49, Record Group 207, Records of the Department of Housing and Urban Development, (formerly General Records of the Housing and Home Finance Agency), National Archives and Records Administration (hereinafter cited as Record Group 207, National Archives).

[22]Doris Ann Krupinski, "Greendale's 'Good Old Days' Are Gone, But Not Forgotten," Greendale Village Life, June 30, 1976.

[23]"Diary on the Milwaukee Project," December 14, 1936, pp. 3–4; Dudley, "Diary on the Milwaukee Project," December 21, 1936, pp. 23–35; Dudley, "Analysis of Milwaukee Land Acquisition," 4–11; Dudley, "Suburban Resettlement Land Acquisition," 2 and 3.

[24]Dudley, "Analysis of Milwaukee Land Acquisition," 8–11; Letter of transmittal from John S. Lansill to W. W. Alexander, Vol. 1, Sec. 1 of Final Report of the Greenbelt Project of the Greenbelt Town Program, 4–5; Arnold, The New Deal in the Suburbs, 60; Dudley, "Suburban Resettlement Land Acquisition," quotation on p. 11.

[25]Dudley, "Suburban Resettlement Land Acquisition, quotation in preface; and "Minutes of Meeting of Visiting European and American Housing Experts Conference Held in Milwaukee, Wisc., September 12, 1934," p. 29, Box 19, Hoan Papers.

Chapter Four

[1]"Plan Federal 'Tugwell Town' on Tract at Hales Corners," Milwaukee Journal, December 4, 1935; "Indicating Area and Type of Houses for 'Tugwelltown' Here," Milwaukee Journal, December 5, 1935.

[2]Frank H. Osterlind to R. G. Tugwell, December 12, 1935, Box 49, Record Group 207, National Archives; Monroe Oppenheimer to Frank H. Osterlind, November 9, 1935; Frank H. Osterlind to Monroe Oppenheimer, November 15, 1935; the latter two items are in Record Group 196, Records of the Legal Division, PHA, National Archives.

[3]"Tugwell Soon to Inspect Site of Town Here," *Milwaukee Journal*, December 16, 1935; also see "Tugwell Town Site Planners Buy Big Farm," *Milwaukee Journal*, December 19, 1935.

[4]See entries for "Zoning and Building Permits," in the *Biennial* and *Quadriennial Reports* of the Milwaukee County Park Commission and the Milwaukee County Regional Planning Department from 1929 to 1936 (Milwaukee: Court House), Milwaukee Public Library. The comment about "bungalow garages" is in the *Quadriennial Report* for 1933–1936, p. 72.

[5]"Garden Town Still on Paper, But Many Seek Homes There," *Milwaukee Journal*, December 18, 1935.

[6]Resettlement officials kept close watch on newspaper coverage in each city. See John Drier to J. S. Lansill, October 28, 1936, attached to a clipping: "Many Interests Helped by Greendale Project," *Milwaukee Journal*, October 25, 1936; and Fred L. Naumer to J. S. Lansill, October 28, 1936, Box 9, Lansill Papers.

[7]"Garden Town Still on Paper, But Many Seek Homes There," *Milwaukee Journal*, December 18, 1935; "Greendale Land Prices," *Milwaukee Journal*, April 29, 1936; "Owner Defends Price of Farm for Greendale," *Milwaukee Journal*, April 29, 1936.

[8]"Tugwell Town Called Boon to Industry Here," *Milwaukee Journal*, January 3, 1936.

[9]Frank H. Osterlind to Victor Rotnem, January 15, 1936, Box 47, Record Group 207, National Archives; John L. Braun to Fred L. Naumer, March 27, 1936, Box 9, Lansill Papers.

[10]"Two Smashing Defeats: Guffy Coal Act and Tugwell Housing Scheme Held Unconstitutional," *Washington Times*, May 21, 1936; and "New Deal Jolted Twice by Courts," *Milwaukee Journal*, May 18, 1936. Despite the overwhelming support given to the Greenbrook proposal by local New Jersey citizens, a small but determined group of opponents succeeded in 1936 in convincing the United States Court of Appeals for the District of Columbia that the project was unconstitutional. For a summary of the events that led to the Court's decision and the abandonment of the project, see Arnold, *The New Deal in the Suburbs*, 61–76.

[11]These were duly noted by Suburban Division officials and relevant articles were clipped from Milwaukee newspapers, presumably to be circulated around offices; for example, "Model Villages All: How the RA Housing Projects Are Progressing," *Milwaukee Journal*, August 2, 1936, Picture Section, was included in Box 9 of the Lansill Papers. A full consideration of the legal implications of resettlement was presented by Daniel M. Schyler, "Constitutional Problems Confronting the Resettlement Administration," in the *Journal of Land & Public Utility Economics*, 12 (August, 1936), 304–306.

[12]"$10,000,000 Home Project Will be Built Here by U.S.," *Milwaukee Sentinel*, December 16, 1935.

[13]*Greendale, Wisconsin: Project History*, Ch. 17, "Public Relations," Box 9, Lansill Papers. Letters and telegrams sent to Suburban Division offices in support of Greendale are also in Box 9 of the Lansill Papers. Senator La Follette read pro-Greendale statements from the Milwaukee Building and Loan Council and the Milwaukee Federated Trades Council into the *Congressional Record*, 74th Congress, 2nd Session, 1936, 80, pt. 6, p. 8090.

[14]Peter J. Banaski to Franklin D. Roosevelt, May 22, 1936, Box 9, Lansill Papers; "Showdown to be Sought on Court Power: Labor Will Fight Housing Tie-up," *Milwaukee Leader*,

May 19, 1936; "Imperiled RA Work Goes On," *Milwaukee Journal*, May 19, 1936; *Summary of Information: Greendale, Milwaukee County, Wisconsin*, p. 10, Box 9, Lansill Papers.

[15]"Parklawn and Greendale are Targets of Lawsuit," *Milwaukee Journal*, August 31, 1936. The legal counsel of the Suburban Resettlement Division advised that the PILOT agreement would undercut the most serious objections raised in the court case by the Milwaukee Building and Loan Association *et al*. vs. R. G. Tugwell *et al*. See the following memoranda regarding property taxes on Greendale: N. S. Boardman to R. G. Tugwell, September 17, 1936, and Nathan Ostroff to Clarence I. Blau, September 3, 1936, Box 48, Record Group 207, National Archives. The *Milwaukee Journal* ("Tugwell Town Is to Be Taxed") reported on December 20, 1935, that Greendale would be subject to local taxes, an important concession to financial and real estate leaders in the city.

[16]U.S. Resettlement Administration, "Information for the Press: Release to Morning Papers of Friday, October 2, 1936," Box 9, Lansill Papers.

[17]Tugwell, "The Resettlement Idea," 163; Charles B. Bennett and Richard B. Fernbach, "Greendale—the General Plan. Discussion," in *Planner's Journal*, 3 (November, 1937), 160.

[18]These derogatory articles were clipped by Resettlement Administration officials in Chicago and sent to Lansill. See, for example, Charles E. Blake, "U.S. Funds Building Communist Town 90 Miles from City," *Chicago American*, October 26, 1936 (included in Box 9, Lansill Papers).

[19]The political difficulties of the greenbelt towns program must, of course, be judged against a background of Supreme Court defeats of many New Deal programs. See Richard Hofstadter, *The Age of Reform: From Bryan to F.D.R.* (New York: Random House, Inc., 1955), 308–314.

[20]Richards, "Summary Chronological History of Greenbelt Project, Greenbelt, Maryland."

[21]"Imperiled RA Work Goes On," *Milwaukee Journal*, May 19, 1936; C. B. Whitnall, "To the Honorable Mayor and Common Council of the City of Milwaukee, Wisconsin" (manuscript of speech), July 30, 1937, p. 1, Box 19, Hoan Papers.

[22]"Row Houses for Rent," in *Architectural Forum*, 66 (May, 1937), 468.

[23]The item cited is an untitled and undated press release from the Office of the Mayor (Milwaukee); it is in Box 19 of the Daniel Hoan Papers.

Chapter Five

[1]Walter E. Kroening, "Across the Manager's Desk," in the *Greendale Review*, May 28, 1948. Kroening was the community manager of Greendale for eleven years.

[2]J. H. Burke to Harold Gelnaw, December 4, 1935, Record Group 196, Records of the Legal Division, PHA, National Archives; Fred Naumer, "Summarized History of the Greendale Project," Vol. 1, Sec. 1, of *Final Report of the Greendale Project of the Greenbelt Town Program*, 1938, p. 1, Box 8, Lansill Papers (also Vol. I of *Greendale Project History*, Record Group 196, Records of the Legal Division, PHA, National Archives); and "Two Housing Jobs Here Pushed Ahead," *Milwaukee Journal*, December 17, 1935.

[3]*Greendale, Wisconsin: Project History*, Ch. 5, "Surveys," p. 1, Box 9, Lansill Papers; Elbert Peets, "Report of the Town Planning Section of the Greendale Planning Staff," Vol. 2 of *Final Report of the Greendale Project of the Greenbelt Town Program*, 1938, p. 138, Box 8, Lansill Papers; Harold Gelnaw to Tilford E. Dudley, February 13, 1936, and Crane and Peets to Frederick Bigger, January 8, 1936, Record Group 196, Records of the Legal Division, PHA, National Archives.

[4]U.S. Resettlement Administration, Suburban Resettlement Division, "Final Budget to Complete Greendale Project, June 3, 1936, in *Greendale, Wisconsin: Project History*, Ch. 17, "Budget Summary," Box 9, Lansill Papers; U.S. Resettlement Administration, *Project Description Book*, June 13, 1936 (see entries for Greenbelt, Maryland; Greenbrook, New Jersey; Greenhills, Ohio; and Greendale, Wisconsin), Box 13, Lansill Papers. Another copy of this report is in Record Group 96, National Archives.

[5]Dudley, "Suburban Resettlement Land Acquisition," 16, Box 1, Lansill Papers; U.S. Resettlement Administration, *Project Description Book* (entries for "Greenbelt, Greenbrook, Greenhills, and Greendale"), Box 13, Lansill Papers.

[6]Naumer, "Summarized History of the Greendale Project," 2–3; "Greendale is Chosen as Name of 'Tugwell Town'," *Milwaukee Journal*, March 24, 1936.

[7]"Questionnaire," Vol. 1, Sec. 4 of *Final Report of the Greendale Project of the Greenbelt Town Program*; "Final Tabulation, Greendale Questionnaires. Income Groups $1000 to $1999," May 20, 1936, Box 9, Lansill Papers.

[8]Memorandum from Clarence S. Stein to John S. Lansill, "Studies of Operation-Maintenance Costs in Suburban Resettlement Communities," December 5, 1935, appended to report by Stein, "Studies of Operation-Maintenance Costs of Local Government, Community Activity and Housing in Suburban Resettlement Communities," Box 2, Lansill Papers.

[9]*Greendale, Wisconsin: Project History*, Ch. 15, "Preliminary Rent Study," pp. 1 and 2; Peets, "Report of the Town Planning Section," quotation on p. 6.

[10]"Final Tabulation: Greendale Questionnaires," Tables 1 and 2, Box 9, Lansill Papers.

[11]*Greendale, Wisconsin: Project History*, Ch. 6, "Planning" (pt. C, "Transportation"), pp. 1–2; "Final Tabulation: Greendale Questionnaires," Table 9, Box 9, Lansill Papers.

[12]Warren Jay Vinton, "Report on Milwaukee, Wisconsin and the Selection of a Site for Suburban Resettlement," Vol. 1, Sec. 2, 1936, of *Final Report of the Greendale Project*, p. 62; "Relationship of Greendale to Milwaukee Regional Planning, April 12, 1937, p. 4, in *Summary Reports and Recommendations*, both items in Box 8, Lansill Papers.

[13]"Final Tabulation: Greendale Questionnaire," Tables 7 and 12; Peets, "Report of the Town Planning Section," 61–66.

[14]"Final Tabulation: Greendale Questionnaires," Table 10.

[15]Jacob Crane, "Greendale—the General Plan," in *Planners' Journal*, 3 (No. 4, 1937), 90; Harry H. Bentley, "Report on Residential and Non-Residential Construction," Vol. 3 of *Final Report of the Greendale Project of the Greenbelt Town Program*, quotation on p. 3; Peets, "Report of the Town Planning Section," 41.

[16]Memorandum from Naumer to Lansill, "Ultimate Area Development," June 15, 1937, in *Summary Reports and Recommendations*, pp. 1–3.

[17]Memorandum from Crane, Peets, Bentley, and Thomas to Lansill, "Immediate Town Development," June 15, 1936, in *Summary Reports and Recommendations*.

[18]*Ibid.*; and Memorandum from Greendale Project Principals to Lansill, "Planting of 5,000 Tree Seedlings," May 1, 1936, in *Summary Reports and Recommendations*.

[19]"Greendale Agricultural Program," Appendix 3 of Henry S. Churchill, *Greenbelt Towns*, pp. 1–3, quotation on p. 2, Box 2, Lansill Papers; Peets, "Report of the Town Planning Section," 78.

[20]Discussions of the greenbelt and the agricultural program are in Peets, "Report of the Town Planning Section," 74–85; Churchill, Appendix 3 of *Greenbelt Towns*; and the following memoranda from the *Summary Reports and Recommendations* for the Greendale project: Crane, Peets, Thomas, and Bentley to Lansill, "Landscaping," December, 1936; and Green-

dale Project Principals to Lansill, "Memorandum of Transmittal re Boarding House," March 31, 1937.

[21]Peets, "Report of the Town Planning Section," 76–78; W. L. Wilson (quoting Elbert Peets) to Jens Jensen, February 15, 1937, in the Jens Jensen Papers, Morton Arboretum Archives, Lisle, Illinois (hereinafter referred to as Jensen Papers); and R. I. Nowell to R. G. Tugwell, January 6, 1936, Box 9, Lansill Papers.

[22]"Home Life of 2 Centuries Contrast in Model Wisconsin Village" (release to *Wisconsin Conservation and Vacation News)*, n.d., Box 9, Lansill Papers; Peets, "Report of the Town Planning Section," quotation on 90–91.

[23]John S. Lansill and Jacob Crane, "Metropolitan Land Reserves As Illustrated by Greendale, Wisconsin," in *American City*, 52 (July, 1937), 55–58; Jacob Crane to John S. Lansill, December 9, 1935, Box 9, Lansill Papers.

[24]The Radburn plan has been explained by Clarence Stein, one of its designers, in Stein, *Toward New Towns for America.* Also see Schaffer, *Garden Cities for America: The Radburn Experience.*

[25]Eugenie Ladner Birch, "Radburn and the American Planning Movement: The Persistence of an Idea," in the *Journal of the American Planning Association*, 46 (October, 1980), 424.

[26]Milwaukee County Park Commission and the Milwaukee County Regional Planning Department, *Biennial Report, 1929–1930* (Milwaukee: Court House, 1930), 45–57. An article that depicts the precedents and applications of the neighborhood unit concept in town and suburban planning and in inner-city philanthropic housing is "The Planned Community," in *Architectural Forum*, 58 (April, 1933), 253–274. In 1932, Perry tried to incorporate his neighborhood concept into a more comprehensive city-planning approach. See Clarence A. Perry, "The Prevention of Slum Conditions Through City Planning," in *Social Forces*, 10 (March, 1932), 382–387. Also see James Dahir, *The Neighborhood Unit Plan: Its Spread and Acceptance. A Selected Bibliography with Interpretative Comments* (New York: Russell Sage Foundation, 1947). Federal housing standards of the mid–1930's are described in Alfred Fellheimer, "Planning Standards for Low-Rent Housing," in *American Architect*, 146 (February, 1935), 12–28.

[27]Peets, "Report of the Town Planning Section," 5. For a similar opinion by a contemporary of Peets, see Tracy B. Augur, "New Towns in the National Economy," in *Planners' Journal*, 3 (January–February, 1937), 38–42.

[28]Peets, "Report of the Town Planning Section," 21–42, quotation on 41; "Greendale is Chosen as Name of 'Tugwell Town' " (quoting Harry H. Bentley), *Milwaukee Journal*, March 24, 1936; Jacob Crane, "Safety Town," in *Public Safety*, 11 (August, 1937), 28–30; John C. Black, "Progress at Parklawn and Greendale," in *Roads and Streets*, 79 (August, 1936), 37–42; communication from Greendale Village Clerk's Office, June 6, 1986.

[29]Peets, "Report of the Town Planning Section," 17.

[30]Bentley, "Report on Residential and Non-Residential Construction," 96–102, quotation on 96. A description of house construction—focusing upon methods and materials—is in Harry H. Bentley, "Greendale, Wisconsin: A Federal Suburban Resettlement Town," in *Monthly Bulletin, Illinois Society of Architects*, 21 (April–May, 1937), 1–2.

[31]Bentley, "Report on Residential and Non-Residential Construction," 98.

[32]Peets, "Report of the Town Planning Section," 18.

[33]*Ibid.*, 35–36, quotation on 49. Peets was an admirer of Camillo Sitte, an internationally renowned architect and town planner, although not his disciple. For a critique of Sitte's civic

design principles, see Elbert Peets, "Famous Town Planners—Camillo Sitte," in *Town Planning Review* (No. 4, 1927), 249–259. Sitte's classic *Der Stadtbau* (1889) has been translated from German into English by George R. Collins and Christiane Crasemann Collins as *City Planning According to Artistic Principles* (New York: Random House, 1965). Also see George R. Collins and Christiane Crasemann Collins, *Camillo Sitte and the Birth of Modern City Planning* (London: Phaidon Press, 1965).

[34]U.S. Resettlement Administration, *Greendale, Wisconsin* (Washington, D.C.: U.S. Government Printing Office, 1936). Peets calculated that no Greendale house was more than five minutes from a park or other open area and no more than a ten-minute walk from the shopping center. See Peets, "Report of the Town Planning Section," 50–51.

[35]Peets, "Report of the Town Planning Section," 148–150. Even today, some architectural and planning theorists contend that "Williamsburg has proved itself not only a compelling history lesson but a textbook for the future." Included among the features they mention is the well established concept of the gridded, axial plan as an ". . . alternative to the arbitrary, winding residential streets and commercial strips of suburbia." See Robert A. M. Stern, *Pride of Place: Building the American Dream* (Boston: Houghton Mifflin Company, 1986), 331–332.

[36]Quotation of Jens Jensen to Henry Wallace, February 16, 1937, Jensen Papers.

[37]Jens Jensen to Henry Wallace, February 16, 1937, Jensen Papers.

[38]W. L. Wilson (quoting Elbert Peets) to Jens Jensen, February 15, 1937, Jensen Papers.

[39]Memorandum from Crane, Peets, Thomas, and Bentley to Lansill, "Landscaping," in *Summary Report and Recommendations*, December 1936, pp. 1–4, quotation on p. 1. James Drought, a local landscape architect, when addressing the Greendale Garden Club in 1940, claimed that the non-native plant specimens found within the community had "no place" in the plan. "These departures from natural grace," he stated, "point the eclectic nature of the plan—the result of compromise." See James Drought, "Landscaping Greendale," *Greendale Review*, January 25, 1940.

[40]Peets, "Report of the Town Planning Section," 23–39; *Greendale, Wisconsin: Project History*, Ch. 7, "Land Preparation."

[41]Peets, "Final Report of the Town Planning Section," 45.

[42]Elbert Peets, "Washington, Williamsburg, the Century of Progress, and Greendale," in Werner Hegemann, *City Planning Housing*, Ruth Nanda Anshen, ed. (New York: Architectural Book Publishing Co., Inc., 1937), 413 and 414, quotation on 413; Peets, "Final Report of the Town Planning Section," 43 and 52–55.

[43]Memorandum from Naumer to Lansill, "Apportionment of Dwelling Unit Types," in *Summary Reports and Recommendations*, February 23, 1937; and Vinton, "Report on Milwaukee, Wisconsin and the Selection of a Site," 35 and 36.

[44]For particular decisions and recommendations of the Greendale staff, see the memoranda in the *Summary Reports and Recommendations*, in the Lansill Papers. The parkway gift to Milwaukee County cleared administrative hurdles in April, 1937. See C. M. Boyle to James D. McGuire, April 15, 1937, Box 47, Record Group 207, National Archives. According to Peets, he wanted basements to be provided for individual housing units at Greendale, but Bentley reportedly vetoed the idea. The houses, however, did have sub-basements or enlarged crawl spaces, and some fifteen houses built into the sides of hills provided an excavated area underneath the house that was approximately the size of a typical basement. It was possible to store some items in the sub-basements, if they were not affected by dampness.

For Peets's observations on the basement issue, see Elbert Peets to Doris Ann Krupinski, November 29, 1960, Greendale Village Collection.

⁴⁵See the *Final Report of the Greenhills Project of the Greenbelt Town Program*, Box 10, Lansill Papers.

⁴⁶Crane resorted to legal counsel in order to ensure that Greendale's lot sizes were not in violation of the state platting statute. See Clarence I. Blau to Daniel F. Margolis, June 15, 1936, Record Group 196, Records of the Legal Division, PHA, National Archives.

⁴⁷Peets, "Final Report of the Town Planning Section," 48. American town planners inveighed against property tax structures which assessed land at its highest and best use and frustrated attempts to consolidate garden-city-size tracts as the British were able to do. See Arthur C. Comey, "An Answer to the Garden City Challenge," in *American City*, 29 (July, 1923), 36–38. ⁴⁸Peets, "Final Report of the Town Planning Section," 46.

⁴⁹*Ibid.*, 41. For a recent review of housing in America, including suburban and public housing examples, refer to Gwendolyn Wright, *Building the Dream: A Social History of Housing in America* (Cambridge, Massachusetts: The MIT Press, 1983).

⁵⁰Bentley, "Report on Residential and Non-Residential Construction," quotations on 97 and 98. Sets of plans for Greendale's housing and public buildings are found in Box 8 of the Lansill Papers, and in the Greendale Village Collection. Also see the descriptions and illustrations of Greendale homes and public buildings in "Greenbelt Towns," in *Architectural Record*, 80 (September, 1936), 227–230; and "Comparative Architectural Details in the Greenbelt Housing," in *American Architect and Architecture*, 149 (October, 1936), 30–33. The greenbelt towns also were profiled in "Farm Security Administration Housing Projects," in *Architectural Forum*, 68 (May, 1938), 415–424.

⁵¹Bentley, "Report on Residential and Non-Residential Construction," 7.

⁵²*Ibid*, 6 and 7; Memorandum from Naumer to Bentley, "Apportionment of Dwelling Unit Types," in *Summary Reports and Recommendations*, February 23, 1937; see especially "Estimate of Direct Costs on a Contract Basis for Houses in Greendale" (Table), Box 9, Lansill Papers.

⁵³Naumer, "Summarized History of the Greendale Project," 7; Bentley, "Report On Residential and Non-Residential Construction," 102; and "Low Cost Furniture," 131–133, quotation on 133.

⁵⁴Bentley, "Report on Residential and Non-Residential Construction," 45.

⁵⁵Letter of transmittal from John S. Lansill to W. W. Alexander, n.d., p. 3, *Final Report of the Greendale Project of the Greenbelt Town Program*; Crane, "Greendale—the General Plan," 90.

Chapter Six

¹See, for instance, the comments of Warren Bishop, "A Yardstick for Housing," in *Nation's Business*, 24 (April, 1936), 29–31, 69–71.

²Peets, "Report of the Town Planning Section," 79–85.

³E. E. Agger to Rexford G. Tugwell, June 6, 1936, Box 48, Record Group 207, National Archives; "Landscaping," in *Summary Reports and Recommendations*, January 12, 1937; Naumer, "Summarized History of the Greendale Project", 8; Peets, "Report of the Town Planning Section," 79.

⁴U.S. Resettlement Administration, Suburban Resettlement Division, Ch. 12, "Labor," pp. 1–2, in *Greendale, Wisconsin: Project History*; Naumer, "Summarized History of the Greendale Project," 3–5.

⁵For early over-estimates of labor to be employed at Greendale, see U. S. Department of Agriculture, Resettlement Administration, *Interim Report of the Resettlement Administration* (Washington, D.C.: U. S. Government Printing Office, 1936), 21; U. S. Resettlement Administration, *Greendale, Wisconsin* (Washington, D.C.: U. S. Government Printing Office, 1936), 1; and "5,000 to Toil at Greendale," *Milwaukee Journal*, May 3, 1936.

⁶*Greendale, Wisconsin: Project History*, Ch. 12, "Labor", 1–2; U. S. Department of Agriculture, Farm Security Administration, *Greendale, Final Report of Project Costs Including Analysis of Actual Construction Costs from Inception of Project to June 30, 1938*, "Exhibit A: Payrolls, Together with Number and Type of Employees," Record Group 96, National Archives.

⁷Capt. R. B. Lord to C. B. Baldwin, March 9, 1937, and Martin G. White to Miss Falke, April 3, 1937, Box 46, Record Group 207, National Archives; *Greendale, Wisconsin: Project History*, Ch. 11, "Overhead," Part C, "Railroad Siding," 7–8.

⁸Naumer, "Summarized History of the Greendale Project," 3–9. See also the relevant items in *Summary Reports and Recommendations* for the Greendale project; and Walter E. Kroening and Frank L. Dieter, "Utility Planning for Greendale, Wisconsin," in *Civil Engineering*, 8 (February, 1938), 94–98.

⁹Naumer, "Summarized History of the Greendale Project," 5 and 6; Arnold, *The New Deal in the Suburbs*, 112–118.

¹⁰Peets, "Report of the Town Planning Section," 147; Sherwood L. Reeder to Major John O. Walker, August 14, 1939, Box 49, Record Group 207, National Archives.

¹¹John S. Lansill to Adrian Dornbush, February 9, 1937; R. I. Nowell to R. G. Tugwell, January 8, 1937; Eleanor Tracy to Adrian Dornbush, January 22, 1937; and Adrian Dornbush to J. S. Lansill, March 6, 1937, all in Record Group 96, National Archives. Background information on the New Deal artists' program, and a detailed account of the post-office murals created by many of these individuals throughout the country, may be found in Karal Ann Marling, *Wall-to-Wall America: A Cultural History of Post-Office Murals in the Great Depression* (Minneapolis: University of Minnesota Press, 1982).

¹²"Alonzo Hauser Interprets Rural Theme in Sculpture," *Greendale Review*, September 10, 1938; "Sculpture with Alonzo Hauser," *Greendale Review*, October 20, 1938; "Mr. Hauser at Work," *Greendale Review*, December 15, 1938. Hauser eventually settled in the Twin Cities of Minneapolis-St. Paul, Minnesota, and also resided in the western Wisconsin community of Prescott, and in New Mexico. Now retired, he taught for several years in the School of Architecture at the University of Minnesota, and had a long and distinguished career as a sculptor.

¹³Quotation in memorandum from M. E. Gilford to G. E. Falke, October 5, 1936; "Visitors at Greendale (Daily and Weekly)" (Table, 9 pp.), both items in Box 9, Lansill Papers.

¹⁴The Greendale guides recorded selected comments of visitors to the Greendale project. Arranged according to topical interest or occupations of commentators ("Town Plan," "Employment of Labor," "House Plan," "Real Estate Dealers," etc.), the visitors' statements were compiled into an untitled report which is in Box 9 of the Lansill Papers.

¹⁵*Ibid.* (quoting Walter Wyrick); Thomas Maras, "Report of the Greendale Guides for the Week Ending March 14, 1937," Box 9, Lansill Papers.

¹⁶Naumer, "Summarized History of the Greendale Project," 8; "Building-Loan Men Back Housing, 'If—'," *Milwaukee Journal*, February 17, 1937.

¹⁷"Mrs. Roosevelt Braves Quiz; Has Praise for Projects Here," *Milwaukee Journal*, November 12, 1936; "After Address Here, First Lady Sees NYA Work," *Wisconsin News* (Mil-

waukee), November 12, 1936; "Building-Loan Men Back Housing, 'If—'," *Milwaukee Journal*, February 17, 1937; untitled report containing Greendale visitors' comments, Box 9, Lansill Papers.

[18]David Margolick, "A Suburb Recalls its New Deal Mission," *New York Times*, June 9, 1985.

[19]Carl C. Taylor to Chester Amers, April 29, 1936, Record Group 96, National Archives. The Resettlement Administration's policy of racial fairness was partly a legacy of the Subsistence Homestead Division which included, for a few months in mid–1934, a special section for the resettlement of Negroes, Mexicans, and Native Americans. Directed by Bruce L. Melvin, the section expired in the midst of dissension from those who wanted to allow "the local community to decide upon racial balance." See the correspondence of the Subsistence Homestead Division, Section of Negroes, Mexicans and Indians, Record Group 96, National Archives.

[20]Naumer, "Summarized History of the Greendale Project," 5; Memorandum from Ralph F. Crane to Project Principals, "Decrease in Size of Greendale, Wisconsin Project from 750 Units to 500 Units," October 7, 1936; Memorandum from Greendale Project Principals to Lansill and Bigger, "Postpone Recommendation to Construct 158 Dwelling Units," October 8, 1936, pp. 1–2 (both of the latter memoranda are in the *Summary Reports and Recommendations.*)

[21]Bentley, "Report on Residential and Non-Residential Construction," 30 (Table 9).

[22]Memorandum from Naumer to Lansill, "Expansion of Present Greendale Village," in *Summary Reports and Recommendations*, January 28, 1937, pp. 1–3, quotation on p. 1.

[23]"Federal Flux," in *Architectural Forum*, 66 (May, 1937), 2; Naumer, "Summarized History of the Greendale Project," 9; U. S. Department of Agriculture, Farm Security Administration, *Greendale: Final Report of Project Costs*, Sec. 5, Plate 1.

[24]Naumer, "Summarized History of the Greendale Project," 9; Albert Miller, "Summary Chronological History, Greenhills Project," Vol. 1, Sec. 1, of the *Final Report of the Greenhills Project of the Greenbelt Town Program* pp. 16–17, Box 1, Lansill Papers; Richards, "Summary Chronological History of the Greenbelt Project, Greenbelt, Maryland."

[25]Peets, "Report of the Town Planning Section," 124.

Chapter Seven

[1]Letter of transmittal from John S. Lansill to W. W. Alexander, Vol. 1, Sec. 1 of *Final Report of the Greenbelt Project of the Greenbelt Town Program*.

[2]Churchill, *Greenbelt Towns*, Ch. 1, "Background," 3.

[3]Memorandum from Monroe Oppenheimer to J. S. Lansill, April 22, 1937, Box 49, Record Group 207, National Archives; "Relationship of Greendale to Milwaukee Regional Planning," in *Summary Reports and Recommendations*, April 12, 1937, p. 5.

[4]Warren Jay Vinton, "Report on Government and Taxes, Eventual Ownership, Operating Budget and Resulting Rents for the Greendale Project at Milwaukee, Wisconsin," 1936, Vol. 1 of *Final Report of the Greendale Project of the Greenbelt Towns Program*, 1–11.

[5]Memorandum from Ralph F. Crane to Project Principals, "Decrease in Size of Greendale, Wisconsin Project from 750 Units to 500 Units," October 7, 1936, Box 8, Lansill Papers; Arnold, *The New Deal in the Suburbs*, 118.

[6]Stein, *Toward New Towns for America*, 8. The first resident manager of Radburn was Herman Emmerich, who, during World War II, became Commissioner of the Federal Public Housing Authority, one of several overseer-agencies for the greenbelt towns program.

[7]"Sherwood Reeder Will be Director of City Planning," *Greendale Review*, July 5, 1944; "Distinguished Guests to Attend Decennial," *Greendale Review*, May 28, 1948; Wallace Richards, "Summary Chronological History of the Greenbelt Project, Greenbelt, Maryland," Vol. 1, Sec. 8, of *Final Report of the Greenbelt Project of the Greenbelt Town Program*.

[8]John Holt, *An Analysis of Methods and Criteria Used in Selecting Families for Colonization Projects*, U.S. Department of Agriculture, The Farm Security Administration and The Bureau of Agricultural Economics Cooperating, Social Research Report No. 1 (Washington, D.C.: U.S. Government Printing Office, 1937), 44; U. S. Department of Agriculture, Farm Security Administration, *Report of Family Selection, Applications, Acceptances, and Occupancies for Units on Projects as of February 1, 1942*, Report No. 22, March 10, 1942, Record Group 96, National Archives.

[9]Mr. Mellett, "Greendale, Wisconsin" (mimeograph), n.d., 9, Box 9, Lansill Papers.

[10]The census of the proposed Greendale Village (July 19, 1938) is in the "Proceedings of the Greendale Village Board" and also includes the minutes of the meetings and resolutions. These "Proceedings" (1938 to 1965) are in the Wisconsin Area Research Center (Milwaukee), a subunit of the State Historical Society of Wisconsin. Hereinafter the minutes are cited as "Minutes of the Greendale Village Board." Also see "Greendale Official Visits Greenhills on Way to Capitol," *Greenhill News Bulletin* (Greenhills, Ohio), January 13, 1939, p. 1; and "Recession Felt by Greendale," *Milwaukee Journal*, May 9, 1938.

[11]U.S. Bureau of the Census, *Sixteenth Census of the United States: 1940. Population and Housing. Family, Tenure, and Rent*.

[12]"Adjust Rents to Meet Large Family Needs," *Greendale Review*, March 11, 1939; Works Progress Administration, *Greendale: Inventory of Local Government Archives*, Village Series No. 141 (Madison, Wisconsin: State Historical Society of Wisconsin and University of Wisconsin, 1941), 4 (hereinafter cited as WPA, *Greendale Inventory*).

[13]"Tenants of Greendale Move Despite Strike," *Milwaukee Journal*, April 30, 1938; "Pro and Con on Greendale," *Milwaukee Journal*, May 1, 1938; Isabel M'Donald, "Greendale's First Residents Arrive; and It's Pretty Fine," *Milwaukee Sentinel*, May 1, 1938.

[14]*Ibid.*; "Pageant Portrays History of Village Up to Present Date," *Greendale Review*, May 4, 1939; John P. Schroeter, "Our Greendale," *Greendale Review*, February 21, 1940.

[15]"Neighbors Out of a Book," *Greendale Review*, July 29, 1939; Pat Knudsen, "Greendale Pioneer Reflects On 28 Years of 'Square Shakes'," *Greendale Village Life*, May 30, 1976; M'Donald, "Greendale's First Residents Arrive"; interviews conducted by the Wisconsin Survey Research Laboratory for the authors of a random sample of Greendale residents in 1978.

[16]John Schroeter, "Public Utilities in the City of Milwaukee" (City of Milwaukee: Committee on Public Ownership, 1932), Greendale Village Collection.

[17]Interview with Christine Kindel, Greendale, Wisconsin, June 13, 1984.

[18]U.S. Bureau of the Census, *Sixteenth Census of the United States: 1940. Population, Vol. 2, Characteristics of the Population, Pt. 7*, "Wisconsin"; Research Section, Suburban Resettlement Division, Resettlement Administration, *Summary of Information: Greendale, Milwaukee County, Wisconsin*, c. 1936, 9, Box 9, Lansill Papers.

[19]Interview with Patricia Goetsch, Greendale, Wisconsin, July 17, 1981.

[20]Leuchtenberg, *Franklin D. Roosevelt and the New Deal*, 271 and 272. Election results were cited in the *Greendale Review*, September 23, 1938. La Follette was unsuccessful in the general election of 1938.

[21]"Progressives and Roosevelt Capture Village Majority," *Greendale Review*, November 12, 1940.

[22]"Manager Loses Race with Stork," *Greendale Review*, October 20, 1938.

[23]A group of Greendale pioneers was interviewed by Dolores Snieg in 1976. See Dolores Snieg, " 'Settlers' Recall the Early Days," *Southwest Post* (West Allis, Wisconsin), Bicentennial Edition, July, 1976.

[24]Hoyt Rawlings, "Hello, Guinea Pig! How Do You Like Life in a Project?" in the *Milwaukee Journal* (Green Sheet), August 15, 1941.

[25]*Ibid.*; "Norwegian Visitor Admires Village," *Greendale Review*, July 29, 1939.

[26]Interviews with two anonymous Greendale residents, 1978, and with Arthur Krueger, Greendale, Wisconsin, June 13, 1984; "War Veteran Looks Back At Early History of the Village," *Greendale Village Life*, May 28, 1976.

[27]Clarence Hackbarth, "Greendale: A Suburban Community Study." (unpublished master's thesis, University of Wisconsin, 1958), 28, 37 and 75; interview with an anonymous Greendale resident, 1978; Philip K. Wagner, "Suburban Landscapes for Nuclear Families: The Case of the Greenbelt Towns in the United States," in *Built Environment* 10 (No. 1, 1984), quotation on 36–37.

[28]"Hard Time Party a Huge Success," *Greendale Review*, October 20, 1938; "Greendale's WPA Project, Or Is It?" *Greendale Review*, April 8, 1939; Hackbarth, "Greendale," 28; *Greendale and the Activities of Its People*, May, 1939 (unpaginated pamphlet in State Historical Society of Wisconsin Library, Madison, and Greendale Village Collection). See also "Tenants Meeting," *Greendale Review*, November 17, 1938.

[29]Sherwood L. Reeder, "A Report on the First Two Years of the Greendale Community," April 30, 1940, pp. 18–19, Box 9, Lansill Papers; Greendale League of Women Voters, *This Is Greendale* (Greendale, Wisconsin: The League, 1948). The nationwide victory garden fad attracted the serious attention of city planners and administrators. See M. T. Wilson, "Victory Gardens in Cities and Suburban Areas," *American City*, 58 (January, 1943), 66–68.

[30]*Greendale and the Activities of Its People.*

[31]Public Service Commission of Wisconsin, *Hearings: In the Matter of a Petition by Sherwood L. Reeder and Prospective Tenants of Greendale, Milwaukee, Wisconsin*, April 22, 1938–July 27, 1938, Record Group 207, National Archives; *Greendale and the Activities of Its People*; "Bus Route. Greendale to Milwaukee Where Greendale Men Worked in 1941–42" (map in Greendale Village Collection).

[32]Irving J. Levy to Dr. W. W. Alexander, October 4, 1938, and Philip Frank to Martin G. White, December 9, 1938, Record Group 207, National Archives; "Minutes of the Greendale Village Board," June 6, 1939, August 31, 1938, and December 1, 1942; "Improve Bus Schedule; Restore Pass," *Greendale Review*, November 29, 1939.

[33]Walter E. Kroening to Major John O. Walker, Record Group 96, National Archives; "These Workers Do It, Why Can't You," *Greendale Review*, November 18, 1942; "Minutes of the Greendale Village Board," August 11, 1939, June 23, 1950, and June 2, 1953; *Greendale and the Activities of Its People.*

[34]Works Progress Administration, *Greendale: Inventory of Local Government Archives*, Village Series No. 141 (Madison: State Historical Society of Wisconsin and University of Wisconsin, 1941), 8–10; Reeder, "A Report on the First Two Years," p. 14; "Greendale Retail Facilities to be Run Cooperatively," *Greendale Bulletin*, August 24, 1938. See also "Greendale Cooperative Association" (a file of leases and subleases entered into by the Farm Security Association, the Greendale Cooperative Association, and various individual les-

sors), Record Group 96, National Archives; *Greendale and the Activities of Its People*; "Greendale Up to Now: A Summary of Events," *Greendale Review*, May 4, 1939.

[35]"Minutes of the Greendale Village Board," April 15, 1941; Greendale Cooperative Association, *Sixth Annual Report, January 1st to August 31st, 1943*, Greendale Village Collection.

[36]The beginnings of the Cooperative Association are summarized in *Greendale and the Activities of Its People*. See also WPA, *Greendale Inventory*, 8–10; and Reeder, "A Report on the First Two Years." For details on the initial linkage with Midland Cooperative of Minnesota, see "H. E. Evans to Confer with Midland Cooperative Wholesale on Project," *New York Times*, October 23, 1938.

[37]"Cooperative Flag," *Greendale Review*, November 3, 1938.

[38]"The Claims of the Cooperative Movement," *Greendale Review*, September 10, 1938; "Professor Cotton Outlines Cooperative Movement," *Greendale Review*, December 15, 1938; Alois A. Washkowiak, "Greendale Co-op Integral Part of Greendale Life," *Greendale Review*, May 4, 1939; "Living in Model Community Builds Desire to be Good Neighbors" (manuscript), 1939, 6, Greendale Village Collection.

[39]Douglas G. Marshall, "Greendale: A Study of a Resettlement Community" (unpublished Ph.D. dissertation, University of Wisconsin, 1943), 49 and 67.

[40]Other than the secondary sources cited previously, the authors have relied heavily upon the *Greendale Review* for this picture of village life. See especially its anniversary number of May 4, 1939.

[41]"Profit and Loss Statement for Period of Sept. 22–Dec. 1, Inc.," *Greendale Review*, December 15, 1938; Greendale Review Publishing Association, *By-Laws*, Greendale Village Collection; "A Thanksgiving Day Tribute to Our President Franklin Delano Roosevelt," *Greendale Review*, November 17, 1938.

[42]"Library News," *Greendale Review*, November 17, 1938; Reeder, *Greendale and the Activities of Its People*, 9.

[43]J. R. Ambruster, "The Changing Concept of Education," *Greendale Review*, September 23, 1938; J. R. Ambruster, "The Greendale School," *Greendale Review*, May 4, 1939.

[44]U.S. Resettlement Administration, *Report of the Administrator of the Resettlement Administration, 1937* (Washington, D.C.: U.S. Government Printing Office, 1937), 19. The Farm Security Administration/Resettlement Administration chose not to build a high school in Greendale, in part, because the West Milwaukee School District was anxious to increase its enrollment following the construction of a new school building. A monthly round trip bus fare of fifteen dollars per student was considered prudent by federal officials. See Thomas Schmidt to Arthur B. Thatcher, September 14, 1938, Record Group 207, National Archives.

[45]Reeder, "A Report on the First Two Years," 6-7, 13, 19; interviews with Christine Kindel, Greendale, Wisconsin, June 13, 1984, and Patricia Goetsch, Greendale, Wisconsin, July 21, 1981.

[46]*Greendale and the Activities of Its People*; "Greendale's Theatre Has Interesting Architectural Treatment; Will Open in the Middle of December," *Greendale Review*, September 23, 1938. A good description of the theater is also in "Inside Story of the Greendale Theatre," *Greendale Review*, October 7, 1939.

[47]"The 'Wise Guide'," *Greendale Bulletin*, August 24, 1938; "Cleveland Officials Visit Greendale," *Greendale Review*, September 23, 1938; "Distinguished Visitors," *Greendale Review*, May 4, 1939; "Greendale to Welcome Secretary Wallace," *Greendale Review*, June 17, 1939; "Wallace Letter Lauds Spirit of Greendale," *Greendale Review*, July 1, 1939.

[48]"Chicago Delegation Invade Greendale and Visit Milwaukee," *Greendale Bulletin*, August 24, 1938; "Park Executives Expected," *Greendale Review*, September 23, 1938; "Display House," *Greendale Review*, November 3, 1938; "Original Model Home Occupied by Nelezens," *Greendale Review*, April 8, 1939.

[49]Interview with Michael Steinberg, Greendale, Wisconsin, November 4, 1977; *Greendale and the Activities of Its People*,; "Greendale Holds Open House," *Greendale Review*, October 20, 1938.

[50]Roy Emerson Stryker and Nancy Wood, *In This Proud Land: America 1935-1943 As Seen in the FSA Photography* (New York: Galahad Books), 7 and 10–14, quotation on 7. The original 270,000 photographs, now pared down to 70,000 images, are on file in the Library of Congress.

[51]"Administration Desires to Make Greendale Self-Governed Community," *Greendale Review*, September 10, 1938; "Minutes of the First Meeting, Citizens' Association Committee," October 14, 1938; Frank W. Klaesing to Mary Haskell, October 16, 1938, Greendale Village Collection.

[52]Greendale Citizens' Association Committee, *By-Laws*, January 10, 1939, Greendale Village Collection.

[53]"Woman's Place in Greendale," *Greendale Review*, March 11, 1939; "Co-op Celebrates," *Greendale Review*, August 26, 1939.

[54]State of Wisconsin Circuit Court, Milwaukee County, *Order of Incorporation, Village of Greendale*, Record Group 207, National Archives; *Greendale and the Activities of Its People*.

[55]Greendale Citizens' Association, "Minutes of Meeting," February 13, 1939, Greendale Village Collection; "Village Board Members a Bit Disgruntled," *Greendale Review*, March 11, 1939.

[56]"National Attention Focused on Manager Plan Vote Here," *Greendale Review*, February 25, 1939; *Greendale and the Activities of Its People*; WPA, *Greendale Inventory*, 17 and 33.

[57]"Reeder is Elected Manager of Village," *Greendale Review*, April 22, 1939; "Kroening Receives Appointment," *Greendale Review*, July 29, 1939; *Greendale and the Activities of Its People*.

[58]"A Community Menace," *Greendale Review*, January 29, 1939; *Report of Family Section*; Marshall, "Greendale," 51–64.

[59]"Living in Model Community Builds Desire to be Good Neighbors," 4; interview with Gerald and Madge Casey, Greendale, Wisconsin, June 13, 1984.

[60]*Helpful Suggestions for Greendale Residents* (pamphlet), Greendale Village Collection; interview with Patricia Goetsch, Greendale, Wisconsin, July 21, 1981. For further examples of intrusions by management into daily life, see "Suggestions to Greendale Housewives," *Greendale Review*, March 11, 1939; and "Will Paint Houses as Weather and Availability Permits," *Greendale Review*, September 18, 1941.

[61]"Minutes of the Greendale Village Board," September 11, 1941.

[62]"Minutes of the Greendale Village Board," February 12, 1941; WPA, *Greendale Inventory*, 33; "Sherwood Reeder Goes to San Diego: Kroening to be Acting Manager," *Greendale Review*, January 8, 1941; Victor J. Jacoby to authors, June 3, 1986.

[63]"!!!Let's be Fair About It!!!" *Greendale Review*, October 20, 1938; Marshall, "Greendale," 34.

[64]Gaston Haxo to John P. Schroeter, February 29, 1940, Greendale Village Collection; Greendale Citizens' Association Housing Committee to U.S. Senator Robert M. La Follette, September 29, 1940, Record Group 96, National Archives.

[65]"Armistice Day Program," *Greendale Review*, November 17, 1938; John P. Schroeter, "To Keep Us Out of War," *Greendale Review*, October 7, 1939; "Minutes of the Greendale Village Board," June 16, September 8, 1941; Hackbarth, "Greendale," 38–39.

[66]"Need is Reported of 3,000,000 Homes," *New York Times*, January 22, 1943.

[67]"Use Big Staff to Run Village of Greendale," *Milwaukee Journal*, January 26, 1943. Farm Security Administration officials complied with a request of the newspaper in verifying the accuracy of this unfavorable account. See Philip Klutznick to James Victory, December 9, 1942, Record Group 196, Records of the Legal Division, PHA, National Archives.

[68]Walter E. Kroening, mimeographed letter to all Greendale residents, February 22, 1943; Roy M. Little to Walter E. Kroening, April 8, 1943 ("Series 3-E," schedule of monthly rentals and income range attached), both items in Greendale Village Collection; C. B. Baldwin to Herbert Emmerich, August 13, 1942, Record Group 96, National Archives.

[69]Roy M. Little to Walter E. Kroening, April 8, 1943; Walter Kroening to James F. Ircink (Village Trustee), memorandum attached to April 8, 1943 letter of Little to Kroening, all in the Greendale Village Collection.

[70]"Rent Increase Stirs Comment," *Milwaukee Journal*, April 11, 1943; "Improvement at Greendale," *ibid.*, April 15, 1943.

[71]"Minutes of the Greendale Village Board," May 4 (Resolution 69), May 11, and June 1, 1943; Greendale Village Board and Executive Board of the Citizens' Association, "Minutes of a Joint Session," May 28, 1943; James Ircink to Hon. Howard J. McMurray, April 14, 1943; Robert La Follette to Raymond J. Miller, April 21, 1943, Greendale Village Collection.

[72]Herbert Emmerich to Hon. Alexander Wiley, April 19, 1943; John P. Schroeter to William Luebke, Jr., May 30, 1943; James T. Gobbel to Walter Kroening (telegram), May 28, 1943, all in the Greendale Village Collection.

[73]See, for example, the following items in the Greendale Village Collection: Martin A. Miller (Greenbelt, Maryland), to John P. Schroeter June 8, 1943; Residents of Greendale to Residents of Greenhills (Ohio), May 9, 1943; and Walter E. Kroening to Board of Trustees and Executive Committees of Citizens' Association, Greendale, Wisconsin, with attachment from Greenhills Citizens' Association Committee, May 31, 1943.

[74]"Greendalers Balk at Rent Raises, Adding Many Other Complaints," *Milwaukee Journal*, April 27, 1943.

[75]Telegram from Al Levy to Wilfred Bosanko, June 10, 1943, Greendale Village Collection; "Minutes of the Greendale Village Board," June 1, 1943; "Ask Greendale Manager Fight Rents or Quit," *Milwaukee Journal*, May 6, 1943; "Rent 'Strike' at Greendale," *Milwaukee Journal*, June 1, 1943.

[76]"Recent Strike" (handwritten synopsis of events leading up to legal proceedings of Roman Kaczmarek and Gordon Hanson), Greendale Village Collection.

[77]Correspondence of the Greendale Citizens' Association, 1943–1944, miscellaneous file in the Greendale Village Collection; Seventh District Federal Court, Chicago, Illinois, Court Case No. 8528 (1944).

[78]"Minutes of the Greendale Village Board," October 5, 1943; "Curfew Ordinance is Tabled," *Greendale Review*, October 13, 1943.

[79]"Problems of Our Youth Can Be Solved by Cooperation," *Greendale Review*, September 1, 1943; "Vandalism Spreads," *Greendale Review*, February 16, 1944; and "Juvenile Disorderly Conduct Cases as of August 9, 1943" (handwritten log), Greendale Village Collection. The perception that young people were fomenting an abnormal amount of mischief was

widespread in America near the end of World War II. See Ernest P. Agnew, "Juvenile Delinquency in the Average Wisconsin City," *Municipality*, 39 (January, 1944), 3 and 4, 16.

[80]"Minutes of the Greendale Village Board," May 11, 1943; "Manager's Position Questioned," *Greendale Review*, March 15, 1944; "Village Manager Reinstated, Withheld Wages Will Be Paid," *Greendale Review*, June 21, 1944; Wisconsin State Senator Allen J. Busby to Stanley G. Samuelson, June 14, 1945, Greendale Village Collection.

[81]"Mrs. Merrill Burke Opposes Bill Before Wisconsin Legislature," *Greendale Review*, May 17, 1945; "New Wisconsin Laws Affecting Cities and Villages," *Municipality*, 40 (September, 1945), 196; "An Open Letter to New Village Manager," *Greendale Review*, January 31, 1947.

Chapter Eight

[1]"Minutes of the Greendale Village Board," May 7 and January 3, 1946.

[2]"Chilean Houser Visits Greendale," *Greendale Review*, February 16, 1944; Richard Dewey, "Peripheral Expansion in Milwaukee County," in the *American Journal of Sociology*, 54 (September, 1948), 118–125, quotation on 125. The latter study was initially prepared as a report to the Milwaukee County Regional Planning Department in 1945; a copy of the report is in the Milwaukee Municipal Reference Library, Milwaukee.

[3]Clarence Stein, "Greendale and the Future," in *American City*, 63 (June, 1948), 106–109, quotations on 107 and 109; also see Elmer Plische, "Greendale," in *Municipality*, 37 (March, 1942), 43; "Minutes of the Greendale Village Board," February 3, 1948; and "Distinguished Guests to Attend Decennial," *Greendale Review*, May 28, 1948.

[4]"What's the Matter With Our Community Spirit?" *Greendale Review*, August 1, 1946; "Candidates Express Views on Political Issues," *Greendale Review*, March 29, 1944; "Community of Good Neighbors Pledged by Civic Group," *Greendale Review*, March 1, 1944.

[5]Lois V. Harlow to Mason C. Doan, December 16, 1947; and Orvil R. Olmsted to Walter E. Kroening, January 16, 1948, Record Group 196, Records of the General Field Office and the Central Office of the PHA Regarding Management and Disposition of Greentown Projects, 1936–61, National Archives and Records Administration (hereinafter referred to as Record Group 196, Records of the General Field Office, National Archives).

[6]Marshall, "Greendale," 51–65; Carl Yost, "Hello Neighbor," *Greendale Review*, April 28, 1950.

[7]"Greendale Co-op Meeting Attracts But 35 members," *Greendale Review*, November 1, 1951; Joseph C. Gray to Board of Directors, Greendale School District, March 25, 1947, Greendale Village Collection; "The Greendale Review to Suspend Publication for Indefinite Period," *Greendale Review*, September 12, 1946.

[8]Roy Little, James T. Gobbel, Lawrence H. Tucker, and Walter E. Kroening to Hon. Herbert Emmerick, March 16, 1944 (letter of transmittal for "Proposal for the Transfer of the Greenbelt Towns From the United States of America to American Communities, Inc."), Record Group 196, Records of the General Field Office, National Archives.

[9]National Housing Agency, Federal Public Housing Authority, *The Disposition and Development of Greendale: A Report*, June 20, 1945, pp. 11, 12, 16 and 35, Record Group 196, Records of the General Field Office, National Archives.

[10]*Ibid.*, 9. Peets later asserted that Richard Ratcliffe, a University of Wisconsin land economist, doubted that Greendale's location would ever attract upper-income families. Peets (rightly, as it turned out) maintained that the parkway site would be a sufficient lure. See Elbert Peets to Doris Ann Krupinski, March 5, 1960, Greendale Village Collection.

[11]National Housing Agency, *Disposition and Development of Greendale*, 6, 7, 9, and 12.

[12]*Ibid.*, 35–36; D. S. Myer to Arthur Marcus, March 10, 1947, Record Group 196, Records of the General Field Office, National Archives; "Minutes of the Greendale Village Board," November 6, 1945; Tenants' Committee on Mutual Housing (correspondence of the members), Greendale Village Collection.

[13]Memorandum from Philip M. Klutznick, to C. Russell Cravens, 1944?; and Oliver Winston to C. Russell Cravens, October 1, 1945, Record Group 196, Records of the General Field Office, National Archives.

[14]Community Manager, Greendale, Wisconsin, "Clover Lane" (sales information and plat map) n. d.; Greendale Design Review Committee, "Information for Purchasers of Lots in Clover Lane Subdivision, Greendale, Wisconsin" (brochure on deed restrictions), October, 1945, Greendale Village Collection; "Village Board Approves Two New Subdivisions," *Greendale Review*, August 16, 1945; "Minutes of the Greendale Village Board," June 20, and July 10, 1945.

[15]Federal Public Housing Administration, *Proposed Provision Pertaining to Appropriation for National Housing Agency, Fiscal Year 1947*, House Doc. 584, 79th Cong., 2nd sess., 1946; "Minutes of the Greendale Village Board," February 5, 1946, June 1, 1948, and December 7, 1948.

[16]Walter E. Kroening to Roy Little, September 16, 1952, Record Group 196, Records of the General Field Office, National Archives (this communique mentions a December 20, 1948, report by Elbert Peets); Elbert Peets, *Explanatory Notes on the Draft for a Zoning Ordinance for Greendale* (Greendale Village Board), quotation on p. 11, copy in possession of Patricia Goetsch, Greendale.

[17]Stein, "Greendale and the Future," 107 and 108.

[18]"Future Expansion Plans for Greendale Outlined at Regular Board Meeting," *Greendale Review*, August 16, 1944; "Greendale Expansion to Proceed in Near Future," *Greendale Review*, August 2, 1945.

[19]Arnold, *The New Deal in the Suburbs*, 230–236.

[20]U.S. Public Housing Administration, *First Annual Report of the Public Housing Administration, 1947* (Washington, D.C., 1947), 17; U.S. Public Housing Administration, *Second Annual Report of the Public Housing Administration, 1948* (Washington, D.C., 1948), 29; U.S. Public Housing Administration, *Third Annual Report of the Public Housing Administration*, 1949), 30.

[21]"Minutes of the Village Board," February 3 and May 4, 1948; Clyde M. Paust to Greendale Village Board, May 3, 1948, copy in possession of Patricia Goetsch, Greendale; "Home Ownership in Greendale," *Greendale Review*, February 20, 1948.

[22]"Offer Is Made for Greendale," *Milwaukee Journal*, February 1, 1948; "Offer Is Made for Purchase of Greendale," *Greendale Review*, February 6, 1948; House Committee on Banking and Currency, *Suburban Resettlement Projects, Hearings Before the Committee on Banking and Currency, House of Representatives on H.R. 2440, A Bill to Authorize the Public Housing Commissioner to Sell the Suburban Resettlement Projects Known as Greenbelt, Md.; Greendale, Wis.; and Greenhills, Ohio, Without Regard to Provision of Law Requiring Competitive Bidding or Public Advertising, March 18 and 19, 1949*, 81st Cong., 1st sess., 1949, p. 20.

[23]"We Still Want to Know!" *Greendale Review*, March 4, 1949; John P. Schroeter to Congressman Clement Zablocki, August 3, 1949, Greendale Village Collection; "Legion Group Meets, Row," *Milwaukee Journal*, August 5, 1950; "Veterans Seek Purchase of Greendale and the City of Milwaukee Cooperates," in *American City*, 64 (January, 1949), 73–74.

[24]Walter E. Kroening, *Recommendations on a Program of Operations and Development and on a Tentative Budget Submitted to the Board of Directors of the American Legion Development Corporation* (confidential), July 22, 1949, Greendale Village Collection; Irving A. Puchner to Robert Eppley, December 10, 1948, copy in possession of Patricia Goetsch, Greendale.

[25]American Legion Development Corporation, *Greendale: An Answer to Veterans' Housing Problems*, Greendale Village Collection.

[26]Orvil R. Olmsted to Egan, December 23, 1948; and R. J. Wadsworth, "Notes on a Conference in OA Conference Room, Washington, D.C., September 22, 1948," both in Record Group 196, Records of the General Field Office, National Archives.

[27]House Committee on Banking and Currency, *Hearings . . . on H.R. 2440*, pp. 2–8, 27, and 36–41; *Congressional Record*, 95 (1949), pt. 5: pp. 5833–5834 and 5980, and pt. 6: p. 7254.

[28]The 1,000-unit addition was, in fact, the first phase of an expansionist plan that was, in turn, a version of the 1945 FPHA development study. See Elbert Peets, "Residential Site Planning Textures," in Spreiregen, ed., *On the Art of Designing Cities: Selected Essays of Elbert Peets*, 202–215.

[29]Real Estate Research Corporation (Chicago, Illinois), for Public Housing Administration, *Village of Greendale, Wisconsin; Appraisal Report*, November 20, 1948, Record Group 196, Records of the General Field Office, National Archives (hereinafter cited as *Greendale Appraisal Report*).

[30]"Minutes of the Greendale Mutual Housing Association," July 23, 1949, Greendale Village Collection.

[31]"Minutes of the Greendale Village Board," December 7, 1948; John L. Fleming to Mr. and Mrs. Greendale (mimeographed letter), July 7, 1949, Greendale Village Collection.

[32]*Greendale Appraisal Report*, "Exhibit 'G,' Tenant Questionnaire Summary"; "An Open Letter to Mayor Frank Zeidler, "*Greendale Review*, July 22, 1949.

[33]"Ballots Spurn Legion Group at Greendale," *Milwaukee Journal*, August 24, 1949; "Minutes of the Greendale Village Board," September 12, 1949.

[34]Virgil H. Hurless to the Honorable Mayor and the Common Council, August 26, 1949, copy in possession of Patricia Goetsch, Greendale; Peets, "Report of the Town Planning Section," 14. Victor Jacoby, a long-time Greendale resident and eight-year veteran of the Village Board, also stated that "only an outsider would have considered that the residents would back the Marcus (ALCDC) plan"; Victor J. Jacoby, to authors, June 3, 1986.

[35]Greendale Village Board, "Resolution No. 49–15," September 12, 1949, copy in possession of Patricia Goetsch, Greendale; John Taylor Egan to Douglas Waier, October 26, 1949, Record Group 196, Records of the General Field Office, National Archives.

[36]"City Wants Its $300,000 Back," *Milwaukee Sentinel*, July 8, 1950; Public Housing Administration, File Memo of D. C. Austin, November 30, 1950, Record Group 196, Records of the General Field Office, National Archives; "Minutes of the Greendale Village Board," October 4 and November 4, 1949; "Legion Group Set to Expire," *Milwaukee Journal*, November 23, 1952.

[37]"G.V.C.H.A. Slate Sweeps Greendale April 4th Election," *Greendale Review*, April 14, 1950; Carl. L. Yost, "We're Tired—Are You?" *Greendale Review*, May 26, 1950.

[38]"War Causes Shifts in Plans for Greendale," *Milwaukee Journal*, August 16, 1950; Carl L. Yost, "We're Froze," *Greendale Review*, August 18, 1950; "Sell Those 'Greentowns'," *Milwaukee Journal*, March 10, 1951.

[39]"Village Board Suspends Operations for May 26," *Greendale Review*, May 26, 1950; "U.S. Moves into Greendale to Get $40,000 Equipment," *Milwaukee Sentinel*, May 27, 1950. A Public Housing Administration file on the extended episode (the dispute continued until early October, 1950) is in Record Group 196, Records of the General Field Office, National Archives.

[40]"Renew Feud at Greendale, *Milwaukee Journal*, June 2, 1950. Manager Eppley resigned shortly after this statement. His letter of resignation was reprinted in the *Greendale Review*, August 18, 1950 ("Manager Eppley Resigns to Enter Private Work").

[41]"Minutes of the Greendale Village Board," November 1, 1949.

[42]"Seeks to Stop Greendale Sale," *Milwaukee Journal*, July 26, 1950; "Test Housing Authority Act," *ibid.*, December 19, 1950; "Housing Bond Offer is Foiled by Court Jam," *ibid.*, April 5, 1951.

[43]C. Russell Cravens to John Dobbs, June 26, 1950, Record Group 196, Records of the General Field Office, National Archives; "Priorities Set in Home Sales for Greendale," *Milwaukee Journal*, August 1, 1951.

[44]Walter E. Kroening to Roy M. Little, May 3, 1951, Record Group 196, Records of the General Field Office, National Archives; "Tell Sale Plan for Greendale," *Milwaukee Journal*, May 24, 1951.

[45]"Lot by Lot Plan Rejected," *Milwaukee Sentinel*, September 23, 1951; Carl L. Yost, "Lottery or Justice?" *Greendale Review*, August 17, 1951; "Greendaler is Crying; He Wants Houses at 1948 Prices," *Milwaukee Journal*, July 26, 1951.

[46]Roy M. Little to Walter E. Kroening, September 30, 1952, Record Group 196, Records of the General Field Office, National Archives; "The Village Hall," *Greendale Review*, February 17, 1950; Carl L. Yost, "An Open Letter to Col. C. Russell Cravens," *Greendale Review*, June 8, 1951; Marshall W. Annis to Hon. Alexander Wiley, reprinted in *Greendale Review*, July 20, 1951.

[47]"Co-op Backed at Greendale," *Milwaukee Journal*, June 25, 1951; "PHA Plan Hit by Greendale," *ibid.*, July 5, 1951; Carl L. Yost, "The Die Is Cast!" *Greendale Review*, September 28, 1951; "Minutes of the Greendale Village Board," July 3, 12, and 18, 1951.

[48]Walter E. Kroening to All Greendale Tenants, January 14, 1952 (sales circular), Greendale Village Collection; "Minutes of the Greendale Village Board," April 15 and 28, 1952. The PHA decided to replat the central residential area (Village Center plan) and to redesign the garages to the adjacent dwellings in order that purchasers of the homes would qualify for federal home loans. See John Taylor Egan to Roman H. Kaczmarek, September 20, 1951, Record Group 196, Records of the General Field Office, National Archives.

[49]"First Drawing for Greendale Lots is Slated for Friday," *Tri-Town News* (Hales Corners, Wisconsin), January 17, 1952; "Draw for Lots at Greendale," *Milwaukee Journal*, January 19, 1952; "Greendale Units Sales Are Near," *Milwaukee Journal*, June 11, 1952; and "Complete Sale at Greendale," *Milwaukee Journal*, July 16, 1952.

[50]"Greendale: Established Prices on Urban Dwelling Units" (Table); Real Estate Research Corporation, *Appraisal Report: Fair Market Value, Village of Greendale, Wisconsin*, July, 1951 (report prepared for Public Housing Administration), September 19, 1951, p. 101, both items in Record Group 196, Records of the General Field Office, National Archives; "Units for Sale in Greendale," *Milwaukee Journal*, September 13, 1951.

[51]*Greendale: Final Report of Project Costs Including Actual Construction Costs from Inception of Project to June 30, 1938*, sec. 3, exhibit A, April 11, 1939, Record Group 96, National Archives; "Minutes of the Greendale Village Board," September 18, 1951.

[52]"Prospective Purchasers for Greendale" (file of correspondence, May 26, 1951, to August 19, 1952), Record Group 196, Records of the General Field Office, National Archives; "Shops Opened at Greendale," *Milwaukee Journal*, September 13, 1952.

[53]"Tenants Fight to Buy Farms," *Milwaukee Journal*, November 18, 1952; "Minutes of the Greendale Village Board," May 27, 1952. According to the realty research firm contracted with the PHA, the farm tenants had not maintained the sound agricultural practices of the original landowners. Consequently, the productivity of the land declined sharply during the period of federal management. Moreover, the research firm concluded that, once the federal government withdrew, property taxes would be too high for the farmers to remain on the land. See *Appraisal Report: Village of Greendale,* November 20, 1948, 85–86; and Real Estate Research Corporation, *Farm Development Land in Greendale* (report prepared for Public Housing Administration), January 21, 1952, Record Group 196, Records of the General Field Office, National Archives.

[54]"Herzfeld Meeting, University Club" (handwritten minutes), October 15, 1952; and quotation of Frank P. Zeidler to Walter Kroening, October 16, 1952, both items in Record Group 196, Records of the General Field Office, National Archives; "Businessmen Make a New Deal Work," in *Business Week* (March 10, 1962), 92–94.

[55]Public Housing Administration, "Greendale, Wisconsin: Analysis of Bids Received on November 19, 1952 on Commercial and Land Areas"; and Walter E. Kroening to Roy M. Little, "Information Regarding Bidders on Greendale Land and Commercial Properties," November 28, 1952, both items in Record Group 196, Records of the General Field Office, National Archives; "Greendale Bid Finds Support," *Milwaukee Journal*, November 21, 1952.

[56]Louis Quarles to John Taylor Egan, November 17, 1952, Record Group 196, Records of the General Field Office, National Archives.

[57]Memorandum from John Taylor Egan to Walter E. Kroening, "Greendale—Sale of Remaining Property to Milwaukee Community Development Corporation," January 19, 1953, Record Group 196, Records of the General Field Office, National Archives.

[58]"Minutes of the Greendale Village Board," April 21 and May 11, 1953; "Check 'Wraps Up' Greendale Purchase," *Milwaukee Journal*, August 25, 1953; "A Good Plan for Greendale," *Milwaukee Sentinel*, November 21, 1952; "W. E. Kroening Gets Schuster Center Post," *Milwaukee Journal*, March 1, 1953.

Chapter Nine

[1]Marygold Shire Melli, "Subdivision Control in Wisconsin," in the *Wisconsin Law Review*, 39 (May, 1953), 447.

[2]For favorably slanted reports on the activity of the MCDC, see N. J. Russell, Jr., "Metamorphosis of a Village," in the *Wisconsin Architect*, 28 (June, 1960), 1–5; Dale R. Johnson, "A 'Greenbelt' Blooms," in *National Civic Review*, 48 (July 1959), 338–342; and "Greendale Being Developed by Private Enterprise," in *American City*, 71 (February, 1956), 133. A series of planning studies for Greendale (1947–1958) may be found in Elbert Peets, "Residential Site Planning Texture," in Spreiregen, ed., *On the Art of Designing Cities*, 202–215.

[3]Assorted items dealing with Greendale's homeowner associations are in the Greendale Development File, Milwaukee County Historical Society, Milwaukee. See also "Greendale Home Owners Steam Ahead on Projects," *Milwaukee Journal*, October 16, 1960.

[4]Greendale was touted as a success story by residents and Milwaukee planning organizations. See Citizens' Governmental Research Bureau, Inc., "Greendale Looks to the Future

on Its 17th Anniversary," *Bulletin Series*, 43 (November 1, 1955); K. W. Bauer, "A Greenbelt Town Grows Up," in *American City* 74 (October, 1959), 143–148; "Greendale Village Is Having a 'Boom'," *Milwaukee Journal*, March 23, 1958; and Doris Ann Krupinski, "Greenbelt Potentials for Suburban Growth" (unpublished manuscript in the Greendale Village Collection).

⁵The details of Greendale's private growth have been gleaned from sources too numerous to list except in a categorical manner. The minutes of the Greendale Village Board have supplied much of the information, as well as the plat records for Greendale subdivisions (Clerk of Courts, Milwaukee County), and records of private home sales in the Greendale Development Files, Milwaukee County Historical Society, Milwaukee. Elbert Peets himself corresponded intermittently with Doris Ann Krupinski, a resident of Greendale who committed the letters to the Greendale Village Historical Collection. The *Milwaukee Journal* and *Milwaukee Sentinel* also published occasional press releases on Greendale's progress. See "Develop Sites in Greendale," *Milwaukee Journal*, September 23, 1956; "Greendale Village Is Having a Boom," *ibid.*, March 29, 1958; and William Janz, "Greendale: Urban Era Pacemaker," *Milwaukee Sentinel*, March 18, 1963 (read into the *Congressional Record* by Congressman Clement J. Zablocki shortly after its publication).

⁶"Minutes of the Greendale Village Board," May 1 and May 10, 1956, and August 7, 1962.

⁷U.S. Bureau of the Census, *Seventeenth Census of the United States: 1950. Population, Vol. 1, Characteristics of the Population, pt. 49, Wisconsin; Census of the Population: 1960, Vol. 1, Characteristics of the Population, pt. 51, Wisconsin;* John M. Kuglitsch, "Greendale: 24 Years of Private Ownership and Development—1952–1976" (unpublished manuscript in the Greendale Village Collection, June 31, 1978). A published synopsis of MCDC plans for Greendale, as well as a general discussion of village government and services (as of 1958), is James Dahir, *Greendale Comes of Age: The Story of Wisconsin's Best Known Planned Community As It Enters Its Twenty-First Year* (Milwaukee: Milwaukee Community Development Corporation, 1958).

⁸Gary Staudacher, "Now Empty Greendale Lab Once Pioneer in Research," *Southwest Post* (West Allis, Wisconsin), September 19, 1979; "Minutes of the Greendale Village Board," September 7, 1965.

⁹The apartment zoning battle raged for months in the fall of 1958. The events were covered by the *Tri-Town News* (Hales Corners, Wisconsin) and by a partisan paper, the *Greendale Times* (see especially the numbers of October and November). Also see "Minutes of the Greendale Village Board," October 17, 1958.

¹⁰"Minutes of the Greendale Village Board," October 21 and November 4, 1958; July 7, 1959; July 5, 1961; March 6 and October 2, 1962; April 6 and September 5, 1963; and April 6, 1966.

¹¹David E. Link, "1100 Acre Greendale Deal," *Milwaukee Sentinel*, November 20, 1964. A few stormy elections in Greendale during the MCDC years yielded an avalanche of circulars and posters. Many are kept in the Greendale Village Collection along with the correspondence of the combatants.

¹²Donald J. Pedo, "Greendale, Wisconsin: Parkways and Progress," in *Concrete Pipe News*, 20 (June, 1968), 43–45; Kuglitsch, "Greendale: 24 Years," 3 and 4; Kurt W. Bauer, "A Backward Glance: Greendale—Garden City in Wisconsin," in *Southeastern Wisconsin Regional Planning Commission Technical Report*, 1 (August/September, 1963), 35.

¹³These density estimates have been based upon several sources and refer primarily to the estates along the parkway and to the Depression-era homes. The sources include: "Develop

Sites in Greendale, *Milwaukee Jour .al,* September 23, 1956; Dahir, *Greendale Comes of Age,* 13–14; and Carl L. Gardner & Associates, Inc., *Preliminary Study, General Plan: Greendale, Wisconsin,* June, 1962 (Greendale: Village of Greendale). The platting record of subdivision activity was consulted in the proceedings of the village board and in the plat books kept by the Clerk of Courts, Milwaukee County.

[14]U.S. Bureau of the Census, *Census of Population and Housing: 1970 Final Report. Milwaukee, Wisconsin SMSA*; U.S. Bureau of the Census, *Census Tracts: Milwaukee, Wis. Standard Metropolitan Statistical Area, 1980 Census of Population and Housing.*

[15]*Ibid.*; U.S. Bureau of the Census, *Sixteenth Census of the United States: 1940. Population, Vol. 2. Characteristics of the Population, Pt. 7,* "Wisconsin".

[16]*Ibid.; Seventeenth Census of the United States: 1950. Population, Vol. 2, Characteristics of the Population, Pt. 49,* "Wisconsin,"; and U.S. Bureau of the Census, *Eighteenth Census of the United States: 1960. Population, Vol. 2, Characteristics of the Population, pt. 51,* "Wisconsin."

[17]*Census Tracts, Milwaukee,* 1980.

[18]*Ibid.; Census of Population and Housing, Milwaukee, 1970.*

[19]*Ibid.*

[20]Citizens' Governmental Research Bureau, Inc., "Greendale Looks to the Future on Its 17th Anniversary," 4; Citizens' Governmental Research Bureau, "Greendale: Commercial and Residential Development Spur Growth of Former Greenbelt Town," *Bulletin,* 61 (May 26, 1973), 2; Harold H. Lutz, Greendale Village Clerk-Secretary, to authors, May 11, 1981.

[21]This breakdown of land use in Greendale has been extrapolated from the platting record on file in the office of the Clerk of Courts, Milwaukee County, and from the Citizens' Governmental Research Bureau, "Greendale: Commercial and Residential Development," 3 and 4; Kuglitsch, "Greendale: 24 Years," 7; and March C. Radtke; Assistant Village Engineer, Greendale, to authors, January 14, 1982.

[22]*Census of the Population and Housing, Milwaukee, 1970; Census Tracts, Milwaukee, 1980*; Cathy Meister, "Will Greendale Welcome Minorities?" *Southwest Post* (West Allis, Wisconsin), December 19, 1979.

[23]Klau-Van Peterson-Dunlap, Inc., "The Greendale Story" (publicity brochure of the Milwaukee Community Development Corporation, n.d.), Greendale Village Collection. The part that developers played in other planned community developments in America was the subject of Marshall Kaplan, "The Roles of Planner and Developer in the New Community," in the *Washington University Law Quarterly* (February, 1965), 88–104.

[24]The adult subjects, 118 in the Center and seventy-eight in Overlook, were selected according to a random sample of house numbers. Fifty of the interviews were conducted in person with Center respondents, while the remaining sixty-eight interviews in the Center and all seventy-eight in the Overlook area were done via telephone by the Wisconsin Survey Research Laboratory. Fifty questions were asked of each respondent concerning family composition, occupation of head of household, number of years in Greendale, and preferences for various features of the residential environments. Several of the latter questions were phrased so as to elicit comparisons between the Center and Overlook. Since the neighborhood plans are so distinctive, the total sample provided a relatively good representation of the socioeconomic range of the village population.

[25]Several studies of resident preferences in American planned communities have been conducted within the past fifteen years. The results of these surveys are comparable only in gross terms because of differing interests, aims, and methods of researchers, the physical and social differences among the new communities studied, and (a less obvious but equally com-

pelling reason), the prevailing academic climates within which the research was undertaken. For conflicting assessments of new towns based upon the resident surveys, compare the following presentations. The first two are supportive, while the last two are critical of the new communities movement. See John B. Lansing, *et al., Planned Residential Environments* (Ann Arbor, Michigan: Survey Research Center, Institute for Social Research, University of Michigan, 1970); Robert B. Zehner, "Neighborhood and Community Satisfaction in New Towns and Less Planned Suburbs," in the *Journal of the American Institute of Planners*, 37 (November, 1971), 379–385; Raymond J. Burby III and Shirley F. Weiss, *New Communities U.S.A.* (Lexington, Massachusetts: Lexington Books, 1976); and Shirley Weiss, "Further Discussion of the University of North Carolina New Town Study," in *Urban Land* 34 (April, 1975), 12–15. A programmatic statement on social research in new towns is offered by Robert W. Marans and Robert B. Zehner, "Social Planning and Research in New Communities," in *The Contemporary New Communities Movement in the United States*, Gideon Golany and Daniel Walden, eds. (University of Illinois Press: Urbana, 1974), 98–108. Sidney Abbot has suggested that federally backed new towns provide important opportunities as living laboratories. See Sidney Abbott, "New Hope for New Towns," in *Design and Environment*, 3 (Spring, 1972), 28–37. Sociologist Herbert Gans proposed the same idea much earlier. See Herbert Gans, "The Sociology of New Towns: Opportunities for Research," in *Sociology and Social Research* 40 (March–April, 1956), 231–239.

[26]Articles in the Milwaukee metropolitan press from the late 1970's and early 1980's reveal many of the concerns and fears felt by Greendalers. See Ann Angel, "Urge Village to Ban Two-Story Additions," *Milwaukee Sentinel*, September 13, 1979; Cynthia Dries, "Central Village Residents Fight Building Restrictions," *Southwest Post* (West Allis, Wisconsin), September 19, 1979; Douglas Rossi, "Greendale May Curb Home Additions," *Milwaukee Journal*, February 6, 1979; "Greendale Center Building Additions Ban Ends," *Milwaukee Sentinel*, March 21, 1979; Gary Staudacher, "Young People, 'Cops' Clash at Root River Parkway," *Southwest Post* (West Allis, Wisconsin), June 27, 1979; and Patrick Knudsen, "Violent Crime Can Happen Here, Police Believe in Being Prepared," *Greendale Village Life*, July 16, 1981. For a more positive assessment of life in Greendale, see Dolores Snieg, "Residents Praise Greendale," *Southwest Post* (West Allis, Wisconsin), Bicentennial Edition, July 1976. A typical comment reported in the latter source is: "The small town atmosphere gave us a comfortable feeling, the clean streets, children playing outside and a minimum of local traffic impressed us."

[27]Stein, "Greendale and the Future," 107; Christiansen, *The American Garden City*, 93.

[28]The ways in which a social identity is created by an urban landscape are examined in Lester B. Rowntree and Margaret W. Conkey, "Symbolism and the Cultural Landscape, in *"Annals of the Association of American Geographers*, 70 (December 1980), 459–474.

[29]Jacob L. Crane, *Urban Planning—Illustration and Reality* (New York: Vantage Press, 1973), 133; Jackson, *Crabgrass Frontier*, 287.

[30]Christiansen, *The American Garden City*, 92.

[31]The design and planning of new towns in Western and Eastern civilizations from ancient to modern times is treated with considerable acumen by Ervin Y. Galantay, *New Towns: Antiquity to the Present* (New York: George Braziller, 1975). The seminal work of Clarence Stein, *Toward New Towns for America*, remains an enduring classic; much of the volume is devoted to a discussion of Radburn, New Jersey. A more recent survey of American "new communities" (a phrase lately used to refer to planned communities in America) is Alan Turner, "New Communities in the United States, 1968–1973: Part I: Historical Background, Legislation and the Development Process," and "Part II: Design Characteristics and

Case Studies," in *Town Planning Review*, 45 (July, 1974), 259–273; (October, 1974), 415–430. For enthusiastic appraisals of the planned communities of the 1960's and 1970's, see "Rise of the New Cities," in *Nation's Business*, 56 (August, 1968), 72–78; Shirley F. Weiss, "New Cities," in *Panhandle Magazine*, 5 (Spring, 1971), 19–22; and Carlos C. Campbell, *New Towns: Another Way to Live* (Reston, Virginia: Reston Publishing Company, Inc., 1976). The physical planning of American new communities is a major focus of James Bailey, ed., *New Towns in America: The Design and Development Process* (New York: John Wiley & Sons, 1973). Policy implications of federal legislation in the early 1970's have been considered by Hugh Mields, Jr., *Federally Assisted New Communities: New Dimensions in Urban Development* (Washington, D.C.: Urban Land Institute, 1973); Letitia C. Langord and Gwen Bell, "Federally Sponsored New Towns of the Seventies," in *Growth and Change*, 6 (October, 1975), 24–31; and William Nicoson, "The United States: The Battle for Title VII," in *New Perspectives on Community Development*, ed. by Mahlon Apgar IV (Maidenhead and Berkshire, England: McGraw–Hill Book Company, Limited, 1976), 38–58.

[32]Examples of the literature critical of new community prospects in America include William Alonso, "The Mirage of New Towns," in *Public Interest*, 19 (Spring, 1970), 3–17; and Leonard Downie, Jr., "The 'New Town' Mirage," in *The Nation*, 214 (May 15, 1972), 617–621.

[33]These issues have been treated by various urban scholars. A relatively recent and comprehensive study is Carol Corden, *Planned Cities: New Towns in Britain and America* (Beverly Hills, California: Sage Publications, Inc., 1977), which pays particular attention to the structural differences between new towns programs in England and the United States. At the root of these differences, Corden discovered contrary attitudes toward centralized political control of residential development. For an earlier and less philosophical comparison of new towns in the two nations, see Shirley F. Weiss, "New Towns—Transatlantic Exchange," in *Town and Country Planning*, 38 (September, 1970), 374–381. Works that venture policy recommendations for new community planning in America are Gideon Golany, "New Communities in the United States: Assessment and Potential," in *The Contemporary New Communities in the United States*, ed. by Gideon Golany and Daniel Walden (Urbana: University of Illinois Press, 1974), 1–22; and Twentieth Century Fund Task Force on Governance of New Towns, *New Towns: Laboratories for Democracy* (New York: Twentieth Century Fund, 1971), 8–24. Authors that have dealt primarily with the issue of public participation in new towns development and administration are Kenneth L. Kraemer, "Developing Governmental Institutions in New Communities," in *Urban Lawyer*, 1 (Fall, 1969), 268–280; and Gans, *Levittowners: Ways of Life and Politics in a New Suburban Community*. Gans, a planner and sociologist, has long been an advocate for social balance in the suburbs and in new communities in particular. Also see Herbert Gans, "How to Succeed in Integrating New Towns," in *Design and Environment*, 3 (Winter, 1972), 28–29, 50 and 52. Robert Whelan, in a recent review of relevant historical and planning literature from an international perspective, has considered the possible demise of the new towns idea. See Robert K. Whelan, "New Towns: An Idea Whose Time Has Passed?" in *Journal of Urban History*, 10 (February, 1984), 195–209. For background information on the demise of the federal government's New Community Development Cooperation, see Andre F. Shashaty, "HUD Terminating Its New Communities Program," in *Urban Land*, 42 (June, 1983), 2–9.

[34]Jackson, *Crabgrass Frontier*, 276.

[35]Stern, *Pride of Place*, 332 (citing Leon Krier). It bears mentioning, however, that all residential lanes in Greendale were recently widened by two feet to help accommodate the automobile.

BIBLIOGRAPHY

Archival and Special Collections

GREENDALE HISTORICAL SOCIETY, Greendale.
GREENDALE VILLAGE LIBRARY, Greendale.
—Greendale Village Collection.
MILWAUKEE AREA RESEARCH CENTER (State Historical Society of Wisconsin),
University of Wisconsin-Milwaukee, Milwaukee.
—Proceedings of the Greendale Village Board, 1938–1965.
MILWAUKEE COUNTY HISTORICAL SOCIETY, Milwaukee.
—Daniel W. Hoan Papers.
—Charles B. Whitnall Papers.
MORTON ARBORETUM ARCHIVES, Lisle, Illinois.
—Jens Jensen Papers.
NATIONAL ARCHIVES AND RECORDS ADMINISTRATION, Washington, D.C.
—Record Group 96: "Records of the Farmers Home Administration."
—Record Group 196: "Records of the General Field Office of the PHA Regarding Management and Disposition of Greentown Projects, 1936–61."
—Record Group 196: "Records of the Legal Division, Public Housing Administration, Regarding Management and Disposition of Greentown Projects, 1935–64."
—Record Group 207: "Records of the Department of Housing and Urban Development: Case Files Regarding the Resettlement Administration and Farm Security Administration."
SPECIAL COLLECTIONS, UNIVERSITY OF KENTUCKY LIBRARY, Lexington, Kentucky.
—John S. Lansill Papers.

Theses

HACKBARTH, CLARENCE. "Greendale: A Suburban Community Study." M.A. thesis. Madison: University of Wisconsin, 1958.
MARSHALL, DOUGLAS G. "Greendale: A Study of a Resettlement Community." Ph.D. dissertation. University of Wisconsin, 1943.
OLSON, FREDERICK I. "The Milwaukee Socialists, 1897–1941." Ph.D. dissertation. Harvard University, 1952.

Public Documents

Comey, Arthur C. and Max J. Wehrly. *Planned Communities, Part 1 of Urban Planning and Land Policies; Volume 2 of the Supplementary Report of the Urbanism Committee to the National Resources Committee.* Washington, D.C.: Government Printing Office, 1939.
Holt, John. *An Analysis of Methods and Criteria Used in Selecting Families for Colonization Projects,* U.S. Department of Agriculture, The Farm Security Administration and the Bureau of Agricultural Economics Cooperating, Social Research Report No. I. Washington, D.C.: Government Printing Office, 1937.
Federal Public Housing Administration. *Proposed Provision Pertaining to Appropriation for National Housing Agency, Fiscal Year 1947.* House Document 584, 79th Congress, 2nd session, 1946.
House Committee on Banking and Currency, *Suburban Resettlement Projects: Hearings Before the Committee on Banking and Currency, House of Representatives on H.R. 2440, A Bill to Authorize the Public Housing Commissioner to Sell the Suburban Resettlement Pro-*

135

jects Known as Greenbelt, MD.; Greendale, Wis.: Greenhills, Ohio, Without Regard to Provisions of Law Requiring Competitive Bidding or Public Advertising. March 18 and 24, 1949, 81st Congress, 1st session, 1949.

Mayer, Albert. *Greenbelt Towns Revisited.* Washington, D.C.: Department of Housing and Urban Development, 1968.

Milwaukee County Park Commission and the Milwaukee County Regional Planning Department. *Biennial Report, 1929–1930.* Milwaukee: Court House, 1930.

Milwaukee County Park Commission and the Milwaukee County Regional Planning Department. *Quadrennial Report, 1933–1936.* Milwaukee: Court House, 1936.

U.S. Bureau of the Census. *Sixteenth Census of the United States: 1940. Population and Housing: Family Tenure and Rent.* Washington, D.C.: Government Printing Office, 1943.

U.S. Bureau of the Census. *Sixteenth Census of the United States: 1940. Population, Volume 2, Characteristics of the Population, Part 7, Wisconsin.* Washington, D.C.: Government Printing Office, 1943.

U.S. Bureau of the Census. *Seventeenth Census of the United States: 1950. Population, Vol. 2, Characteristics of the Population, Part 49, Wisconsin.* Washington, D.C.: Government Printing Office, 1952.

U.S. Bureau of the Census. *Eighteenth Census of the United States: 1960, Population, Vol. 2, Characteristics of the Population, Part 51, Wisconsin.* Washington, D.C.: Government Printing Office, 1963.

U.S. Bureau of the Census. *Census of Population and Housing: 1970 Final Report. Milwaukee, Wisconsin SMSA.* Washington, D.C.: Government Printing Office, 1972.

U.S. Bureau of the Census. *Census Tracts: Milwaukee, Wis. Standard Metropolitan Statistical Area, 1980 Census of Population and Housing.* Washington, D.C.: Government Printing Office, 1983.

U.S. Department of Agriculture, Resettlement Administration. *Interim Report of the Resettlement Administration.* Washington, D.C.: Government Printing Office, April, 1936.

U.S. Farm Security Administration. *Greenbelt Communities.* Washington, D.C.: Government Printing Office, 1940.

U.S. Public Housing Administration. *First Annual Report of the Public Housing Administration.* Washington, D.C.: Government Printing Office, 1947.

U.S. Public Housing Administration. *Second Annual Report of the Public Housing Administration.* Washington, D.C.: Government Printing Office, 1948.

U.S. Public Housing Administration. *Third Annual Report of the Public Housing Administration.* Washington, D.C.: Government Printing Office, 1949.

U.S. Resettlement Administration. *Greenbelt Towns: A Demonstration in Suburban Planning,* Washington, D.C.: Government Printing Office, September, 1936.

U.S. Resettlement Administration. *First Annual Report, Resettlement Administration.* Washington, D.C.: Government Printing Office, November 1936.

U.S. Resettlement Administration. "What the Resettlement Administration Has Done." Washington, D.C.: Government Printing Office, November 1936.

U.S. Resettlement Administration. *Greendale, Wisconsin.* Washington, D.C.: Government Printing Office, 1936.

U.S. Resettlement Administration, "Homes for Workingmen." Washington, D.C.: Government Printing Office, n.d.

U.S. Resettlement Administration. *Annual Report of the Administration, 1937.* Washington, D.C.: Government Printing Office, 1937.

Works Progress Administration. *Greendale: Inventory of Local Government Archives.* Village Series No. 141. Madison: State Historical Society of Wisconsin and University of Wisconsin, 1941.

Interviews

Gerald and Madge Casey, Greendale, June 13, 1984.
Patricia Goetsch, Greendale, July 17, 1982.
Christene Kindel, Greendale, June 13, 1984.
Arthur and Leona Krueger, Greendale, June 13, 1984.
Linus Lindberg, Greendale, June 13, 1984.
Michael Steinberg, Greendale, November 4, 1977.

Correspondence

Victor J. Jacoby, June 3, 1986.
Harold H. Lutz, Greendale Village Clerk-Treasurer, May 11, 1981.
Mark C. Radtke, Assistant Greendale Village Engineer, January 14, 1982.

Newspapers

Greendale Review.
Milwaukee Journal.
Milwaukee Sentinel.
Southwest Post (West Allis).
Tri-Town News (Hales Corners).
Greendale Village Life.

Published Articles, Books, and Reports: Greendale

American Legion Community Development Corporation. *Greendale: The Answer to the Veterans' Housing Problem.* Greendale: The Corporation, 1948.
Bauer, Kurt W. "A Backward Glance: Greendale—Garden City in Wisconsin." *Southeast Wisconsin Regional Planning Commission Technical Record,* 1 (August/September, 1964), ii, 8, 17, 18, 32–35.
Bauer, K. W. "A Greenbelt Town Grows Up." *American City,* 74 (October, 1959), 143–148.
Bennett, Charles B., and Richard B. Fernbach. "Greendale—the General Plan. Discussion." *Planner's Journal,* 3 (November–December, 1937), 160–161.
Bentley, Harry H. "Greendale, Wisconsin: A Federal Suburban Resettlement Town." *Monthly Bulletin, Illinois Society of Architects,* 21 (April–May, 1937), 1–2.
Black, John C. "Progress at Parklawn and Greendale." *Roads and Streets,* 79 (August, 1936), 37–42.
"Businessmen Make a New Deal Idea Work." *Business Week* (March 10, 1962), 92–94.
Citizens' Governmental Research Bureau. "Greendale Looks to the Future on Its 17th Anniversary, November 1, 1955." *CGRB Bulletin,* 43 (November 1, 1955), 1–8.
Citizens' Governmental Research Bureau. "Greendale: Commercial and Residential Development Spur Growth of Former Greenbelt Town." *CGRB Bulletin,* 61 (May 26, 1973), 1–9.
Crane, Jacob. "Greendale—the General Plan." *Planners' Journal,* 3 (No. 4, 1937), 89–90.

Crane, Jacob. "Safety Town." *Public Safety*, 11 (August, 1937), 28–30.

Dahir, James. *Greendale Comes of Age: The Story of Wisconsin's Best Known Planned Community As It Enters Its Twenty-First Year*. Milwaukee: Milwaukee Community Development Corporation, 1958.

Eden, Joseph A., and Arnold R. Alanen. "Looking Backward at a New Deal Town: Greendale, Wisconsin, 1935–1980." *Journal of the American Planning Association*, 49 (Winter, 1983), 40–58.

Greendale and the Activities of Its People. Greendale, Wisconsin, 1939.

"Greendale Being Developed by Private Enterprise." *American City*, 71 (February, 1956), 133.

Greendale Decennial Committee. *This is Greendale*. Greendale: The Committee, 1948.

Johnson, Dale R. "A 'Greenbelt' Blooms." *National Civic Review*, 48 (July, 1959), 338–342.

Kroening, Walter E., and Frank L. Dieter. "Utility Planning for Greendale, Wis.: A Demonstrational Suburban Housing Project by the Resettlement Administration." *Civil Engineering*, 8 (February, 1938), 94–98.

Lansill, John S., and Jacob Crane. "Metropolitan Land Reserves as Illustrated by Greendale, Wisconsin." *American City*, 52 (July, 1937), 55–58.

League of Women Voters of Greendale. *Presenting Greendale*. Greendale: The League, 1964.

Pedo, Douglas. "Greendale, Wisconsin: Parkways and Progress." *Concrete Pipe News*, 20 (June, 1968), 43–45.

Peets, Elbert. "Washington, Williamsburg, the Century of Progress, and Greendale." In Werner Hegemann, *City Planning Housing*. Edited by Ruth N. Anshem. New York: Architectural Book Publishing Co., Inc., 1937.

Peets, Elbert. "Studies in Planning Texture and Housing for a Greenbelt Town," and "Greendale." *Architectural Record*, 106 (September, 1949), 130–137.

Peets, Elbert. "Residential Site Planning Texture." In *On the Art of Designing Cities: Selected Essays of Elbert Peets*. Paul O. Spreiregen, editor. Cambridge, Massachusetts: The M.I.T. Press, 1968.

Plische, Elmer. "Greendale." *Municipality*, 37 (March, 1942), 43.

Russell, N.J., Jr. "Metamorphosis of a Village." *Wisconsin Architect*, 28 (June, 1960), 1–5.

Stein, Clarence S. "Greendale and the Future." *American City*, 63 (June, 1948), 106–109.

Vance, Mary. *Greendale, Wisconsin*. Council of Planning Librarians Exchange Bibliography No. 4. Monticello, Illinois: Council of Planning Librarians, 1958.

"Veterans Seek Purchase of Greendale and the City of Milwaukee Cooperates." *American City*, 64 (January, 1949), 73–74.

Published Articles, Books, and Reports: General

Abbott, Sidney. "New Hope for New Towns." *Design and Environment*, 3 (Spring, 1972), 28–37.

Agnew, Ernest P. "Juvenile Delinquency in the Average Wisconsin City." *Municipality*, 39 (January, 1944), 3–4, 16.

Alanen, Arnold R., and Thomas J. Peltin. "Kohler, Wisconsin: Planning and Paternalism in a Model Industrial Village." *Journal of the American Institute of Planners*, 44 (April, 1978), 145–179.

Allen, Irving Lewis, editor. *New Towns and the Suburban Dream: Ideology and Utopia in Planning and Development*. Port Washington, New York: Kennikat Press Corporation, 1977.

Alonso, William. "The Mirage of New Towns." *Public Interest*, 19 (Spring, 1970), 3–17.

"Alphabets and Architects." *American Architect*, 148 (January, 1936), 17–23.

Apgar, Mahlon, editor. *New Perspectives on Community Development*. Maidenhead and Berkshire, England: McGraw Hill Book Company, Limited, 1976.

Arnold, Joseph L. *The New Deal in the Suburbs: A History of the Greenbelt Town Program, 1935–1954*. Columbus: The Ohio State University Press, 1971.

Augur, Tracy B. "New Towns in the National Economy." *Planners' Journal*, 3 (January–February, 1937), 38–42.

Bailey, James, Editor. *New Towns in America: The Design and Development Process*. New York: John Wiley & Sons, 1973.

Berger, Bennet M. "Suburbia and the America Dream." In *New Towns and the Suburban Dream: Ideology and Utopia in Planning and Development*. Irving Lewis Allen, editor. Port Washington, New York: Kennikat Press Corporation, 1977.

Binford, Henry C. *The First Suburbs: Residential Communities On the Boston Periphery, 1815–1880*. Chicago: University of Chicago Press, 1985.

Birch, Eugenie Ladner. "Advancing the Art and Science of Planning: Planners and Their Organizations." *Journal of the American Planning Association*, 46 (January, 1980), 22–49

Birch, Eugenie Ladner. "Radburn and the American Planning Movement: The Persistence of an Idea." *Journal of the American Planning Association*, 46 (October, 1980), 424–439.

Bishop, Warren. "A Yardstick for Housing." *Nation's Business*, 24 (April, 1936), 29–31, 69–71.

Burby, Raymond J., and Shirley F. Weiss, *et al. New Communities U.S.A.* Lexington, Massachusetts: Lexington Books, 1976.

Campbell, Carlos C. *New Towns: Another Way to Live*. Reston, Virginia: Reston Publishing Company, Inc., 1976.

Christianson, Carol A. *The American Garden City and the New Towns Movement*. Ann Arbor, Michigan: UMI Research Press, 1985.

Chudacoff, Howard P. *The Evolution of American Urban Society*. Englewood Cliffs, New Jersey: Prentice-Hall, 1981.

Churchill, Henry S. "America's Town Planning Begins." *New Republic*, 87 (June, 3, 1936), 96–98.

Collins, George R. and Christiane Crasemann Collins. *Camillo Sitte and the Birth of Modern City Planning*. London: Phaidon Press, 1965.

Comey, Arthur C. "An Answer to the Garden City Challenge." *American City*, 29 (July, 1923), 36–38.

Committee on Housing Exhibition. "The Planned Community." *Architectural Forum*, 58 (April, 1933), 253–274.

"Comparative Architectural Details in the Greenbelt Housing." *American Architect and Architecture*, 149 (October, 1936), 20–36.

Conkin, Paul K. *Tomorrow a New World: The New Deal Community Program*. Ithaca, New York: Cornell University Press, 1959.

Corden, Carol. *Planned Cities: New Towns in Britain and America*. Beverly Hills, California: Sage Publications, Inc., 1977.

Crane, Jacob. "Russian Planning Norms." *City Planning*, 8 (July, 1931), 168–169.

Crane, Jacob L. *Urban Planning—Illusion and Reality*. New York: Vantage Press, 1973.

Creese, Walter L. *The Search for Environment—The Garden City: Before and After*. New Haven, Connecticut: Yale University Press, 1966.

Cutler, Phoebe. *The Public Landscape of the New Deal*. New Haven, Connecticut: Yale University Press, 1985.

Dahir, James. *The Neighborhood Unit Plan: Its Spread and Acceptance. A Selected Bibliography with Interpretative Comments*. New York: Russell Sage Foundation, 1947.

Dewey, John. "The Influence of Darwinism on Philosophy." In *American Thought: Civil War to World War I*. Edited by Perry Miller. New York: Rinehart & Company, Incorporated, 1954.

Dewey, Richard. "Peripheral Expansion in Milwaukee County." *American Journal of Sociology*, 54 (September, 1948), 118–125.

Downie, Leonard, Jr. "The 'New-Town' Mirage." *The Nation*, 214 (May 15, 1972), 617–621.

Draper, Earle S. "Shall We Plan the Future?" *Landscape Architecture*, 25 (July, 1935), 183–186.

Drier, John. "Greenbelt Planning: Resettlement Administration Goes to Town." *Pencil Points*, 17 (August, 1936), 400–419.

Edelman, Murray. "New Deal Sensitivity to Labor Interests." In *Labor and the New Deal*, Milton Derber and Edwin Young, editors. Madison: University of Wisconsin Press, 1957.

Eliot, Charles W. "Welfare and Happiness in Works of Landscape Architecture." *Landscape Architecture*, 1 (April, 1911), 145–153.

"European Experts Now Touring the United States." *American City*, 49 (September, 1934), 99.

"Farm Security Administration Housing Projects." *Architectural Forum*, 68 (May, 1938), 415–424.

"Federal Flux." *Architectural Forum*, 66 (May, 1937), 2.

Fellheimer, Alfred. "Planning Standards for Low-Rent Housing." *American Architect*, 146 (February, 1935), 12–28.

Friedmann, John, and Clyde Weaver. *Territory and Function: The Evolution of Regional Planning*. Berkeley: University of California Press, 1979.

Galantay, Ervin Y. *New Towns: Antiquity to the Present*. New York: George Braziller, 1975.

Gans, Herbert J. "The Sociology of New Towns: Opportunities for Research." *Sociology and Social Research*, 40 (March–April, 1956), 231–239.

Gans, Herbert. *Levittowners: Ways of Life and Politics in a New Suburban Community*. New York: Pantheon Books, 1967.

Gans, Herbert J. "How to Succeed in Integrating New Towns." *Design and Environment*, 3 (Winter, 1972), 28–29, 50, 52.

Geddes, Patrick. *Cities in Evolution: An Introduction to the Planning Movement and to the Study of Civics*. New York: Howard Fertig, Inc., 1968.

Goist, Park Dixon. *From Main Street to State Street: Town, City, and Community in America*. Port Washington, New York: Kennikat Press Corp., 1977.

Golany, Gideon. "New Communities in the United States: Assessment and Potential." In *The Contemporary New Communities in the United States*. Gideon Golany and Daniel Walden, editors. Urbana: University of Illinois Press, 1974.

Golany, Gideon and Daniel Walden, editors. *The Contemporary New Communities Movement in the United States*. Urbana: University of Illinois Press, 1974.

Goldfield, David R. "The New Regionalism." *Journal of Urban History*, 10 (February, 1984), 171–186.

Goodman, Paul and Percival. *Communitas: Means of Livelihood and Ways of Life*. New York: Vintage Books, 1947.

"Greenbelt Towns." *Architectural Record*, 80 (September, 1936), 215–234.

Hadden, Jeffrey K. and Josef J. Barton. "An Image That Will Not Die: Thoughts on the History of Anti-Urban Ideology." In *New Towns and the Suburban Dream: Ideology and Utopia in Planning and Development*. Irving Lewis Allen, editor. Port Washington, New York: Kennikat Press Corporation, 1977.

Hegemann, Werner, and Elbert Peets. *The American Vitruvius: An Architects' Handbook of Civic Art*. New York: The Architectural Book Publishing Company, 1922.

Hill, Howard C., and Rexford Guy Tugwell. *Our Economic Society and Its Problems: A Study of American Levels of Living and How to Improve Them*. New York: Harcourt, Brace and Company, 1934.

Hofstadter, Richard. *The Age of Reform: From Bryan to F.D.R.* New York: Random House, Inc., 1955.

Hofstadter, Richard. *Social Darwinism in American Thought*. Boston: Beacon Press, 1955.

Howard, E.A. "Milwaukee County Plan Successful." *City Planning*, 8 (October, 1932), 237–238.

Howard, Ebenezer. *Garden Cities of To-morrow*. Cambridge, Massachusetts: The M.I.T. Press, 1965. (First published in 1898 as *Tomorrow: A Peaceful Path to Real Reform*.)

Hubbard, Henry. "Annual Report of the President, American Society of Landscape Architects." *Landscape Architecture*, 25 (April, 1935), 159–162.

Jackson, Kenneth T. *Crabgrass Frontier: The Suburbanization of the United States*. New York: Oxford University Press, 1985.

Jakle, John A. *The American Small Town: Twentieth Century Place Images*. Hamden, Connecticut: Shoestring Press, 1982.

Kaplan, Marshall. "The Roles of Planner and Developer in the New Community." *Washington University Law Quarterly*, 1965 (February, 1965), 88–104.

Kraemer, Kenneth L. "Developing Governmental Institutions in New Communities." *Urban Lawyer*, 1 (Fall, 1969), 268–280.

Langord, Letitia C. and Gwen Bell. "Federally Sponsored New Towns of the Seventies." *Growth and Change*, 6 (October, 1975), 24–31.

Lansing, John B., Robert W. Marans, and Robert B. Zehner. *Planned Residential Environments*. Ann Arbor: Survey Research Center, Institute for Social Research, University of Michigan, 1970.

Lapping, Mark B. Review of Joseph L. Arnold, *The New Deal in the Suburbs: A History of the Greenbelt Town Program, 1935–1954*. In *Journal of the American Institute of Planners*, 39 (January, 1973), 64.

Leuchtenberg, William E. *Franklin D. Roosevelt and the New Deal*. New York: Harper and Row, 1963.

Lilienthal, David. *TVA: Democracy on the March*. New York: Harpers, 1944.

Lingeman, Richard. *Small Town America: A Narrative History, 1620—The Present*. New York: G.P. Putnam's Sons, 1980.

"Low Cost Furniture." *House Beautiful*, 79 (April, 1937), 131–133.

Lubove, Roy S. "New Cities for Old: The Urban Reconstruction Program of the Thirties." *Social Studies*, 53 (November, 1962), 201–213.

Lubove, Roy S. *Community Planning in the 1920's: The Contribution of the Regional Planning Association of America*. Pittsburgh: University of Pittsburgh Press, 1963.

Lubove, Roy. *The Urban Community; Housing and Planning in the Progressive Era*. Englewood Cliffs, New Jersey: Prentice-Hall, 1967.

Lubove, Roy. "Housing Reform and City Planning in Progressive America." In *Cities in American History*. Kenneth T. Jackson and Stanley K. Schultz, editors. New York: Alfred A. Knopf, 1972.

Marans, Robert W. and Robert B. Zehner. "Social Planning and Research in New Communities." In *The Contemporary New Communities Movement in the United States*. Gideon Golany and Daniel Walden, editors. Urbana: University of Illinois Press, 1974.

Marling, Karal Ann. *Wall-to-Wall America: A Cultural History of Post-Office Murals in the Great Depression*. Minneapolis: University of Minnesota Press, 1982.

Mayer, Albert. "Green-Belt Towns for the Machine Age." *New York Times Magazine* (February 2, 1936), 8–9, 18.

Mayer, Albert. "The Greenbelt Towns: What and Why." *American City*, 51 (May, 1936), 59–61.

McFarland, John R. "The Administration of the New Deal Towns." *Journal of the American Institute of Planners*, 32 (July, 1966), 217–225.

McKelvey, Blake. *The Urbanization of America, 1860–1915*. New Brunswick, New Jersey: Rutgers University Press, 1963.

McKelvey, Blake. *The Emergence of Metropolitan America, 1915–1966*. New Brunswick, New Jersey: Rutgers University Press, 1968.

Melli, Marygold. "Subdivision Control in Wisconsin." *Wisconsin Law Review*, 39 (May, 1953), 389–457.

Mields, Hugh, Jr. *Federally Assisted New Communities: New Dimensions in Urban Development*. Washington, D.C.: Urban Land Institute, 1973.

Miller, Zane L. *Suburb: Neighborhood and Community in Forest Park, Ohio, 1935–1976*. Knoxville: University of Tennessee Press, 1982.

Mumford, Lewis. "The Fourth Migration." *Survey Graphic*, 54 (May, 1925), 130–133.

Myrha, David. "Rexford Guy Tugwell: Initiator of America's Greenbelt New Towns, 1935–1936." *Journal of the American Institute of Planners*, 40 (May, 1974), 176–188.

"New Wisconsin Laws Affecting Cities and Villages." *Municipality*, 40 (September, 1945), 185–188, 196–201.

Nicoson, William. "The United States: The Battle for Title VII." In *New Perspectives on Community Development*. Mahlon Apgar, editor. Maidenhead and Berkshire, England: McGraw-Hill Book Company, Limited, 1976.

Nolen, John. "The Landscape Architect in Regional and State Planning." *Landscape Architecture*, 25 (June, 1935), 199–202.

Odum, Howard W. *The Regional Approach to National Social Planning*. New York and Chapel Hill, North Carolina: Foreign Policy Association and University of North Carolina Press, 1935.

Peets, Elbert. "Famous Town Planners—Camillo Sitte." *Town Planning Review*, 12 (No. 4, 1927), 249–259.

Peets, Elbert. "L'Enfant's Washington." *Town Planning Review*, 15 (No. 3, 1933), 155–164.

Perry, Clarence A. "The Prevention of Slum Conditions Through City Planning." *Social Forces*, 10 (March, 1932), 382–387.

Petersen, William. "The Ideological Origins of Britain's New Towns." *Journal of the American Institute of Planners*, 34 (May, 1968), 160–170.

Purdom, C.B. "New Towns for Old: I, Garden Cities—What They Are and How They Work. *Survey Graphic*, 54 (May, 1925), 169–172.

Reiss, R.L. "American Green Belt Towns." *Town and Country Planning*, 6 (January, 1938), 16–18.

Reps, John W. *The Making of Urban America: A History of City Planning in the United States*. Princeton, New Jersey: Princeton University Press, 1965.

Reps, John W. *Cities of the American West: A History of Frontier Urban Planning*. Princeton, New Jersey: Princeton University Press, 1979.

Rifkind, Carole. *Main Street: The Face of Urban America*. New York: Harper & Row, Publishers, 1977.

"Rise of the New Cities." *Nation's Business*, 56 (August, 1968), 73–78.

Robbins, Ira S. "Resettlement Administration Only Partially Unsettled." *American City*, 51 (June, 1936), 5.

"Row Houses for Rent." *Architectural Forum*, 66 (May, 1937), 468–470.

Rountree, Lester B., and Margaret W. Conkey. "Symbolism and the Cultural Landscape." *Annals of the Association of American Geographers*, 70 (December, 1980), 459–474.

Rowlands, W. A. "Possibilities of Rural Settlement in Wisconsin." *Agricultural Engineering*, 17 (June, 1936), 251–253.

Schaffer, Daniel. *Garden Cities for America: The Radburn Experience*. Philadelphia: Temple University Press, 1982.

Schaffer, Daniel. "Ideal and Reality in 1930s Regional Planning: The Case of the Tennessee Valley Authority." *Planning Perspectives*, 1 (January, 1986), 27–44.

Schuchardt, William. "The Milwaukee County Highway and Park Plan." *American City*, 28 (April, 1923), 363–364.

Schuyler, Daniel M. "Constitutional Problems Confronting the Resettlement Administration." *Journal of Land & Public Utility Economics*, 12 (August, 1936), 304–306.

Scott, Mel. *American City Planning Since 1890*. Berkeley and Los Angeles: University of California Press, 1969.

Seckler, David. *Thorstein Veblen and the Institutionalists: A Study in the Social Philosophy of Economics*. Boulder, Colorado: Associated University Press, 1975.

Seidel, Emil. "Garden Homes Steps Out." *Historical Messenger of the Milwaukee County Historical Society*, 28 (Summer, 1972), 73–78.

Selznick, Philip. *TVA and the Grassroots: A Study in the Sociology of Formal Organization*. Berkeley: University of California Press, 1949.

Shashaty, Andre F. "HUD Terminating Its New Communities Program." *Urban Land*, 42 (June, 1983), 2–9.

Shillaber, Caroline, "Elbert Peets: Champion of the Civic Form." *Landscape Architecture*, 72 (November–December, 1982), 54–59, 100.

Slichter, Gertrude Almy. "Franklin D. Roosevelt's Farm Policy as Governor of New York State, 1928–1932," *Agricultural History*, 33 (October, 1959), 167–176.

"Site Plans of Greenbelt Towns." *American City*, 51 (August, 1936), 56–59.

Sitte, Camillo. *City Planning According to Artistic Principles*. (Translated from the German into English by George R. Collins and Christiane Crasemann Collins.) New York: Random House, 1965.

Sorden, L. G. "The Northern Wisconsin Settler Relocation Project, 1934–1940." *Transactions of the Wisconsin Academy of Sciences, Arts, and Letters*, 53 (1964), 135–138.

Spreiregen, Paul D. Editor. *On the Art of Designing Cities: Selected Essays of Elbert Peets*. Cambridge, Massachusetts: The M.I.T. Press, 1968.

Stein, Clarence S. *Toward New Towns for America*. Cambridge, Massachusetts: The M.I.T. Press, 1957.

Stern, Michael C. "Regionalism in the Great Depression." *Geographical Review*, 73 (October, 1983), 430–446.

Stern, Robert A. M. *Pride of Place: Building the American Dream*. Boston: Houghton Mifflin Company, 1986.

Sternsher, Bernard. *Rexford Tugwell and the New Deal*. New Brunswick, New Jersey: Rutgers University Press, 1964.

Stilgoe, John R. "The Suburbs." *American Heritage*, 35 (February/March, 1984), 20–36.

Still, Bayrd. *Milwaukee: The History of a City*. Madison: State Historical Society of Wisconsin, 1948, reprinted, 1965.

Sussman, Carl, Editor. *Planning the Fourth Migration: The Neglected Vision of the Regional Planning Association of America*. Cambridge, Massachusetts: The M.I.T. Press, 1976.

Teaford, Jon C. *City and Suburb: The Political Fragmentation of Metropolitan America, 1850–1970*. Baltimore: Johns Hopkins University Press, 1979.

Tugwell, Rexford G. *The Battle for Democracy*. New York: Columbia University Press, 1935.

Tugwell, Rexford G. "The Meaning of the Greenbelt Towns." *New Republic*, 90 (February 17, 1937), 42–43.

Tugwell, Rexford G. "The Sources of New Deal Reformism." *Ethics*, 64 (July, 1954), 249–276.

Tugwell, Rexford G. "The Resettlement Idea." *Agricultural History*, 33 (October, 1959), 159–164.

Tugwell, R. G., and E. C. Banfield. "Grassroots Democracy—Myth Or Reality?" *Public Administration Review*, 10 (Winter, 1950), 47–55.

Turner, Alan. "New Communities in the United States: 1968–1973. Part I: Historical Background, Legislation and the Development Process." *Town Planning Review*, 45 (July, 1974), 259–273.

Turner, Alan. "New Communities in the United States: 1968–1973. Part II: Design Characteristics and Case Studies." *Town Planning Review*, 45 (October, 1974), 415–430.

Twentieth Century Fund Task Force on Governance of New Towns. *New Towns: Laboratories for Democracy* New York: Twentieth Century Fund, 1971.

Wagner, Philip K. "Suburban Landscapes for Nuclear Families: The Case of Greenbelt Towns in the United States." *Built Environment*, 10 (November, 1984), 35–41.

Weiss, Shirley F. "Further Discussion of the University of North Carolina New Town Study." *Urban Land*, 34 (April, 1975), 12–15.

Weiss, Shirley F. "New Towns—Transatlantic Exchange." *Town and Country Planning*, 38 (September, 1970), 374–381.

Weiss, Shirley F. "New Cities." *Panhandle Magazine*, 5 (Spring, 1971), 19–22.

Whelan, Robert K. "New Towns: An Idea Whose Time Has Passed?" *Journal of Urban History*, 10 (February, 1984), 195–209.

Whitnall, C. B. "By Regional Planning The Milwaukee of Tomorrow Conserves Nature's Attributes." *Park and Recreation*, 6 (March–April, 1923), 279–286.

Wilson, M. T. "Victory Gardens in Cities and Suburban Areas." *American City*, 58 (January, 1943), 66–68.

Wright, Gwendolyn. *Building the Dream: A Social History of Housing in America*. Cambridge, Massachusetts: The M.I.T. Press, 1983.

Zehner, Robert B. "Neighborhood and Community Satisfaction in New Towns and Less Planned Suburbs." *Journal of the American Institute of Planners*, 37 (November, 1971), 379–385.

TABLE 1

POPULATION BY AGE GROUPS, GREENDALE AND MILWAUKEE, 1940

Age Group (years)	Greendale (n = 2527) %	Milwaukee City (n = 587,572) %
0-4	18.0	6.7
5-14	24.8	14.4
15-19	4.3	8.2
20-24	4.1	8.8
25-34	28.7	17.4
35-44	14.6	36.4
Over 44	5.6	36.4
Total	100.0	100.0

SOURCE: U.S. Bureau of the Census, *Sixteenth Census of the United States: 1940. Population, Vol. 2, Characteristics of the Population, Part 7, Wisconsin.*

TABLE 2

LEVEL OF EDUCATIONAL ATTAINMENT FOR ADULTS 25 YEARS OF AGE AND OVER IN GREENDALE AND MILWAUKEE, 1940

Educational Level	Greendale (n = 1231)	Milwaukee City* (n = 363,740)
High School Graduates	20.4%	13.4%
Attended College	16.0%	8.8%
Median Number of School Years Completed	10.4	8.7

*White adults only.
SOURCE: U.S. Bureau of the Census, *Sixteenth Census of the United States: 1940. Population, Vol. 2, Characteristics of the Population, Part 7, Wisconsin.*

TABLE 3

NUMBER OF PERSONS IN DIFFERENT AGE GROUPS, GREENDALE AND THE MILWAUKEE SMSA, 1970 AND 1980

Age Groups	Greendale 1970 No.	%	1980 No.	%	Milwaukee SMSA 1970 No.	%	1980 No.	%
Under 5	1,645	10.9	965	5.7	122,121	8.7	100,963	7.2
5-19	5,401	35.8	5,269	31.2	421,106	30.0	346,276	24.9
20-24	709	4.7	1,125	6.6	106,680	7.6	132,390	9.5
25-44	4,587	30.4	4,719	27.8	332,674	23.7	383,534	27.4
45-64	2,218	14.7	3,722	22.1	286,352	20.4	278,732	19.9
Over 64	528	3.5	1,128	6.6	134,754	9.6	155,248	11.1
Total	15,088	100.0	16,928	100.0	1,403,687	100.0	1,397,143	100.0

SOURCE: U.S. Bureau of the Census, *Census Tracts: Milwaukee, Wis. Standard Metropolitan Statistical Area, 1980 Census of Population and Housing.*

TABLE 4

SELECTED SOCIO-ECONOMIC AND HOUSING CHARACTERISTICS
FOR GREENDALE AND THE MILWAUKEE SMSA, 1980

Socio-economic Characteristics	Greendale	Milwaukee SMSA
White Collar Workers (%)	80.2	66.7
Blue Collar Workers (%)	19.8	33.3
Persons 25 Years of Age and Older Having at Least One Year of College Education	48.8	33.3
People Below Poverty Line (%)	1.3	6.3
Black Population (%)	.1	10.8
Median Age (Years)	32.2	29.8
Median Family Income	$26,327	$23,635
Housing Characteristics	**Greendale**	**Milwaukee SMSA**
Median Number of Rooms	6.1	5.2
Persons Per Household	3.15	3.3
Median Housing Value	$78,000	$60,200

SOURCE: U.S. Bureau of the Census, *Census Tracts: Milwaukee, Wis. Standard Metropolitan Statistical Area, 1980 Census of Population and Housing.*

TABLE 5

SOCIO-ECONOMIC AND HOUSING CHARACTERISTICS
FOR CENSUS TRACTS IN GREENDALE, 1980

	Census Tract	
Characteristics	Village Center-East Town	Overlook
Population	13,811	3,117
Median Family Income	$25,882	$ 33,588
Number of Housing Units	4,466	946
Median Housing Value	$73,400	$119,800

SOURCE: U.S. Bureau of the Census, *Census Tracts: Milwaukee, Wis. Standard Metropolitan Statistical Area, 1980 Census of Population and Housing.*

TABLE 6

OCCUPATIONAL GROUPS IN THE VILLAGE CENTER AND
OVERLOOK NEIGHBORHOODS OF GREENDALE, 1978

	Neighborhood			
	Village Center		Overlook	
Groups	No.	%	No.	%
White Collar	35	29.7	55	68.8
Blue Collar	52	44.1	20	25.9
Retired	31	26.2	4	5.3
Total	118	100.0	79	100.0

SOURCE: 1978 Survey Questionnaire. (The number of respondents represents a *sampling* of Greendale residents.)

TABLE 7

REASONS FOR MOVING TO GREENDALE IN THE VILLAGE CENTER AND
THE OVERLOOK NEIGHBORHOODS OF GREENDALE

| | Neighborhoods | | | |
| | Village Center | | Overlook | |
Reasons for Moving	No.	%	No.	%
Social	46	39.3	10	13.3
Economic	34	29.1	23	31.7
Community Image	17	14.5	30	40.0
Community Plan	8	6.8	6	8.0
Other	12	10.3	6	8.0
Total	117	100.0	75	100.0

SOURCE: 1978 Survey Questionnaire. (Sampling of residents.)

TABLE 8

COMMUNITY FEATURES OF GREENDALE MOST APPRECIATED IN THE
VILLAGE CENTER AND THE OVERLOOK NEIGHBORHOODS, 1978

| | Neighborhoods | | | |
| | Center | | Overlook | |
Features	No.	%	No.	%
Esthetics	35	29.9	24	30.8
Friendliness	33	28.2	21	26.9
Convenience	23	19.6	13	16.7
Traffic Safety	16	13.7	8	10.3
Open Space	3	2.6	4	5.1
Other	7	6.0	8	10.2
Total	117	100.0	78	100.0

SOURCE: 1978 Survey Questionnaire. (Sampling of residents.)

TABLE 9

EVALUATION AND USE OF NEIGHBORHOOD OPEN SPACE AREAS IN GREENDALE IN THE VILLAGE CENTER AND OVERLOOK NEIGHBORHOODS, 1978

Neighborhood	Primary Values/Benefits										Frequency of Use			
	Play Areas for Children		Esthetic Qualities		Walking		Other		None		Daily or Several Times Per Week		Once a Week or Less	
	No.	%	No.	%	No.	%	No.	%	No.	%	No.	%	No.	%
Village Center	37	31.4	37	31.4	27	22.9	5	4.2	12	10.1	63	53.4	55	46.6
Overlook	26	33.4	35	44.9	5	6.4	2	2.5	10	12.8	26	33.3	52	66.7
Total	36	32.2	72	36.7	32	16.3	7	3.6	22	11.2	89	45.5	107	54.5

SOURCE: 1978 Survey Questionnaire. (Sampling of residents.)

TABLE 10

MOST FREQUENT USES OF OPEN SPACE IN GREENDALE IN THE VILLAGE CENTER AND OVERLOOK NEIGHBORHOODS, 1978

Neighborhood	Types of Open Space Uses					
	Active (Sports, Games)		Passive (Hiking, Biking)		Reflective (Looking, Nature Study)	
	No.	%	No.	%	No.	%
Village Center	50	42.7	43	36.8	24	20.5
Overlook	58	75.3	17	22.1	2	2.6
Total	108	55.7	60	30.9	26	13.3

SOURCE: 1978 Survey Questionnaire. (Sampling of residents.)

TABLE 11

EVALUATIONS OF TOWN PLANNING AND OPEN SPACE FEATURES IN THE VILLAGE CENTER
AND OVERLOOK NEIGHBORHOODS OF GREENDALE, 1978

		Evaluation							
		Own Neighborhood Better		Both Neighborhood The Same		Other Neighborhood Better		Don't Know	
Feature	Neighborhood Where Respondents Resided	No.	%	No.	%	No.	%	No.	%
Layout and Planning	Village Center	45	(38.1)	28	(23.7)	21	(17.8)	24	(20.4)
	Overlook	43	(55.1)	27	(34.6)	2	(2.6)	6	(7.7)
Open Space	Village Center	47	(39.8)	26	(22.0)	22	(18.7)	23	(19.5)
	Overlook	30	(38.5)	25	(32.1)	20	(25.6)	3	(3.8)

SOURCE: 1978 Survey Questionnaire. (Sampling of residents.)

TABLE 12

GREENDALE POPULATION, 1940-1985

Year	Population
1940	2,527
1950	2,752
1960	6,843
1970	15,088
1980	16,928
1985 [est.]	16,770

SOURCE: Figures for 1940–1980 from U.S. Censuses. Estimate for 1985 from Applied Population Laboratory, University of Wisconsin–Madison.

INDEX

support for and opposition to Green-
dale, 21-24, 56; resigns New Deal posi-
tion, 24
"Tugwelltowns," 6, 21
United Taxpayers Cooperative
Association (Milwaukee), 22
University of Chicago, 63
University of Wisconsin, 46, 49, 62, 66,
75, 90
Unwin, Sir Raymond, 1, 13, 43, 64
Urban Growth and New Community Act
of 1970 (Title VII), 101
Vachon, John, 65
Vandenberg, Arthur, 22
Village Center (Greendale), 86, 91-94, 96-
99, 103
Vinton, Warren J.: 6-7, 10, 12, 24;
planning of Greendale, 14-17, 29, 31,
53, 76, 87
Wagner-Ellender Act, 78
Wallace, Henry, A., 40, 51, 64
Warren, Robert Penn, 2
Washington, D.C., 1, 12-13, 16; directives
for and relationships to Greendale, 17-
18, 21-25, 26, 48-50, 64, 71, 78, 80, 84,
87

Washington Highlands (Milwaukee), 9
Welwyn, England, 2
West Allis, Wisconsin, 43, 55-56
White, Stanley, 41
Whitnall, C. B., 13-14, 25
Wiley, Alexander, 71
Willkie, Wendell, 57
Winston, Oliver, 76, 78, 80
Williamsburg, Virginia, 10, 40, 42, 64, 103
Wisconsin Building and Loan League, 22
Wisconsin State Forestry Department, 32
Wisconsin State Supreme Court, 85
Wooden, William, 3
Works Progress Administration (WPA):
8, 11; work at Greendale, 46-48, 60, 62,
64
World War II, 100
Wright, Frank Lloyd, 40
Wright, Henry, 2-3, 7, 13, 20
Wyrick, Walter, 49
Zablockin, Clement, 82, 85
Zeidler, Frank, 81, 83, 87

THE AUTHORS

ARNOLD R. ALANEN, Honorary ASLA, is an emeritus professor of landscape architecture at the University of Wisconsin-Madison, where he served as the co-founder of *Landscape Journal* and was chairperson for five years. He has received numerous research and communication awards from the American Society of Landscape Architects, the Council of Educators in Landscape Architecture, the Society for Architectural Historians, the Pioneer America Society, Finlandia Foundation National, and several other organizations. The University of Wisconsin Alumni Foundation also recognized him with its outstanding teaching award in 1984. Dr. Alanen, who received a Ph.D. in cultural geography from the University of Minnesota, continues to write about planned communities, company towns, landscape history, vernacular architecture, and ethnic settlements of the upper Midwest. His most recent book is *Morgan Park: Duluth, U.S. Steel, and the Forging of a Company Town* (2007).

JOSEPH EDEN (SHIFLETT), after graduating from Wittenberg College in Ohio, spent two years as a Peace Corps volunteer in Malaysia. He subsequently earned M.A. degrees in anthropology from Ohio's Miami University, and in Southeast Asian Studies from Ohio University. After teaching at Warren Wilson College in North Carolina he enrolled in the Department of Landscape Architecture at the University of Wisconsin-Madison, where he completed a M.A. research thesis (1981) that featured the early planning of Greendale. Upon his acceptance into the geography Ph.D. program at the University of North Carolina, Mr. Eden returned to his earlier interests in Malaysia and its people. His dissertation, a study of the urban social geography of Malaysian women, was completed in 1989. Prior to his unexpected death in 1998, Dr. Eden taught in California and Thailand.